SPIRITUALITY DEMYSTIFIED

YOUR ROADMAP TO PERSONAL FULFILMENT

RAJIV R. GUPTA

JAICO PUBLISHING HOUSE

Mumbai Delhi Bangalore Kolkata
Hyderabad Chennai Ahmedabad Bhopal

Published by Jaico Publishing House
121 Mahatma Gandhi Road
Mumbai - 400 001
jaicopub@vsnl.com
www.jaicobooks.com

© Rajiv R. Gupta

SPIRITUALITY DEMYSTIFIED
ISBN 978-81-7992-755-7
(This book is a revised edition of *Spirituality Unplugged*)

First Jaico Impression: 2007

Printed by
Anubha Printer
B-48, Sector-7, Noida-201301

REVIEWS IN LEADING NEWS PAPERS, MAGAZINES AND BY CORPORATE LEADERS

The author examines the spiritual quest from the standpoint of the seeker who pursues spiritual goals, yet does not wish to give up ambitions for the fulfilment of other personal and professional goals.

— Life Positive

The book also sheds light on the more popular methods of developing one's spiritual self. It first provides information on these methods and then – in tabular form – lists the advantages of adopting each method.

— JETWINGS

The book helped me find practical ways to identify methods and approaches that help to bust the inevitable stress that comes in when you have an irregular and unpredictable schedule.

— Riya Sen (Celebrity Model, Actress)

The book clears misconceptions and contradictions, thereby removing some of the intellectual roadblocks on the spiritual path.

— DNA

Spirituality as a concept is wrapped in layers of myths and obfuscation. This book makes an attempt to demystify spirituality.

— The Tribune

The book is targeted at those people who want to pursue this path but are dissuaded by its complex and confounding principles.

— Navbharat Times

The book provides a great juice for emotional thirst.

— Celina Jaitly (Miss India 2001, Model & Actress)

Given the increasing stress & anxieties at work and in the social context, the timing of this book is good. The subject has been treated in a manner so that an educated & qualified manager would not shy away from reading it. Having read it, one should be able to develop one's own specific path for nurturing this important dimension.

N.K. Goila
Human Resources Director, Honda Siel Cars India Ltd.

The book has been an eye opener. It is pragmatic, crisp and shows how to be a Guru of your own destiny by shunning away the myths and paradigms through our own experiences and experimentation.

A.V. Suresh, COO, Eureka Forbes

The book brings a unique approach to the issue of spirituality— that of a scientific and rational person. It does not pander to those who turn to blind spiritual concepts because of some psychological trauma. The author's approach is refreshing for someone like I, who is sceptical of traditional religious ideas, but does have some, albeit ineffable, spiritual beliefs. This book has a treasured place on my bookshelf.

Alif N. Shirali, Graduate from Harvard College —
Student of   Nobel Prize Winner (2005) in Economics

DEDICATED TO:

My father,

Shri Radhey Shyam Gupta

(26.11.1940 to 29.11.1992)

Whose presence is felt at all moments.

Who lived 200 years, in a life spanning just 52.

Who demonstrated that living with passion is

the only way to live and that

material success & compassion can co-exist.

This book is meant for those who want to make a success of their lives in the real world and yet want that something "extra" to fill the void within. It is also for those who do not want to follow any system based on belief or blind faith, but would rather take each step towards spirituality with caution and conviction. For those who would like to assimilate spirituality into their lives provided it is in sync with their rational minds and their worldly aspirations. Those desirous of methodically selecting the spiritual path and meditation technique and monitoring their progress along the way.

This book will take you beyond merely providing "inspiration" or curiosity towards the path of spirituality. It will try to take you to the "Next Level" by answering the What – Why – How – When – and How Much about how to get started on a spiritual path and remain on it to make tangible progress.

The book aims at helping you build a specific and actionable roadmap by:

1. Removing intellectual bottlenecks that emerge from doubts, myths, misunderstandings, and contradictions around spirituality.
2. Helping you to choose the path or technique that is most suitable to you.
3. Giving you tools to help you evaluate your progress.

The above three aspects should help address self-doubt, which is a major cause of seekers leaving the spiritual path after having initially dabbled with it.

CONTENTS

PREFACE   x

ACKNOWLEDGEMENTS   xii

GETTING STARTED

- Why Do People Seek The Spiritual Path, But
  Never Commit Themselves To It?   xv

- The Stages Of Different Seekers   xviii

- Making The Intellect An Aid, Not A Bottleneck   xxvi

PART I – CONCEPTUAL FRAMEWORK

1. Do I Need A Meditation Technique Or A Formal
   Method To Progress On The Spiritual Path?   2

2. Do I Need A Guru?   7

3. The Three Pillars Of The Spiritual Quest-Mind,
   Meditation And Karma   14

4. The Role Of Meditation In The Spiritual Quest   17

5. Mind And Its Ever Dissatisfied Nature   21

6. Karma And Principles Associated With It   27

7. Basic Fundamentals Of What Meditation Wssentially Is   32

8. What Can Meditation Specifically Do For A Seeker?   39

9. How Much Time Should I Spend In Meditation?   45

10. Re-Look At The Key Concepts   49

11. Can Spirituality, Then, Be Your Cup Of Tea?   55

PART II – SELECTING A TECHNIQUE

1. Why All The Fuss About The 'Right Method' When
   All Methods Are Bound To Lead Us To The Same Goal?   60

2. Overview Of Some Meditation Paths & Techniques   62

3. Selecting The Most Suitable Path   77

PART III – CHALLENGES ALONG THE COURSE

1. Started Meditating, But Still Feeling Low....?   86

2. I Was Promised Ananda, Then Where Does
   Suffering Come From?   101

3. You May Have Learnt The Method, But Persistence Is
   The Key   107

PART IV – WE NEED MORE THAN JUST SPIRITUALITY
TO FIND FULFILMENT

1. Is Spirituality The Means As Well As The End?   114

2. All Other Dimensions Are Just As Critical As Spirituality 122

3. Living The Four Dimensions   149

PART V – CONTRADICTIONS & INTELLECTUAL
BOTTLENECKS

1. Spirituality Is Anti-Materialistic   152

2. Self-Control And Repression Are Critical To
   Spiritual Growth   157

3. Meditation Is Nothing But Concentration   165

4. Spirituality Encourages A Fatalistic, Destiny Driven Mindset
   And Not Aggression To Create One's Own Destiny   169

5. Spirituality Talks Of Dispassion, While All
   Achievements And Successes Are Built Through Passion 175

6. Spirituality Talks Of Focusing Solely On Karma (And Not
    Results) Whereas Professional Life Is Results-Oriented   177

7. How Can I Be Thankful All The Time, As The
    Spiritualists Suggest, When Everything Is Ordinary And
    I Am Aspiring To Be Extraordinary   180

8. Living In The Present Moment Is A Very Important
    Prerequisite For Spiritual Growth   182

9. Rituals, Religious Ceremonies, Idolatry Are An Integral
    Part Of Spirituality   184

PART VI – WRAPPING UP AND SIGNING OFF

1. The Spiritual And Material Quest... The Yin & Yang
    Of Happiness   188

2. Some Of The Don'ts For Seekers   194

3. Eighteen Important Tips For Any Seeker   197

APPENDIX

Detailed Overview Of Some Of The Spiritual Paths &
Meditation Techniques   204

Glossary Of Terms   242

Seekers Interviewed   247

Bibliography   249

PREFACE

A rational, educated, and ambitious seeker who searches for spirituality in order to find deeper meaning and purpose is bombarded with so many messages from books, scriptures, and sermons. Many of these messages may seem contradictory, mystical or complex, and thus difficult to digest. Unable to find convincing answers, many such seekers may quit the pursuit by deciding that spirituality began burdening their minds rather than simplifying their lives. A number of those who do take the next step and get started with a particular technique get disillusioned at a later stage because the answers they receive from their teachers or from published literature may not survive rational scrutiny in any modern and educated mind.

The sole purpose of this book is to help guard gullible seekers from choosing a path that is incapable of facilitating their spiritual growth. Additionally, this book serves to provide a rational framework for doubting and questioning minds so that such seekers do not turn away from spirituality just because it does not seem to measure up to their standards of scrutiny.

This book will not try to convince you to follow a particular path or technique. It has no alignments to any sects or masters or techniques. What it will do, however, is introduce some of the popular techniques and suggest tools to help the seeker find the most suitable one from the list, as well as from other methods not discussed. It shall not teach any method or generic way of meditation, as the author believes this needs to be done under the personal guidance and supervision of a trained teacher of a respective path.

Finally, the book discusses how meditation is necessary but not sufficient or complete in itself for spiritual growth. It emphasises that intellectual understanding of the concepts, gaining experience through practice and nurturing a compassionate heart are all equally critical for rapid growth and fulfilment.

The book makes no claims of having been written by an enlightened person, nor by one who has achieved the goal of spirituality. The author is just another seeker who has treaded the path for some time and studied it from the scientific and practical viewpoints of a modern individual. The aim is to help people avoid having to learn each lesson 'the hard way'. This, in turn, can help reduce the 'dropout rate' from spirituality by providing tools to overcome some of the stumbling blocks that appear along the way.

This book is not a fable. It does not read like a storybook. It has been written in a structured way in subject-centric chapters with the aim of providing a method and giving sense to so many concepts and theories that a seeker may be harbouring within himself.

ACKNOWLEDGEMENTS

THE FIRST EDITION

(Published in 2006 by Jaico under the title 'Spirituality Unplugged')

First and foremost, I wish to express my gratitude to Shri. Surendraji Srivastava, who acted as a mentor and guide through the initial years, when I was battling with several doubts on the path of spirituality. Without his guidance, it is unlikely that I would have persisted in my pursuit. Surendraji has spent many years in close association with Maharishi Mahesh Yogi and has dedicated his life to Transcendental Meditation and other activities of the organization.

Mr. Akash Shah, my publisher, who took a serious look at my work. I first shared the manuscript with him in 2003, when it consisted only of Part I. He explained how more could be written on the subject, which is what led to the development of the book in its current form.

The following institutions have been kind enough to provide their inputs, guidance, as well as permissions to quote from their websites, and published materials.

1. Maharishi Institute of Management, Maharishi nagar, Noida (for Transcendental Meditation as taught by Maharishi Mahesh Yogi); www.tm.org; www.maharishi.org

2. Art of Living Foundation, Udayanpura, Bangalore (for Art of Living as taught by Sri Sri Ravi Shankarji); www.artofliving.org

3. Osho International Foundation, Koregaon Park, Pune (for the path shown by Osho); www.osho.com

4. Adavaita Ashram, Delhi Entally Road, Kolkata (for path taught by Swami Vivekanda); www.advaitaonline.com

5. Vipassana Research Institute, Igatpuri (for Vipassana as taught by Sri S N Goenkaji); www.vri.dhamma.org

6. Yogoda Satsang Society (YSS), Ranchi (for Kriya Yoga as taught by Sri Yogananda Paramahansa); www.yoganandasrf.org

7. Life Eternal Trust, Mumbai (for Sahaj Yoga, taught by Shri Mataji, Nirmala Devi); www.sahajayoga.org

8. ISKCON – International Society for Krishna Consciousness and A.C. Bhakti Vedanta Trust founded by His Holiness Swami Prabhupada; www.iskcon.com

My cousin, Shailesh Agarwal, proprietor of Chotiwala Foods & Hotels at Swargashram (Rishikesh), who introduced me to my first teacher, Shri. Surendraji Srivastava.

My closest friend and conscience Keeper, Anil Kumar Bhatia, who is a non-believer, but nevertheless embodies complete selflessness, compassion and love for one and all.

My dost, Jagadeesh R. Kini, who has been a successful critique of my English writing 'skills' and has taught me how to laugh at myself. Jaya Agarwal, who introduced me to the Art of Living Foundation and Sudarashan Kriya, and who is a trained teacher at the Foundation. Anuj Hariraj Gupta for all his coordination work to facilitate the release of this book. My family, whose belief in me has kept me going and whose support has been crucial at every stage.

THE MAKING OF THE SECOND EDITION

I am grateful to the following people whose invaluable feedback resulted in re-editing and revising this book under a new title "Spirituality Demystified".

1. Mr. Parveen Chopra of the DNA group and erstwhile editor of Life Positive Magazine. He was the first one to publish a

review of my book. He has also been kind enough to provide me with guidance from time to time.

2. Mr. Vithal C Nadkarni, of the Times of India group, whose intellectually stimulating articles on science, technology, human spirit, and psychology in the Economic Times and the Times of India are a reader's delight. Interacting with him was a journey into the discovery of my own aims and objectives for the book, thus it set the base for the second edition.

3. My old friends, Shaily & Naveen Gupta, who told me that while shopping for a meditation method, they found my book quite relevant. Based on their inputs, the finer details of meditation methods have been moved to the Appendix in this edition. They also advised me that the book must have author's recommendations regarding the methods. Thus, a chapter on Important Tips for Any Seeker was added.

4. Deepak Khanolkar, who earlier was brand manager at Loksatta and who was the first one to make me realize how to give the book more impact.

5. Dr. Brij Lal Santoshi (Vikasnagar) and Rashmi deedi, who have been kind enough to agree to translate the book into Hindi. Their sharing of their own experiences on this path helped me to restructure the book.

6. Ajay Goyal, Vinod Menon, Shashank and Neeti Jain, Dhananjay & Shivani Balodi, Rajiv Sulekh, Pratibha & Ashok Ratawal, Deepti Gharat, Abhishekh Bhatia, Abhinav for their invaluable feedback on how I could make the book more reader-friendly and free-flowing so that it did not weigh as "heavy as the subject".

7. Anuradha Iyer, Kiran Kurwade and a few other friends with whom I interacted, who taught me that seekers are not only confused about which method to follow, but also about "whether they need a formal method at all". Thus, a new chapter entitled 'Do I Need a Method' was added.

GETTING STARTED

WHY DO PEOPLE SEEK THE SPIRITUAL PATH, BUT NEVER COMMIT THEMSELVES TO IT?

There are several reasons people choose the spiritual path:

1. Personal pain, hurt and suffering

   Any persistent pain, either physical or emotional, can create a sense of hopelessness and dejection in a person. Ill health, physical suffering, the loss of a loved one, non-attainment of objects of desire, intense hurt, or insult are some of the events that drive people to seek solace in spirituality.

2. High stress levels

   With stress and anxiety ruling high in most people's lives, the promise that meditation will reenergize and soothe the nerves is appealing.

3. Curiosity

   The desire to know more about the true nature of existence and the Self. Many people, including those from the realm of science, turn to spirituality for the questions modern science is unable to answer.

4. The desire to be different

   The desire to add another dimension to life that will set a person apart from the rest; something that will make the individual feel different from the masses.

5. Family & Friends

   The religious and spiritual orientation of family and friends can be a factor. A chance meeting with a guru or a spiritually evolved person may also act as a driver.

6. As a means of livelihood

For some, the spiritual path may become a means of livelihood, for example, employees or volunteers in an ashram or a spiritual institution, who may also be practicing and promoting the path.

7. A desire to live a more fulfilling life

A number of people seek this path, not for solutions to specific problems or for nirvana, but rather to help them lead more fulfilling lives by nurturing their inner beings. Some also hope to find a deeper meaning and purpose to their existence through this path.

In today's times, a more common reason for exploring spirituality is to see if it can help relieve us from stress, anxiety, clutter, or even hurt, loneliness, or hollowness. The reason for looking to spirituality for solace is the intrinsic promise that all masters, gurus, and paths provide bliss and redemption from sorrow and suffering. In fact, masters with 'ananda', meaning bliss, as a suffix to their name will give you a clear assurance of this.

Despite the promise of bliss or ananda, a lot of people still choose to keep away from spirituality as it is often associated with complex, mysterious, and mystical forces; forces that are irrational and that do not appeal to a scientific mind. There are so many images and aspects associated with spirituality that my rationality refuses to digest:

Saadhus, Babas, Swamis, Pandits... some of whose ways seem absurd... scores of them bathing on the ghats of Ganges... smoking chillam, ashes applied to their naked bodies... long hair like ropes... eyes without a sparkle of intelligence or awakening...

Not only this, but anything that is mystical, mythical, metaphysical, or abstract easily gets classified under the term 'spirituality':

- Rituals
- Tantra, Mantra
- Astrology, Astronomy, Palmistry, Numerology
- Feng shui, Vaastu, Oracle, Tarot cards
- Ayurveda, Alternative medicine, Panchkarma
- Reiki, Past life therapy, Chakras, Auras

And the list goes on...

As a result, a modern, scientific person, who is intrigued by the realm of spirituality abstains from taking the plunge by concluding that **'spirituality is certainly not my cup of tea.'** Thus, even before exploring any further what spirituality is really all about, **scores of people dump it aside as something not meant for them.**

@ *Spirituality is too esoteric for a common man like me*

I find meditation and sanyas beyond my comprehension. It is too profound for me. I believe in living a normal life in the world that I know. I cannot even be certain of the existence of a world beyond the material one. Hence, all of this is not for me.

@ *I am an educated and rational person and I therefore do not believe in spirituality*

Spirituality is for the gullible man. None of the people who talk about spirituality can offer a scientific explanation for it. Everything has to be taken at face value. Soliciting **'belief'** from an educated and rational person like me is asking for too much.

THE STAGES OF DIFFERENT SEEKERS

The figure below displays some of the typical stages and mind frames at which various types of seekers may be:

Stage	Frame of mind of the seeker

Stage 0: Unaware & Uninterested
→ What is spirituality?

Stage 1: Vaguely aware; may or may not be keen to know more
→ Yes, I have heard about it, but don't really know much.
→ It's not my cup of tea

Stage 2: Interested and has made conscious efforts to learn more
→ Seems interesting; let me check it out through books, lectures, etc.

Stage 3: Outcome of initial study or research in the subject – put off or wants to know more
→ Type A: Sounds too absurd, mystical and complicated for me. ◄─► Type B: I want to know in specific terms how to develop my roadmap to personal fulfilment

Stage 4: Wants to know how to get started
→ Do I need meditation? Why? What about a guru?

Stage 5: Concerned about making choices so as to avoid getting stuck with an unsuitable path
→ How do I select the right meditation method, spiritual path, or guru?

Stage 6: Adopts a path, but not sure if making adequate progress.
→ How do I ensure I am making progress? My experiences are not too tangible.

Stage 7: They seem to tell me that spirituality is the means and the end. Will I get fulfilment from meditation alone?
→ Is spirituality enough or do I need anything else to find fulfillment in life?

Stage 0 people are those who do not understand the word spirituality. They may have vaguely heard about spirituality, but have never bothered to find out what it means.

Stage 1 people are those who vaguely know what it is about. Some may not be keen to learn any more based on their preconceived notions. These are the types discussed towards the end of the previous chapter. There is a second type who does want to know more; they are indicated by having reached Stage 2.

The seekers of **Stage 2** delve deeper into the subject by reading books, listening to sermons, or talking to other friends on the path. The typical queries that a seeker has at this stage are:

- What is spirituality?
- Does spirituality make sense?
- Can it complement my dynamic and rational life?
- Will it really give me peace of mind as promised, or is it a farce?
- Is it really a panacea for anxiety and depression?
- How can I get a quick overview without having to go through bulky scriptures or visiting ashrams?
- Will I have to learn how to meditate? How long will it take? Where do I learn?
- I want to be successful and happy, and that's it. Does spirituality fit into this basic scheme of life?

A number of people (Type A) get disillusioned at this point and walk out at **Stage 3**. The primary reasons are the disconnects that they feel during the initial study and exploration:

- A modern seeker infers from his tryst with the subject that *spirituality is against the material world.*

  The world is an illusion (*mithya*). Sensual gratification is not good. Abstinence is important. All success and achievements are ultimately futile. The goal of life is to attain nirvana. You are baffled. You came to this way to find ways to de-stress and reenergize yourself so that you can take the world on with greater vengeance, energy, passion, and a killer instinct. But here you are being asked to renounce, abstain, overcome, deny, ignore the very important things you wish to conquer and rule over, on which you wished to leave your mark.

- It seems to be driving us towards a *dull, non pleasurable existence.*

  Non-indulgence, non-gratification, abstinence, and conquering desire seem to be fundamental tenets. This concerns us because we wonder what an insipid existence that might be. Those who have gone through a patch where they were feeling low and blue would reckon that in such phases, even sensual gratifications did not seem to provide any great relief. 'The inability to enjoy pleasures' was concomitant with 'feeling low'. "Wouldn't abandoning them make you dull," you wonder. "No, thank you. I am better off with all my vices," you conclude.

- **Spirituality and Religion:** This whole inner-peace spiel is about religious teachings. Religion has taken so many innocent lives across the world. How can I identify myself with such teachings or viewpoints?

- **Scriptures:** Scriptures are outdated. While they may have been important guiding lights in a bygone era, they are perhaps no longer relevant. Nobody can be certain that their content is really the Almighty's own words; they could well be the work of authors with extraordinary conceptual skills, intuition, and insight. Besides, I don't know how and where to start. The Gita talks about abandoning the desire for the fruits of one's labour. Well, if I were not 'results-oriented', I would not have arrived this far in life. I feel lost in this labyrinth.

- Rituals: Dogmas, rituals, superstitions, and servility to godmen - for what? To seek some favours and blessings in return? How weak are we? All of this just puts me off.

They do not like to spend any further time on this as in their own reckoning:

"I want to be successful in life but spirituality suggests renouncing the material world. I am ambitious and driven and I cannot renounce everything that I have worked so hard to achieve. Why should I take sanyas? After all, I have my own dreams to fulfil as well as duties to my family, friends, and society to perform."

Those who do get past all of the above issues are keen to know more in specific terms – how-when-what they should do to progress on the path. In Stage 3, these are demonstrated by Type B people. They typically face the following dilemmas:

Stage 4: Why Meditation?

I hear a lot about meditation these days but will it really help me? Is it worth investing so much time in it? Are there any negative side effects? What is a good, reliable method? I have heard of so many methods – Kriya Yoga, Sahaj Yoga, Hatha Yoga, Transcendental Meditation, Art of Living, Sudarshan Kriya, Japa, Concentration, Kundalini, Reiki, Satsang, Naam Sumiran and Vipassana. Which should I choose, and how? Is there an evaluation method? Where do I go to seek expert advice? How do I ensure that I do not choose the wrong system for me? Can a wrong choice adversely affect my mind?

Stage 5: Which path?

- "None of them seem convincing enough".
- Most spiritual people I have met appear "abnormal"
- Most people who seek spirituality seem to be on a different plane of existence. It is so difficult to relate to them. Many of them speak of things that make little sense to me. While some insist on rituals and prayers, others are full of superstitions and inflexible mindsets. I have also seen a few who have been practicing meditation, mantra, and yoga for a long time, but haven't evolved spiritually. They are still irritable and often irrational. Some have even lost their sanity and their families have suffered.
- Many godmen are frauds – even criminals. I constantly hear of such men allegedly being associated with exploitation, sexual

indulgence, underworld activities, drugs, and the like. Many even enjoy political patronage. So what is the guarantee that the individual I choose will not eventually turn out to be a fraud? Isn't it best to just keep away from them?

- I can't bow to a human being who claims to be God
- Many of these men eventually turn out to be nothing more than self-proclaimed masters. They may not be enlightened at all, but rather good orators who have researched and studied the subject. Yet we see hordes of people falling at their feet. I just can't bring myself to eulogize them.
- I find it impossible to believe that a human being can be God or a demigod. The fact that thousands of people follow a particular man does not prove the latter's spiritual evolution or greatness. Even politicians and celebrities have huge fan followings but that does not make them divine. I feel most of these men are self-proclaimed masters. After all, God can't be so blatant as to admit and publicly accept that he is God. The servility with which people desperately try see, touch and get the blessings of the holy man puts me off.

Stage 6: Am I progressing?

If they do start out on a specific path under a master or mentor, there is a fair probability of quitting halfway through, as the experience did not meet their expectations: "I do not seem to be benefiting or making progress. Is it really worth the effort and time? Am I practicing it the right way?"

If they do try out an alternative path (or method or meditation technique) and do not receive much satisfaction by it either, they might quit spirituality for good. "All paths are the same. None can really help in transformation. I am okay without any of these".

Stage 7: What else should I do?

They tell me that the spiritual path is both the means and the end. The fact that I am actively pursuing it makes me eligible to leave aside everything else and focus on this as the primary goal of life.

The inability to get satisfactory answers causes seekers to drop out at each stage. It is like a multi-stage filtration process where only a few make it to the each subsequent stage due to:

- Non-resolution of doubts, concerns
- Not finding the motivation to learn a technique or follow a system or a guru.
- Finding a technique but not being motivated to continue because
    - They are not having any tangible or good experiences
    - They are experiencing negative emotions or having a negative experience

The aim of this book is to arrest the high drop-out rate of genuine seekers who quit because they did not find convincing answers to their doubts or concerns along each stage of the path. It attempts to do this by:

- Developing a theoretical framework, which a rational-questioning-doubting intellect can fathom. This is relevant for people who develop an inertia and aversion to taking any further steps to pursue spirituality because of intellectual roadblocks and unanswered queries.
- Introducing some of the popular techniques in their pristine form ("Official Description"). A non-prejudicial analysis of each technique has been included based on interactions with practitioners.
- Suggesting objective methods and tools, both qualitative and quantitative, that can help the reader select the spiritual path or meditation technique that is most appropriate for him or her.
- Developing realistic expectations so that if miracles or blissful experiences do not occur within weeks of starting meditation, this does not become a reason to quit the method or spiritual path.
- Being prepared for the definite trials and tribulations that will occur along the way – because 'ananda' does not come free. It helps to be prepared to tread the razor's edge.

- Knowing how to measure and evaluate progress. This can prevent the seeker from both remaining stuck with an unsuitable path or quitting prematurely.

By attempting to do the above, this book aims to address the queries and concerns of people like these so that there might be a higher conversion rate from the stage of 'casual interest' to 'dedicated practice'. This, in turn, would help save and nurture the positive energies that seek to know the Truth and the Self.

What purpose would the above serve? Would it be worth the time and effort being spent by busy people who are always under pressure to excel in their professional and personal lives?

The book might help steer efforts and pursuits in such a manner that disillusionment and drop-out rates are reduced, thereby helping a greater proportion of seekers reach awakening. With people from all walks of life, such as students, corporate managers, professionals, CEOs, industrialists, the rich and famous, stars, and celebrities becoming intrigued by this realm, generic advice on "what" is no longer enough. This creed may not be willing to take in dosages of gyan with heads nodding in reverence. They would like to question, debate, dissect, and challenge and would want specific answers on the how-what-when-where, and how much. They will not take a 'leap of faith' or 'leave everything to the master' – at least not a delicate thing like their mind. They would like to know the *process, time-lines, input to output ratio*. But can they dare ask such questions? Will such blasphemy be tolerated? Should they therefore necessarily cede their rationality in order to get initiated and endowed with the secret 'mantra' – their vehicle for spiritual transformation?

Is there hope for those who are seeking fulfilment through spirituality in this world? For those who would like to live in and enjoy this world rather than actively seek out nirvana? Those who would like to associate with the divine, but not by forsaking their aspirations and dreams; rather seeking divine help to make a mark on this planet, in this very life, in this very human form?

Is it that those who are coming with such selfish, superficial objectives will never make it or gain any spiritual evolution? Are the paths of the monk and the materialist mutually exclusive?

If my main motive is not moksha, am I barking up the wrong tree by turning to spirituality? Will a person like me have to tread a sub-optimal, sub-standard, 'kindergarten-level; path?

The good news, which this book will try to argue, is that whether seekers are just trying to reenergize and de-stress in order to take the world on more effectively, or are seeking redemption from the cycle of rebirth, they can find fulfilment of these divergent goals on this path. But there are conditions, for example, following all the precepts of the path exactly as advised.

Even better news is that most of the popular paths today do take into account lifestyles, work pressures, social obligations, ambitions, aspirations, and the need for continuing intellectual stimulation of seekers. Hence, without getting overwhelmed with the baggage or negative images that a seeker may have gathered based on reading, talking, listening, or observing this realm, he should resolve to give it another chance by focusing on only ***one critical aspect of spirituality, which is self-development and personal fulfilment.*** The reader is advised to keep aside, for the time being, the absurd and indigestible theories, images, and impressions that he may have about this subject. He can rest reassured that he will not have to forsake either his rationality or his material aspirations and dreams in order to effectively pursue this path.

MAKING THE INTELLECT AN AID, NOT A BOTTLENECK

This book, being targeted at rational, ambitious, and educated people, will dwell a lot on conceptual clarity about the subject. The intellect may still not be satisfied until it gets to see evidence, proof, and research findings. It will want to know how and why it should accept any aspects of a spiritual journey, whether it be:

- The rejuvenating and de-stressing benefits of meditation
- The existence of a pure consciousness, i.e. the realm of the Absolute and the Divine
- The Law of Karma, or any others

But what they can usually expect for an answer is: "All of these things were beyond the realm of intellect. They transcended it. Therefore, one has to rely on belief first until one evolves and experiences the truth himself. They cannot be known without becoming. To become, you have to tread the path. But you need someone to show you the path. If you do not want to tread the path and become, then you will never know. And no one can prove to you conclusively that the path will lead you to the goal."

Hence, it boils down to trust and faith. They will tell you to keep your mind and intellect outside, just as you had removed your slippers before entering the room where the master was teaching. You cannot fathom it through the mind. It is a bottleneck. You have to transcend the mind. You have to go beyond it. Asking too many questions or too direct questions like "how do I know for sure that the master was enlightened" will be seen as sacrilege.

While this might, in fact, be true, a seeker should be advised to keep his intellect handy with him and not do things that go against it. There is a difference between something being irrational and something that cannot be explained with all the rigours of rationality. Keeping our judgment, discerning power, discretion, and questioning and doubting mind at each stage of the journey are important. There is no need to submit or surrender it. However, we must not allow the non-resolution of doubts at a given stage of our journey to become a bottleneck that prevents us to graduate to the next stage. Doubts can be parked, not surrendered; the quest of the intellect can be put on hold, not vanquished. As we start out on the path, give it adequate time, follow all the mandates, keep your eyes-ears-intellect open, give yourselves a chance to experience it firsthand – the answers will come. Then, proofs will no longer matter.

This book may make you experience the Truth. That requires time, patience, and practice. But it will help encourage the seeker to keep moving to subsequent stages of the journey by clarifying as many doubts as possible, purely at the level of the intellect/rationale, and providing a convincing indication that, over time, the answers to even the most residual doubts will be found.

Thus, before we start out on this journey, adopting this perspective can help keep impatience at bay.

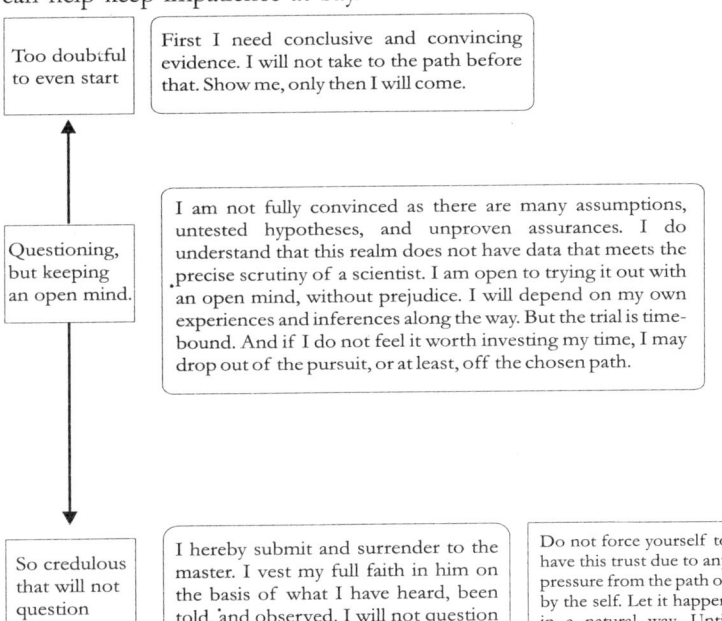

Too doubtful to even start

First I need conclusive and convincing evidence. I will not take to the path before that. Show me, only then I will come.

Questioning, but keeping an open mind.

I am not fully convinced as there are many assumptions, untested hypotheses, and unproven assurances. I do understand that this realm does not have data that meets the precise scrutiny of a scientist. I am open to trying it out with an open mind, without prejudice. I will depend on my own experiences and inferences along the way. But the trial is time-bound. And if I do not feel it worth investing my time, I may drop out of the pursuit, or at least, off the chosen path.

So credulous that will not question

I hereby submit and surrender to the master. I vest my full faith in him on the basis of what I have heard, been told, and observed. I will not question or doubt, no matter what.

Do not force yourself to have this trust due to any pressure from the path or by the self. Let it happen in a natural way. Until then, follow the path while parking doubts for future resolution.

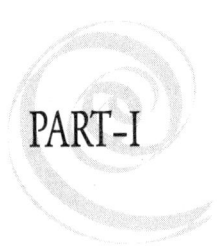

PART-I   CONCEPTUAL FRAMEWORK

(Basic fundamentals for any seeker)

As discussed earlier, the first and foremost doubts that a seeker who decides to sincerely pursue this path are:

1. Do I need a formal method or path to progress effectively?

2. Does it also mean having a master or guru?

3. Will I have to surrender to the guru?

4. Most of the godmen seem to be lecturing on the importance of spirituality in our lives and thereby motivating seekers to follow their path. Is this the right way?

5. What is meditation? Is it common for all? i.e. Is there one generic type like yoga, or does each guru have his own way? How do I choose the right one?

6. Is meditation necessary? Is it sufficient?

The chapters that follow take up these fundamental doubts and concerns.

DO I NEED A MEDITATION TECHNIQUE OR A FORMAL METHOD TO PROGRESS ON THE SPIRITUAL PATH?

"The concept of spirituality in the west is quite different from what it is in India. In the latter, they feel that in order to qualify as being spiritual, one must have a guru or master and must practice some technique," she said and then continued explaining her own view on the subject "However, my own belief and experience is different. I can be in meditation when listening to music, while reading, while sitting by the seaside, or when deeply involved in my work. I do not need to sit down separately to focus on it. It sounds so unnatural and pretentious."

"True, but will you be able to consistently experience this trance, day after day. I mean, will it not be too sporadic and uncontrolled," I offered.

"How does it matter? Will I get to that state when seated in that posture, day after day? That it is controlled and well-managed is more of a placebo. Because you feel you are doing something concrete. Whereas I can experience that state for maybe even a longer duration than what I would in that seated posture. Because the trigger or the stimulus for that state may come at any time."

Her logic was formidable. How does one compare and measure whether the feeling of peace-relaxation-poise while we are doing some of the daily activities we love is closer to 'pure consciousness' than what one experiences while practicing the technique. Which one is accurate or closer? How does one know? With regards to the latter approach being more controlled managed, regular and tracked, the argument is still not invincible. Because one could

experience that day after day and perhaps for longer times if one
allocates sufficient time in the course of a day to things that trigger
that feeling?

There is no foolproof argument that practicing the former
technique is better. But then, are the two approaches mutually
exclusive? Why could we not pursue our professions, passions, and
good acts while adding on a formal method that accelerates
spiritual growth?

"But are we hung up on a formal system? That, precisely, is my
point – why should I do one at all?" she retorted. "Why are we
slaves to this mindset that we must do something tangible and
concrete like the gym routine to remove our guilt."

"Why was she so against a formal system?" I wondered. "Had she
suffered from any bad experiences while pursuing this path?"

Like her, a number of seekers wonder if they need a formal
method at all. They are unable to digest why individuals cannot
evolve through their:

• Work, profession, fulfilment of duties

• Passions, dreams, hobbies, DNA; their calling

• Care for their family

• Good acts, community service

• Interaction with like-minded people

• Prayers

• Reading, listening to sermons

They are unable to accept why they need a formal method like
meditation that asks them to sit in a particular posture for a certain
time every day.

"I do not think one really needs to sit down in a particular posture
and practice a particular methodology in order to experience the
meditative state. I am in such a state when absorbed in my work,
when listening to music, when I feel I have done something
worthy. It is just a way of life. Why should I follow an organized

sect or path with all its tenets and conditions? I would like to be free and experience it naturally, as I tread along the course of my life."

The contention cannot be argued against. Yes, we do experience such meditative states during the course of our work or while we unwind, and it is not only a meditation technique that can provide this experience of pure consciousness. In fact, when an object of desire that we have been anxiously longing for is granted to us, we experience pure and unbounded joy. This state is quite close to what one may experience in samadhi. In fact, even in physical union with a partner whom one loves, in trysts with the deeply loved one with whom one might have been separated, in doing good for the poor and needy, one may experience this state. If so, why, then, get into any organized form of meditation or path, or surrender my freedom to any master?

Besides the realization that we can progress on a spiritual path without a formal method, the aversion to a meditation technique may be because of the following factors:

- Too many techniques, gurus, or masters, leading to confusion as to whom to trust. Seekers are unsure if they will end up selecting the right method. Hence they feel like abstaining from it completely rather than risking a wrong choice.
- Assumed inseparability of
  - Master or guru to whom one needs to surrender and under whom one needs to seek refuge, and
  - Meditation Technique or Path
- Many seekers believe in their particular God and cannot think of bringing another entity into their hearts and souls under whom to seek refuge. It would almost be like distrusting their own almighty God, whom they have trusted all along.
- Non-acceptance of the concept that a human being can be a master or guide.
- No belief in God or in any divine force.

Hence, it is often not the rejection of the very idea of the meditation method that keeps seekers wary and at bay. Rather, it is the baggage of masters and techniques, their inseparability, and the absence of any objective way to select the method and monitor progress that makes them opt out of any formal pursuit.

Pursuing spiritual path without a systematic method can be compared to going to the gym without a set schedule, and using the treadmill or doing other exercises. Its benefits would be evident, in terms of physical fitness, weight loss, cardio training, and the like, but having a personal trainer helps us by:

1. Providing a pre-tested method evolved out of experiences with many individuals

2. Checking if we are doing the exercises properly, and suggesting interventions

3. Monitoring our progress

In today's world, where a storehouse of **validated information** is available on the internet, in audio visual aids, self help manuals, books, and CDs, why do we still enrol in structured programs if we are serious about learning something? Having a formal technique can be likened to this:

- It is an aid.
- It is more guided, controlled, organized, systematic and less sporadic.
- We can know it was effective. Better cause-effect inferences can be drawn as to what was helping us and what was not.
- The chances of success are more as one can rely on the experiences of others who have tread the path before. We can learn useful Dos and Don'ts.
- It helps to connect with other seekers along the path, with whom one can talk, discuss, share dilemmas, and exchange views.

The inherent risks associated with getting stuck with a wrong method or guru are no justifications for keeping away from taking the plunge. Yes, it is risky. But as long as we keep our intellect, rational mind, and judgment in tact, and approach the subject with open eyes, we can mitigate the risks and launch ourselves on a path than can give us lasting fulfilment. In Part II, we will discuss tools to ensure we choose the right method, and in Part III, we will see how and when mid-course corrections can help.

DO I NEED A GURU?

In being able to effectively pursue spirituality, how important and necessary is it to have guru? This is one of the first doubts that strikes seekers. Why does this not get belaboured in other pursuits such as academics, sports, or martial arts, where we naturally accept the need for a guide, teacher, or master? It is perhaps because we look at such teachers, coaches, and guides as facilitators or even mentors who have more knowledge than us about the given field, who are thus equipped to improve our knowledge and skill level. There is no question of blind faith or surrendering one's intellect, will, or doubts at their feet. We are only supposed to pay them the respect that is due to them on account of their having better knowledge or expertise, qualifying them to be our coach. We do not start questioning them from the get go. We listen and pay attention to what they have to say. If they do not live up to the mark, we may not make much hue and cry. We might look for another teacher. But when it comes to accepting someone as our spiritual master, our resistance is very high. This is because surrender to the one showing us the way seems to be the norm in the realm of spiritual development.

"Guru brahma asmi," say the scriptures, meaning that the stature of a guru is similar to that of the creator.

A prayer that any saadhak utters before going into meditation is "Guru Brahma, Guru Vishnu, Gurudev Maheshwara; Guru saakshaat param brahma, tasmaye shree guruey namah", which means that the Guru is the true face of the Supreme and the Almighty Lord, who is the Creator- Preserver-Destroyer; I bow to him in humility and pay my honours at his feet."

The other reason is that a seeker is usually overwhelmed by so many methods and masters, he does not know how to choose the right one. He tries to rationalize that there was no need to follow any formal method or system. He is not comfortable with the idea of becoming a part of any sect or clan of saadhaks (seekers) without having thoroughly examined the credentials of the path. Such an examination is not only difficult, but it is sacrilege to even talk about it. "Trust," the followers will say, "is the starting point. If you do not have it, keep away." Watching thousands of frontrunners on the path, who were obsequiously bowing to the master and yearning for his darshan, eye contact, or touch confounds him. He wonders if he was not better off aspiring to evolve spiritually just by doing his karma, duties, and noble acts for the good of everyone rather than get into this guru-making business.

Therefore, when we ask, 'Do I need a guru?' we are basically asking:

- Will I have to accept a godman as my master?
- Will I have to trust him and vest my full faith in him? Will I have to surrender to him? Will I have to have an emotional bond with him?
- Will I have to treat him virtually as my God?
- Can I not learn meditation without accepting a guru?
- Can I not learn it from a friend or a book or a CD or any website?

If we could look at those who can teach us meditation as mentors and coaches without any mandate to deify or hero-worship them, it may be that much easier. Our propensity to place spiritual teachers on such a high pedestal stems from following beliefs:

- No spiritual growth can happen without the grace of the guru
- To get a guru's grace, I must vest my faith in him. Why? Because any relationship is based on the principle of 'reap as you sow'. So if you continue to doubt, how can grace flow to you. Faith moves mountains. It infuses power into a statue of

the divine. Hence, to solicit the guru's blessings, our feeling towards him are crucial.

- There is no such thing as partial faith. Either you trust fully or you don't. It has to be 100%. Anything short of that means a doubting mind. And that is the sure recipe for failure.

The outcome of the above belief system is that love and surrender to the guru are prerequisites. A rationalist faces a unique dilemma. How can he suddenly equate his God, to whom he has prayed and with whom he has bonded for so long, with someone whose meditation technique he was planning to learn? It's too sudden. It's too demanding. Thus, even though aspiring to seriously explore spirituality in order to de-stress or to find a greater meaning to life, he gets dissuaded as he cannot come to grips with the prospect of becoming a chela (follower).

The way out of this dilemma for such individuals is to:

- Carefully and objectively choose the meditation technique. The tools and factors mentioned in Part II may come in handy.

- Practice the precepts, regimens, and instructions religiously. Even if you are unable to feel a bond with the master, do not worry. Do not let the oozing love and falling at guru's feet by other fellow seekers make you anxious. Your not falling will not disadvantage you as long as the chosen technique is right and suitable for you, and you were practicing it with all sincerity.

- Understand that faith in the master or the creation of a bond with him might happen over a period of time, depending on your individual experiences. Even if it does not happen, you could still evolve and transform with time and practice. You might think of discounting the vast majority who were happy to surrender by telling yourself that they were gullible simpletons and people who were only waiting for something to fill their void. There is no need to condemn them because you did not feel the same way. There is no need for you to rationalize how your lack of feelings was right.

- Most of the popular methods like those mentioned in Part II and in the Appendix have institutionalized the process of teaching meditation by having trained teachers. Many of them have a certification program after which the person is authorized to teach others. So, while many of these teachers may be in awe of the guru and may tend to express this awe, a good training program provides the teacher with standard templates and talking points so that they do not colour the message being given to new seekers with their own individual experiences. In learning from such teachers, one would be saved from the hassle of surrender or veneration to the master. The teacher will be perceived as a coach rather than as someone divine.

Notwithstanding what has been stated above, there are distinct advantages to having a guru:

a. It facilitates the learning of a technique.

b. It also helps in the discussions and resolution of doubts. This can be done directly with the master, if one has access to him, or with other people who have been taught by the master.

c. One becomes a part of a community of people who are following a particular technique. One can relate with others. This can help provide an opportunity to exchange thoughts, ideas, queries, experiences, and thus progress along with one another.

d. Surrendering to a guru helps one dissolve one's ego to a great extent. The very feeling of surrender is a strong aid in the path to spiritual evolution. This works irrespective of whether or not the chosen guru is, in fact, enlightened or capable of showing us the way. This is because the surrender of the ego of a subject (seeker) is of far greater consequence than the qualification of the object (master, guru, or teacher).

e. The guru holds the hands and supports the saadhak as he progresses along this difficult path. He provides the required impetus to walk on *the razor's edge*. The guru guides and monitors the seekers' progress. The seeker has the opportunity to receive the guru's grace. While each one of us has to suffer the consequences of our karma, the flow of the guru's grace (or God's grace through the guru), can make the suffering more bearable. (For those who doubt this and cannot seek such protection or refuge, the other four advantages will still hold).

Just like any other field requiring expert opinion and help, meditation must be learned under the personal instruction and supervision of a qualified person to do the job. Learning it on one's own through self-learning books, or audio or video tapes is not impossible, but the personal instruction of an expert is a definite aid. In meditation, we deal with sensitive issues such as consciousness and mind. The stakes are very high. Doing it accurately is critical, and help from a master, or a teacher who has trained under a master, is helpful, as he can observe and correct or guide us.

The only possible downside of having a guru is that one could get stuck with a master who is incapable of guiding one through the path. To avoid this, or at least to minimize the chances of its occurrence, one should exercise all care and due diligence in adopting the right technique in the first place. And if an individual is not experiencing any positive changes, he can look to change his course, as discussed in Part III.

Let us look at a counter viewpoint of a seeker who was so immersed in his quest that nothing seemed to matter. When one of the fellow seekers asked how he was so sure that the guruji (the master) would lead him to the light, he said, "I have wasted so many lives earlier that it does not really matter if one more gets wasted due to my having chosen a master who cannot lead me to the light. However, what if I am right in my choice of gurus? It is certainly worth the risk." But such a commitment to the path and the guru is not common. A rationalist need not feel guilty or disadvantaged if such a commitment is not forthcoming in the initial stages of the pursuit.

Here is an anecdote on the guru's grace:

Once, on a very cold, winter night, a master and his followers were sitting around a makeshift fireplace. The guru was speaking words of wisdom and the followers were listening intently. All of a sudden, the guru called one of his old and sincere disciples and made him sit beside him while continuing to talk. Suddenly, unprovoked, the guru caught this disciple's hand and thrust it into the burning fire. Both the disciple's and the guru's hands were considerably burnt in the process. Seeing this, the other disciples stood up in shock and started protesting against this gruesome and illogical act. The guru kept quiet and did not react. The disciples, too, cooled down after a while. The guru then began to speak gently: "Would you have rather seen his entire arm being burnt?"

The disciples did not understand. The guru went on to explain: "This disciple was ordained to suffer severe burning of his entire arm due to his past karma. However, he has been allowed to let go with the moderate burning of his hand. No one, including me, could save him from the suffering of this burning. But, by grace, he has been fated to go through it in a much more bearable manner."

It may be noted in the above story that the guru had to partake some of the suffering of the disciple by burning his own hand. This is another dimension of the guru's grace. *Often, in trying to protect or save the followers from suffering, the masters have to suffer themselves.* Jesus Christ went through some of the worst pain and suffering ever known to mankind so that others could live. He took their sins upon himself and suffered for them.

While it can be argued that one could accomplish a similar result by surrendering to the Divine directly, rather than to a guru, it is purely a matter of personal choice. A number of people find it easier to surrender to someone whom they can see, feel, touch, and talk to in human form. Others feel the opposite and find it difficult to surrender to a living person. Nonetheless, even if one is unable to surrender, it is a definite aid to have the guidance of a master, a trained and experienced teacher (i.e. an 'expert') along the path.

SUMMARY:

There are obvious advantages to having a guru, just as there are in learning any new skill or subject:

- It facilitates learning the finer nuances of a technique
- It enhances the ability to share doubts, experiences, and feelings
- The surrender to an expert helps in the dissolution of the ego
- It provides a guide who can hold our hand through the formidable path of spirituality

The disadvantage is the possibility of being stuck with a system that is incapable of completely taking one through the spiritual path. An objective evaluation based on what has been suggested earlier, as well as relying on one's own experiences can be of help in this regard.

Rational, educated seekers are unable to surrender, hero-worship, or deify the master. An understanding that this is a prerequisite, and observing other fellow seekers falling at the feet of the guru, dissuades them from seriously starting out on the pursuit. Their education and experience has taught them to be guarded and not accept anything at face value without adequate experience, reliable references, or credible evidence. The author urges them not to abstain from actively pursuing the spiritual path just because of this mental block. They must maintain their rationality and questioning mind, but remember that it is important to follow the method and all its precepts exactly as taught, *without any innovations or prejudices* in order to reap the full benefits.

THE THREE PILLARS OF THE SPIRITUAL QUEST-MIND, MEDITATION AND KARMA

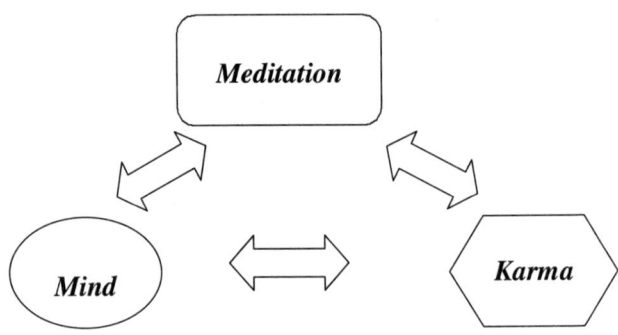

Before progressing further, it is useful to examine the relationship between spirituality and meditation particularly imponderables such as 'Is meditation necessary or sufficient?' Is 'anything else' also required? What is the difference between meditation and yoga? Do I need both yoga and meditation?

Since mind-management is integral to spirituality, we will study the relevant characteristics of the mind that makes it so restless and insatiable. The mind's intimate relationship with spirituality is not only because of the stress that we feel or the clutter of thoughts that we want to control. The mind is the repository of our consciousness, and consciousness is very closely intertwined with each step of the spiritual journey.

One of the goals of the spiritual pursuit is freedom from bondage. Bondage from what? From our accumulated karma and its residue or impression within us. But why should I seek such freedom at all? On the one hand, we are told that it is karma that counts most. On the other hand, we are saying that we need to be free from it. Does freedom mean abandoning the karma? Is this feasible? Is it desirable? One may say that life is good, so who is interested in nirvana? It is not really a matter of the choice of giving up on efforts or pursuits. These are the questions that we will seek to answer. But at this stage, we can only state that freedom from karma is a critical prerequisite of the journey.

Meditation, or any other specific spiritual technique, influences our mind, karma, and our being. The first part of this book will include a framework for studying the subject of spirituality, and will include the bare essentials for a seeker of this path:

- The nature of the mind and consciousness and its relevance to spiritual growth.
- How can the spiritual journey free us from bondage to karma?
- Exactly what is meditation, and is there is only one generic type (like yoga) or are there different methods and techniques?
- Do I really need a formal method? What are the advantages as compared to progressing by simply doing my duties?
- Can one actively pursue material aspirations while being a serious seeker of spiritual growth?

In Part II, we will move on to discuss specific techniques and methods for selecting the most appropriate meditation technique. We will also look at tools that could help us evaluate if we are on the right track.

In Part III, we will look at the challenges that may occur during the course of our learning. It is useful to acknowledge that the spiritual pursuit is not only about ananda or bliss; there are challenges and pitfalls to be wary of. Knowing this helps the individual to persist without getting dissuaded.

In Part IV, we examine how service to mankind is an important element of the spiritual journey. We will also look at practical ways to do something in this sphere rather than this remaining a mere aspiration.

In Part V, we dissect various contradictory and confusing messages that the study of spirituality seems to teach. We will clear myths, misconceptions, and doubts that sometimes become intellectual roadblocks along the way.

Part VI, is one of the most crucial sections of the book which summarises the Dos and Dont's of pursuing the spiritual path.

Details of specific techniques, including their official description, published with permission, are included in the Appendix. This section also contains information on how and where to learn the techniques, what to expect, the author's critique, and where to obtain additional information. It is recommended that readers keen on knowing the details of various popular paths and techniques go through these.

THE ROLE OF MEDITATION IN THE SPIRITUAL QUEST

To most people, meditation is associated with a method used for concentration and driving away thoughts, taking diksha and surrendering to a guru, and committing oneself to a lifestyle of abstinence and self control. As such, many seekers find it rather complex and mystical. They look at it as a ritual whose benefit cannot be objectively explained.

In this context, the following broad principles are being stated. Their reason, rationale, and basis will be discussed at several points in the chapters that follow. However, until then, the reader is requested to take these as *hypotheses or broad principles* that will be supported with arguments later.

- Meditation is a crucial component in making the spiritual quest effective. It can make a sizeable difference to the speed, efficacy, and results of the pursuit by providing method, structure, and an important facilitation tool.

- A right method is a key to spiritual growth. But then, one may wonder, are there any wrong methods or bad methods? There may not be. But some may be better equipped to lead you to the goal than others, just as, among qualified professionals like doctors or lawyers, some may be more capable than others, or some may work better for us than others.

- A study of Patanjali's Yoga Sutras indicates that Meditation is the seventh rung or step in the eight step ladder of Yoga. (*Yoga here is used in the broad sense of the word, which means union with True, Absolute Self and Being*):

  1. Yama (self restraint).

2.   Niyama (religious observation).

3.   Asana (posture).

4.   Pranayama (restraint or regulation of breath).

5.   Pratyahara (abstraction or withdrawal of the senses).

6.   Dharana (concentration).

7.   Dhyana (meditation)

8.   Samadhi (super conscious state or blissful union with the supreme self).

With regard to the six steps preceding meditation, a seeker may wonder when he would be ready to take the seventh steps i.e. Meditation. This is because preceding steps like self restraint, religious observation and withdrawal of senses are difficult and without any definitive time frame in which these could be achieved. Should one therefore focus on practicing these before taking the plunge into meditation? It may thus mean a long wait till we can hope to reach stage 7. The good news is that most systems today teach us to take the plunge into meditation straightaway, without waiting to be adept in the first six steps. They do not look at the earlier steps as prerequisites. Different systems will emphasize one or more of the above 8 steps. Since steps 1, 2 and 5 are difficult, a good way is to start practicing the technique and let your experiences help you to accomplish skills in these three steps over time.

- In terms of what one needs to do in the physical sense, there are three elements:
- Asana (posture)
- Pranayama (regulation of breath)
- Dhyana (meditation)

The other five elements can be a result of the sincere and regular practice of the above, coupled with a commitment to avoid indulgences, not with forced repression, but rather, gentle avoidance.

Many people consider yoga asanas or postures as being 'complete yoga' in itself. Similarly, a number of those who practice any type of pranayama feel that meditation is no longer required. They view pranayama (breath regulation technique) as being complete in itself. This is more common when the chosen pranayama method includes exercises that require keeping the eyes closed, as this is like being in meditation. However, as can be seen above, postures, breath regulation, and meditation are 3 distinct elements of yoga. *(Note: There are some meditation methods that involve the observation of the breath. However, these may not be pranayama by definition, but very much meditation methods that were only deploying breath as a tool to help one transcend to higher/deeper states of consciousness. There are other methods that may apply any other tools, such as a word, a mantra, an image, bodily sensations, or thoughts. There are others that may use an entirely different approach, and Part II of the book deals with these.)*

A better approach would be to take the plunge with the religious practices of steps 3, 4, and 7 concurrently through proper methods and allow other things to happen to your being. ***Avoiding mindsets*** like, "I am not yet ready for meditation. I need to progress somewhat before I start meditating" is a good approach, as we can do something concrete right away to prepare and start treading rather than wait for the opportune time to come.

- Is having a guru an integral part of meditation? Is surrender necessary? What if I am unable to look at any of the gurus as my masters and my mind is full of doubts and questions? Should I force the trust by annulling my questioning mind? Is there hope for me?

Why do we worry so much about this? It is partly because we are genuinely concerned about not getting stuck on a path that is wrong for us. But this may be driven by our own ego that refuses to accept anyone else as a guide. More important than worrying about becoming an underdog or a faithful servant of a master (or man of God), one needs to realize that if meditation plays an important role in spiritual growth, then one has to learn it from somewhere; and it better be from a good and reliable source. Whether or not that will entail submitting oneself at the feet of the guru is not as crucial as finding the right way. However, to put the reader's anxiety on this front to rest, the answer to this question is simply that *there are many methods and spiritual foundations that do not stress upon surrender to or hero-worship of the guru.* While some are against the very idea of a guru or someone to hold your hand and show you the path, they can take solace in the fact that there are teachers who emphasize the regular practice of the method, precisely as taught, irrespective of what feelings you have for the originator of the technique (or the master). The aspect, 'Whether rapid progress is feasible without faith', is discussed in an earlier chapter entitled, "Do I need a guru?"

MIND AND ITS EVER DISSATISFIED NATURE

As mentioned in the earlier chapter, obtaining a quick and basic overview of those aspects of mind, thoughts, and consciousness that are relevant to spirituality is useful. Let us look at some of these in this chapter.

1. THE MIND IS ALWAYS WORKING

It works like a perpetual machine during the course of one's life. Even while sleeping or in the state of dreaming, the mind is working continuously.

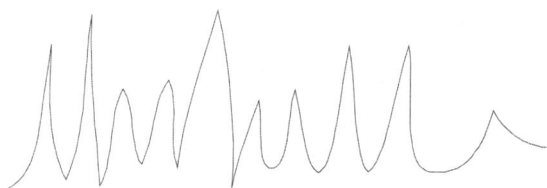

Note: This is an artistic/imaginary illustration of thoughts passing through the mind – not an actual Electroencephalogram (EEG) of the brain.

The mind may be working to a greater or lesser degree at different times, but it is always on the job.

2. THE MIND WORKS IN A CONTINUUM

There are **no breaks** in the mind's functioning. It goes on in a continuum.

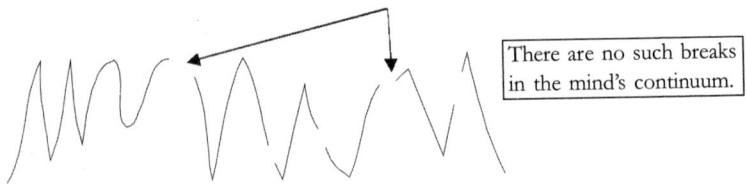

There are no such breaks in the mind's continuum.

3. THE MIND IS ALWAYS JUMPING FROM ONE THOUGHT TO ANOTHER

All of us have experienced how the mind rapidly moves from one subject to another, even when we are engaged in an activity. For example, when listening to someone, innumerable thoughts and ideas constantly cross the mind.

4. THE MIND IS ALWAYS LOOKING FOR MORE

The mind is constantly in search of more. It works harder when tense, anxious, or craving. Achievement relaxes it. It is like a respite. It still works, but in a state of calmness and poise. But this state does not last long. It again ramps up its activity level, driven by a new desire or stress.

Let us take an example.

(i) The mind is working under pressure for an exam.

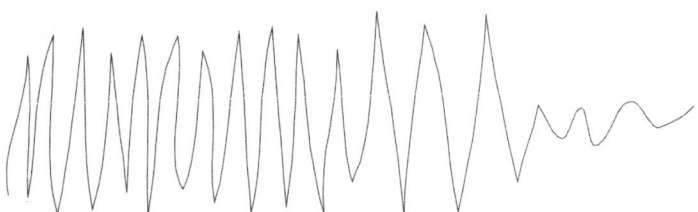

High Level of anxiety/stress
(thought waves are closer)

Note: More compressed waves are representing higher level of stress in the mind (artistic impression only; not actual EEG)

(ii) After the exam, the mind is stressed in anticipation of the results of the exam.

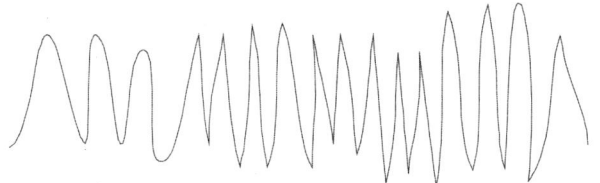

High Level of anxiety/stress
(but slightly lesser than in (i) above)

(iii) If the person obtains excellent marks and a good rank, it results in a sense of fulfilment. The stressful energy is released and the mind is relaxed. Contact with the field of happiness is established.

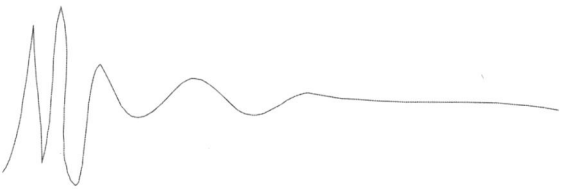

Anxiety   Relaxation/Happiness/Bliss

(iv) The joy lasts for some time, but then the desire to get admitted into a premier college creates anxiety again.

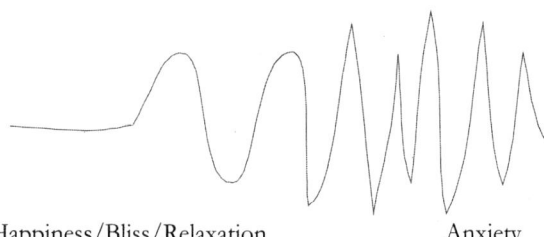

Happiness/Bliss/Relaxation   Anxiety

If the person gains admission to a college of choice, the joy re-appears.

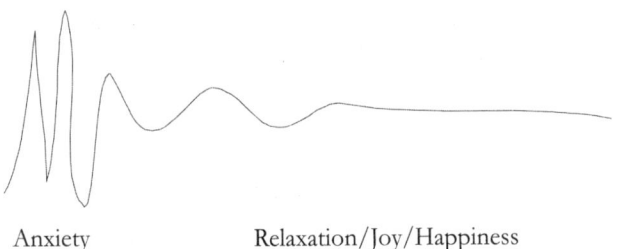

Anxiety   Relaxation/Joy/Happiness

(v) Soon, the person starts worrying about doing well in college, financing the education, and then getting a job. The joy is forgotten.

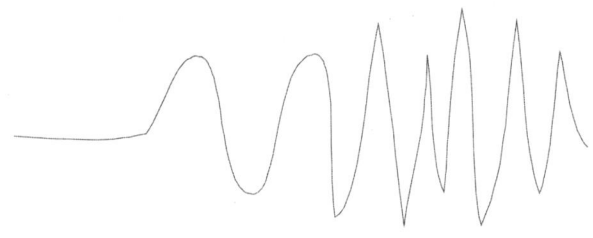

Happiness/Bliss/Relaxation   Worry/Anxiety

And the cycle goes on...

The process can be analyzed as follows:

(a) Whenever one achieves the object of one's desire, the mind is relaxed and one experiences joy.

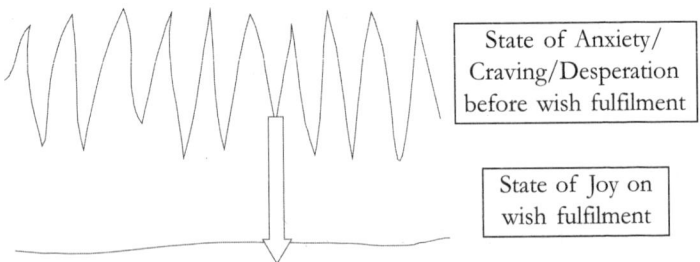

State of Anxiety/Craving/Desperation before wish fulfilment

State of Joy on wish fulfilment

This state of relaxation/happiness/joy is like establishing contact with the field of pure consciousness that is vested deep inside each one of us.

(b) The experience of this joy is short-lived because thoughts and worries soon set in and the mind begins to hanker for more.

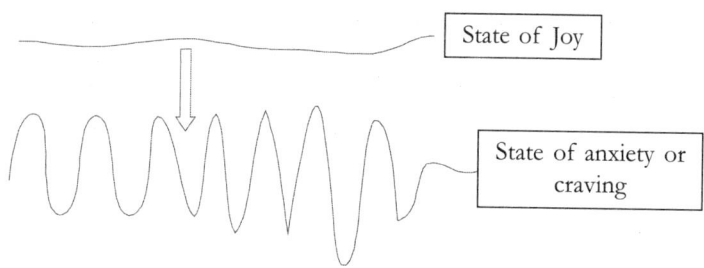

State of Joy

State of anxiety or craving

Contact with the field of pure joy is broken, and the mind is back in its craving/anxious mode.

Hence, a very wealthy man may be just as unhappy with his wealth as a middle-class person is with his limited resources. Both want more. Before earning his money, the rich man's mind may think: "If only I could make this much money, I would be happy forever." However, after achieving the goal, it is no longer capable of sustaining the happiness. Soon, the mind is discontent and wants more.

5. THE MIND CAN BE DIVIDED INTO 3 PARTS

The conscious mind forms only 5-10% of the total potential of the mind. Hence, unlimited potentiality exists in the subconscious and unconscious mind.

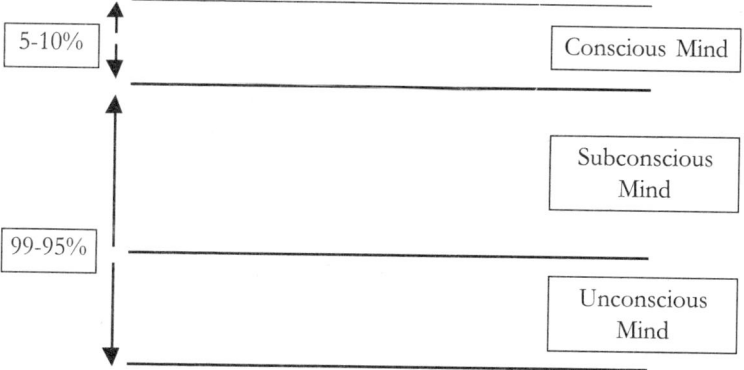

5-10%

Conscious Mind

Subconscious Mind

99-95%

Unconscious Mind

6. THE CONSCIOUS MIND IS FULL OF THOUGHTS, WHICH ARE LIKE BUNDLES OF ENERGY

Thoughts may emerge from the subconscious or unconscious realms of the mind, but they are experienced only when they reach the conscious mind. Thoughts are like little bundles of energy. A measure of the *power* of a thought is its ability to manifest itself into action.

SUMMARY

The mind is always working and moving in the direction of obtaining more happiness. This eternal quest makes the joy of past achievements short-lived. Hence, if a means can be found to calm the mind or to submerge it in a source of joy, then happiness can be a constant reality.

And where would this source be?

- We know that the mind experiences joy, even if for a short duration, when we attain the object of our desire. Therefore it seems like the mind has established contact with *a source of joy within ourselves* on such occasions.

- The fact that the mind is so full of thoughts virtually all the time, and that these thoughts abound in energy, indicates that there is a *source of unending energy somewhere deep within ourselves*.

Both joy and energy are experienced by the mind through the thoughts that emerge from it. If a reverse journey of the thought could be undertaken to its source, then the mind could possibly establish contact with this source of unlimited joy and energy. Meditation, as we shall see in later chapters, is one such tool to establish contact with this source.

6 KARMA AND PRINCIPLES ASSOCIATED WITH IT

Having touched some aspects of our mind and thoughts, let us look at Karma, which finds continuous reference as one pursues spirituality. Even an initial attempt to try and understand the theory of karma exposes us to seemingly contradictory views. At times, we are told that karma is supreme in our existence and our duties. At other times, we learn that getting redemption from past karma and from bondage to future karma is one of the most crucial goals of spirituality. But even while an individual wonders why he should seek redemption from karma if it is supreme, more doubts and questions may emerge:

- Is Karma the only important thing in life?
- Can I get material success and spiritual joy by doing enough Karma?
- What type of Karma is binding?
- Can my good Karma offset my consciously or unconsciously effected bad Karma? If so, can I then do enough good Karma to redeem myself of my bad Karma?
- If the Gita tells us that we have the right to do Karma, but not to determining the results, then who determines the results – fate, luck, or fortune? Who creates fate? If God creates fate, on what basis does he do so?

Here are some postulations on the theory of Karma:

1. It is impossible not to do Karma at any given moment.

    "Truly none can ever rest for even an instant, without

performing action; for all are made to act helplessly indeed, by the Gunas born of Prakriti."

(Bhagwad Gita: Ch. III/5)

– Karma is manifested as action, and even to sustain basic bodily functions such as eating, drinking, and bathing, 'karma' is an essential act. We may try to be as passive as possible, but even then, we cannot avoid 'doing' karma even for a moment.

– We may try to avoid Karma by not undertaking any extra effort or to perform our:

  • Routine jobs

  • Social or work-related duties

  • Things extending beyond normal routine or duty

However, by avoiding that extra effort, we cannot possibly stop doing Karma.

"Do thou perform obligatory action; for action is superior to inaction and even the bare maintenance of body would not be possible if thou art inactive."

(Bhagwad Gita: Ch. III/8)

– One should keep in mind that avoiding Karma is a wasted effort, as even the acts of 'not doing' or 'trying not to do' are forms of Karma.

2. Doing active karma is better than trying not to do karma.

Since we end up doing some Karma anyway, it is better to do 'active' Karma. Trying to avoid active karma sets a bad example for others and can become an impediment in performing our natural duties or *svadharma*.

3. There is no mechanism to offset the bad Karma from the good.

(This is purely the author's hypothesis. It is used later to explain some of life's phenomena, e.g. why bad things happen to good and innocent people. This view may not be endorsed in any scriptures)

Simply put, one has to reap the results of both the good (or positive) Karma and the bad (or negative) Karma. We cannot hope to escape the consequences of bad Karma, by offering our good Karma as a trade-off.

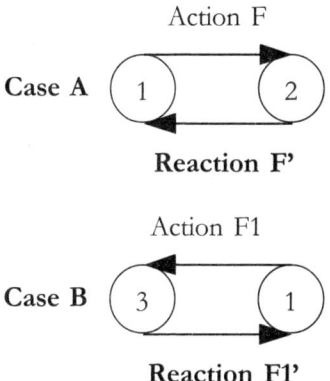

The theory of Karma can be explained by the law of Physics that states that "every action has an equal and opposite reaction." This law postulates that both the forces 'action' and 'reaction', though equal, act on different bodies.

For the sake of simplicity, let us take Body 1 as the doer and Case A and Case B as the performance of good and bad Karma respectively. Body 1 has to suffer both the reactions F' and F1'.

It is a different issue that Body 1 may not move

- If F' and F1' are equal, opposite, and simultaneous, or
- Are too small in comparison to the mass or weight of Body 1

Yet it does not mean that Body 1 does not suffer these reaction forces.

This brings forth two points:

(i) The consequences of negative karma have to be suffered just as the rewards of positive karma can be reaped.

(ii) It makes sense to invest in good or positive Karma

because, even though it may not help offset the negative side of the balance sheet, it will yield positive returns later.

4. Both Positive and Negative Karma are binding

Since we have to suffer or reap the consequences of both positive and negative Karma, they are therefore binding in nature. The vicious cycle thus continues.

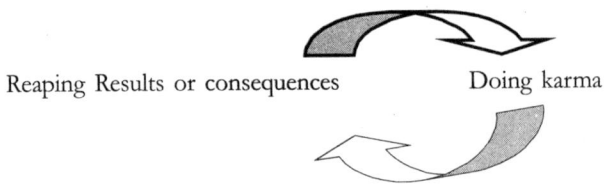

Reaping Results or consequences   Doing karma

Does that mean that while continuing to perform 'active' karma, the more karma we do, the more bound we get? Logically speaking, if all karma is binding, then to free ourselves from karma and its consequences, we should get rid of karma itself.

Hence, to come out of this cycle we need to:

(a) Either stop doing karma (both positive and negative), or

(b) Do karma in a manner that we do not have to suffer its consequences.

The option (a) of discontinuing doing karma is not possible as has been discussed earlier. Option (b) is not possible in the normal manner in which we do karma. Hence, a technique where *we do karma* and *yet do not get bound* by it has to be found.

The scriptures, particularly the Gita, teach us the following:

- For any Karma performed, one has to bear the consequences.
- However, if the karma is done in conjunction with Yoga, then one does not need to face the consequences of the karma.

Hence, the Gita suggests that the way out of not being bound by any karma is by performing karma, while being established in Yoga:

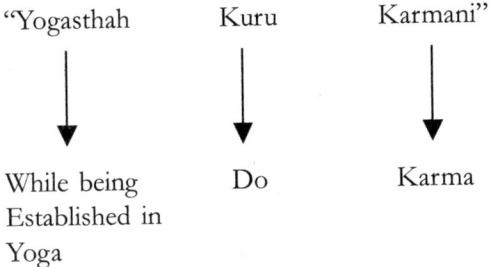

"Being steadfast in Yoga, O Dhananjaya, perform actions..."

(Bhagwad Gita: Ch. II/48)

In the teachings of the Transcendental Meditation technique of Maharishi Mahesh Yogi, reference is often made to this shloka from the Gita.

But what is Yoga? How does one 'get established' in Yoga? We shall examine that in the next chapter.

SUMMARY

The renunciation of karma is neither desirable nor possible. In fact, doing active karma is better than being passive or avoiding karma altogether. The consequences of both negative karma and positive karma have to be borne since our negative karma cannot be offset by our positive karma. While both positive and negative karma are therefore binding, there is a way by which we can be freed from the fruits of our karma, and that is by doing karma while being established in yoga. An explanation of yoga and the skill or secret behind doing karma while not being bound by it will be studied in next chapter.

BASIC FUNDAMENTALS OF WHAT MEDITATION ESSENTIALLY IS

In the last chapter, we saw that the way out of the confusing theory of karma is to continue doing active karma in such a way that one is not bound by its consequences. A possible solution we learned is 'doing' karma while being 'established' in Yoga. Let us try to figure out what yoga is all about.

The literal meaning of the word Yoga is a union with one's true Self or Being. This true self or being is the field of the absolute, free, and pure consciousness that lies deep within ourselves. We had concluded in chapter III that there exists deep within us:

- A source of joy
- A source of unlimited energy

We also saw that since both joy and energy are experienced in the mind, there should be a way through which the mind can establish contact with this source. This source of all energy is known by several names such as:

1. The field of Reality/Absolute/Truth or *Sat*
2. The field of pure consciousness or *Chita*
3. The field of pure joy or *Ananda*
4. The fourth state of consciousness (the other three being sleeping, waking, and dreaming)
5. The Self or Being
6. The Atman or Soul
7. The Field of Divine or Divinity

While this field of absolute consciousness transcends the mind, the *thoughts in the mind* can be used as vehicles to take us to this state of consciousness.

Meditation is a technique that helps us establish contact with *this field of consciousness – with ananda*. The ultimate goal of meditation is to make this field permanent so that even while one is engaged in going about one's daily living, this consciousness permeates through us and through the other 3 states of consciousness – sleeping, waking, and dreaming.

While enlightenment is the ultimate goal, the process of establishing contact recurrently with this source of energy, weakens the binding link to the consequences of one's Karma. It thus sets us on the path of working out our own Karma.

Thus, by enabling us to experience this state of consciousness, regular meditation can help us to:

(a) Work out our karma by establishing contact with this source

(b) Satiate the thirst of the mind for more joy.

The important thing is that this happens "progressively" until one reaches the ultimate state of enlightenment, from where one need not go any further.

How does meditation really work? Is it all about controlling thoughts or concentration?

According to the scriptures and the writings or words of gurus, there are over a hundred known ways to meditate. While the goal of each technique is the same, various techniques use different approaches to reach there.

Meditation techniques can be broadly categorized as follows:

1. Concentration-based techniques

- Essentially, this means concentrating on an object which may be:
    - Any given point.
    - The centre of the forehead.
    - A source of light that is real or imagined.

- Concentrating on a word or a string of words, such as a mantra.
- Concentrating on a particular image.

2. Contemplation-based techniques

- Contemplating thoughts and images of the divine.
- Trying to evoke feelings of love, devotion, and surrender from within oneself.
- The above two techniques may be combined with the continuous chanting of a 'name' or mantra, or perhaps even singing and dancing while reciting the mantra.
- A variation of this method would be to think deeply about our existence and to raise the question "Who am I?" This is similar to one of the approaches for self-knowledge taught by the great saint of Tiruvalluvar, Bhagwan Ramana Maharishi.
- Another variation would be to imagine the death of a dear one or to imagine our own death and how different people that we know would react to it.

3. Breathing- or 'prana'- (life-force) based techniques

For example

- Pranayama.
- Rhythmic breathing or Sudharshan Kriya, such as the technique taught in the Art of Living course of Sri Sri Ravi Shankar ji.

    Note: The Art of Living is much more than a breathing technique. It is included here for simplicity and convenience.

- Kriya Yoga, in conjunction with yogic and physical exercises.

4. Natural Thought-based techniques

- These are neither concentration – nor contemplation-based techniques, nor do they involve breathing exercises. They are based on relaxing the mind in a natural way, without obstructing the natural flow of thoughts, ideas, or emotions.

Transcendental Meditation, taught by Maharishi Mahesh Yogi, can be broadly understood as one such technique that differs from all of the categories described earlier.

5. Self-Observation techniques

- Vipassana is an important technique that can be placed in this subset.

- A variation of this technique is to become a detached observer of one's thoughts without evaluating them. To watch them rise from nowhere and disappear into nowhere in a continuous manner.

6. Others

- Other methods include variations of the methods listed above, or totally different methods.

The above are broad categorizations made solely for the sake of understanding and convenience. Many people who practice these techniques may use more than a single technique in their practice. For example, one can do Pranayama, followed by concentration on a mantra, or practice a self-observation method along with a breathing technique.

Each technique has its own merits and limitations. To recommend any one of them would not be right because all are valid paths to the ultimate destination. However, with so many options available, it may be useful for a beginner to look at the suggested approach to selecting a technique at the end of this chapter.

Part II of this book discusses this subject in more specific terms by suggesting the process, and the qualitative and quantitative parameters for technique selection.

SUMMARY

The trick is to do karma while being established in yoga. Yoga means union or synthesis and refers to the union with one's own Being, i.e. the realm of pure consciousness, which is *Sat* (existence/absolute), *Chita* (consciousness) and *Ananda* (bliss).

A Suggested Approach to Meditation Technique Selection

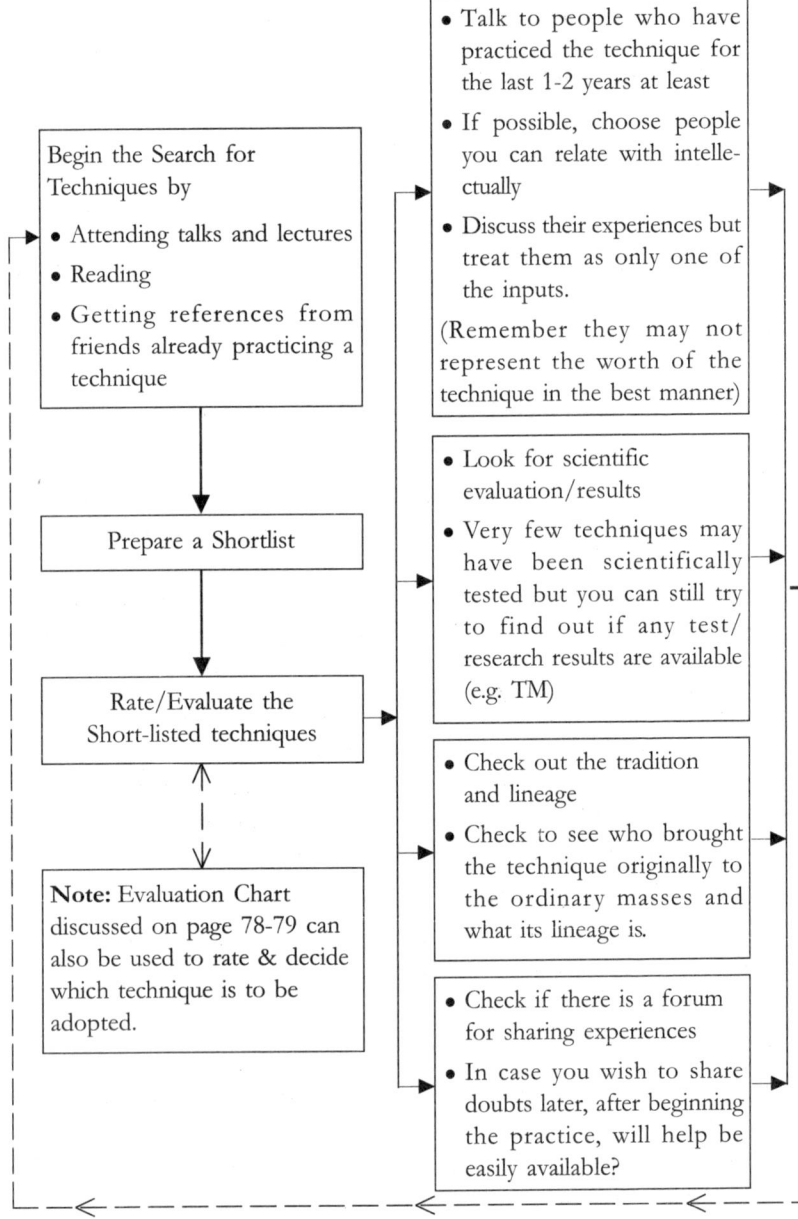

Begin the Search for Techniques by

- Attending talks and lectures
- Reading
- Getting references from friends already practicing a technique

Prepare a Shortlist

Rate/Evaluate the Short-listed techniques

Note: Evaluation Chart discussed on page 78-79 can also be used to rate & decide which technique is to be adopted.

- Talk to people who have practiced the technique for the last 1-2 years at least
- If possible, choose people you can relate with intellectually
- Discuss their experiences but treat them as only one of the inputs.

(Remember they may not represent the worth of the technique in the best manner)

- Look for scientific evaluation/results
- Very few techniques may have been scientifically tested but you can still try to find out if any test/ research results are available (e.g. TM)

- Check out the tradition and lineage
- Check to see who brought the technique originally to the ordinary masses and what its lineage is.

- Check if there is a forum for sharing experiences
- In case you wish to share doubts later, after beginning the practice, will help be easily available?

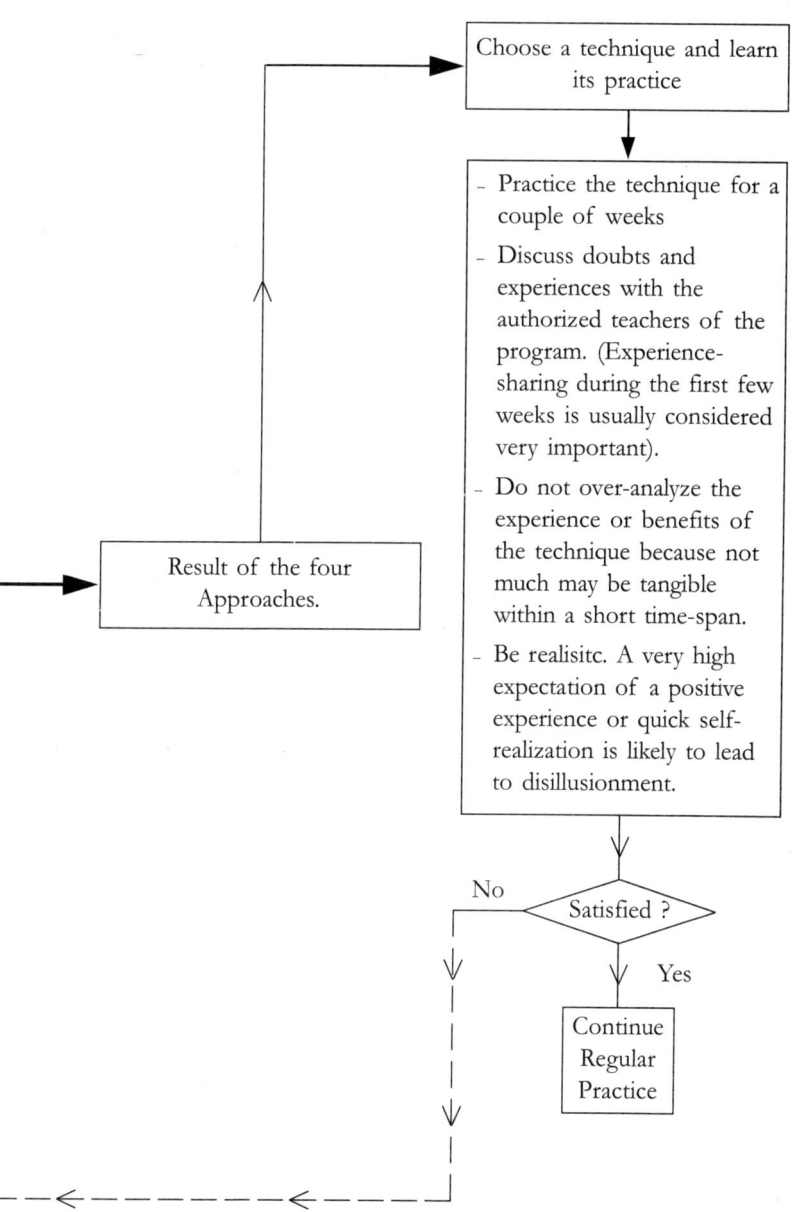

Meditation is a technique that can help us to establish contact with this realm of pure Being or consciousness, and eventually, through recurrent contacts, help us become established in this consciousness.

There are various known techniques of meditation that can be broadly classified as concentration-based, contemplation-based, breathing-based and self-observation-based methods. Each has its own merits. One can decide which to adopt in order to tread on this path of spiritual awakening.

"Renunciation of action, O mighty-armed, is hard to attain to without performance of action; the man of meditation, purified by devotion to action, quickly goes to Brahman."

(Bhagwad Gita: Ch. V/6)

We started this chapter by saying that skill is to do karma while being established in Yoga. We explained that meditation was the way to do this. But then came the obvious doubts – that if yoga is meditation, then what are the asanas that are taught by my yoga teacher. If I do that, can I be freed from having to engage in meditation? I also heard one of the famous gurus teaching pranayama as the yoga for good health and spiritual development. That brings us to doubts as to whether Yoga (with physical postures or asanas), meditation (with eyes closed), and pranayama (breathing-related) have the same effect, and are actually alternatives to choose from, or whether one needs to do more than one of these for better results.

WHAT CAN MEDITATION SPECIFICALLY DO FOR A SEEKER?

Meditation, as we saw in previous chapters, is a technique that can help us establish contact with the field of Absolute Existence.

The practice of meditation helps us experience a fourth state of consciousness, which is both different from and beyond the three normally-experienced states of consciousness (i.e. waking, sleeping, and dreaming).

In this chapter we will try to take a look at the benefits or impacts of meditation in our spiritual journey.

1. Working out karma

The Gita teaches, as we saw in chapter IV, that in order to do karma and not be bound by its fruits or results, it must be performed by being established in Yoga. Meditation helps in such a 'union' or establishment. This, in turn, leads to:

(a) Not being bound by *future* karma

(b) Accelerating the process of working out the *past* karma.

This does not mean that as one begins to meditate, one is immediately freed from the bondage of past and future karma. Rather, **meditation acts as a catalyst** to accelerate the process of working out one's past karma. While one can do this simply by suffering the results of both the positive and negative karma, meditation and the spiritual journey shorten the time frame in which these are to be worked out. One thus experiences the consequences sooner, rather than later, so that the weight of one's past karma is made lighter at a quicker pace.

For subsequent or future karma, the principles are the same. *The rate of addition* of new karma gets decelerated. The *impact, intensity, and extent of karmic bondage* tends to decrease by practicing meditation.

"As blazing fire reduces wood into ashes, so, O Arjuna, does the fire of knowledge reduce all karma to ashes."

(Bhagwad Gita: Ch. IV/37)

2. Achieving Enlightenment:

Enlightenment, which is the ultimate goal of the spiritual journey, can be achieved through meditation in the following way:

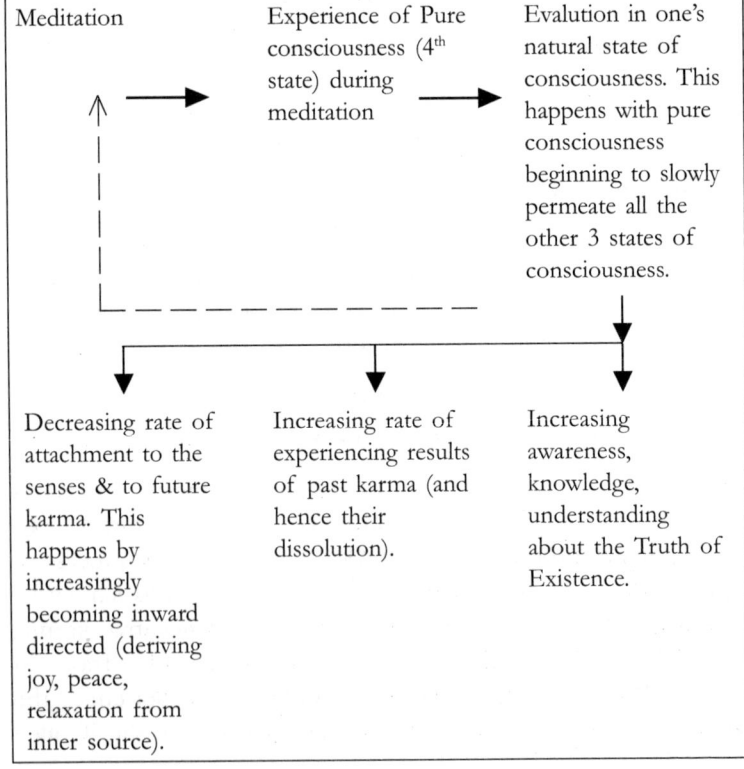

With continuing practice and evolution, one could achieve the ultimate state of enlightenment wherein:

(i) The Pure consciousness remains permanently established and permeates through all the other 3 states of consciousness. In such a state, one experiences the absolute truth of existence, unbound and pure consciousness, and a state of bliss at all times.

(ii) One gets complete redemption from past karma.

(iii) One has complete freedom from subsequent karma.

(iv) One is in complete control of his or her senses, desires, and emotions.

The continuous and permanent experience of pure consciousness may sound discomforting. What will happen to the other three states, we may wonder? How will this fourth state make me look or feel? Will it mean that I will no longer sleep? How will this state of permanence affect my existence and the other three states of waking, sleeping, and dreaming?

The state of **continued experience** of pure consciousness is nothing but achieving enlightenment. In such a case, one does not stop sleeping or dreaming. The pure consciousness **does not replace or substitute** the other three states. It pervades through them so that even when one is sleeping, is awake, or is dreaming, that experience of divinity and ananda persists.

The Gita describes a person who is enlightened as one who is propelled towards doing karma even though he or she may not gain or lose anything by doing or not doing it. Such a person is driven towards doing or performing karma in order to:

• Render a service to society (Lok Kalyan).

• Set an appropriate example for others.

"But the man who is devoted to the Self, and is satisfied with the self, and content in the self alone, has no obligatory duty."

(Bhagvad Gita: Ch. III/17)

"He has no object in this world (to gain) by doing (an action), nor (does he incur any loss) by non-performance of action...nor has he (need of) depending on any being for any object."

(Bhagwad Gita: Ch. III/18)

"Whatever the superior person does, that is followed by others. What he demonstrates by action, that people follow."

(Bhagwad Gita: Ch. III/21)

"I have, O son of Prtha, no duty, nothing that I have not gained; and nothing that I have to gain, in the three worlds; yet I continue in action."

(Bhagwad Gita: Ch. III/22)

3. Saturating the mind with what it hankers after

The mind is always yearning for more and is always dissatisfied, as we saw in Chapter 3. Any achievement or happiness is short-lived.

Thus, we need to take the mind to the state where it can experience pure and unbounded bliss that can satiate its eternal thirst.

As the mind increasingly experiences this state of pure consciousness, it begins to get its diet of happiness and joy from it. As this happens at an increasing rate, the mind's desperate thirst for material objects, events, and sensory gratifications correspondingly decreases. As the mind begins to experience this joy or *ananda* more directly through meditation, a couple of things begin to happen:

- It learns of an erstwhile unknown source
- This joy is more fulfilling and unbound
- It is more permanent by its very nature

Hence, naturally, without effort, repression, forced control of one's senses, or sacrifice of material objects and desires, our restlessness and cravings diminish. We learn to drink and derive joy from a deeper inner source.

"Objects fall away from the abstinent man, leaving the longing behind. But his longing also ceases, who sees the supreme."

(Bhagwad Gita: Ch. II/59)

"With the heart unattached to external objects, he realizes the joy that is in the Self. With the heart devoted to the meditation of Brahman, he attains undecaying happiness."

(Bhagwad Gita: Ch. V/21)

THIS CAN BE EXPLAINED FURTHER

We often hear from spiritual teachers to look inwards for happiness. They say that the world is an illusion (*mithya*) and that happiness is not in the external world but within us. They tell us that sensual pleasures are undesirable. However, we know from our experience that the world is real and that it is capable of giving joy and gratification. On the other hand, many of us may not have experienced any joy from an "inner source".

Unless one actually experiences the joy from within oneself, day after day, it is virtually impossible to not look for fulfilment outside, in the objects of the real world. Our efforts to suppress the craving for the latter may not be too successful and will thus lead us to feelings of guilt. Meditation helps connect us with this internal source of joy and helps us to experience it firsthand. As this experience deepens and becomes more and more perceptible, the gap between happiness from internal and external sources will reduce. There may come a time, if one's search and practice is sincere, when inner bliss outweighs the satisfaction obtained from external objects and indulgences. At such a time, sermons about looking inwards will no longer be required. The mind and the senses will naturally redirect their quest inwards.

SUMMARY

The practice of meditation helps us to establish contact with the fourth state of consciousness, which is also referred to as pure consciousness or one's Absolute Being. This contact helps accelerate the process of "working out" one's past karma.

"Working out" essentially means the dissolution of or being freed from. Meditation acts like a catalyst for working out past karma and also helps reduce the accumulation of new karma.

The mind is always thirsting for more joy and happiness. Meditation can help saturate the mind with pure and unbounded joy by making the mind experience pure consciousness. This helps the mind naturally turn inwards *without forced self-control*, repression, or sacrifice of material dreams.

As the practice of meditation enhances, the experience of pure consciousness becomes deeper and more refined. There may thus come a time when pure consciousness remains permanently established in one's being and permeates through all the other three states of consciousness. This is the state of enlightenment.

9   HOW MUCH TIME SHOULD I SPEND IN MEDITATION?

"With the mind not moving towards anything else, made steadfast by the method of habitual meditation, and dwelling on the Supreme, Resplendent Purusa, O son of Prtha, one goes to him."

(Bhagwad Gita: Ch. VIII/8)

From what has been said in the earlier chapters, it appears that the key to spirituality is Meditation and that, by itself, can lead to enlightenment. But this brings up the following doubts:

1. Meditation – is that it? Is there nothing more that is required?
2. How much meditation is enough? Can I get enlightenment quickly if I meditate continuously for long stretches?
3. How do I check whether I am progressing? How do I measure my rate of progress?

Let us try to address these:

1. Meditation – is that it?

A number of meditation techniques, in fact, teach precisely that. They say that it is enough to simply meditate, and other things will follow naturally. They do not prescribe any specific regimen of diet, exercises, yoga, dress code, or lifestyle. They permit individuals to continue their everyday life and routines as they had been. They profess that whatever requires correction will happen naturally as the mind evolves and transforms appropriately with meditation. Others take an even more aggressive stand and challenge those who meditate to indulge as much in worldly things as they can or wish to, but the prerequisite is to continue the practice of meditation. The urge to indulge, they say, will recede naturally, as one meditates more and more.

Many people ask whether they will have to turn vegetarian, abstain from sex, or avoid late nights in order to begin meditation. This depends entirely upon the chosen technique or system. A number of techniques or paths prescribe a certain code of conduct and discipline, which aids in experiencing higher states of consciousness through meditation. Many others, as stated earlier, leave the seekers free from any such regimen.

However, experience shows that people who maintain a healthy lifestyle benefit more from meditation because *less of the positive energy of meditation is consumed towards trying to correct the imbalances in their system created due to an unhealthy lifestyle.* Thus, a disciplined routine, with a balanced diet, adequate sleep, rest, and exercise is an aid.

2. How much meditation is enough?

Each technique prescribes its own recommended time span for meditation. While no general rule can thus be stated, typically techniques prescribe

- Twice daily (Morning/Evening) practice of 20 to 45 min each,
- Once daily (Early Morning or Evening) practice of 30 or 60 or 90 minutes, or
- Variations of the above

Typically, a serious seeker is expected to allocate 60-90 minutes to meditation in a 24-hour schedule, which might be split into morning and evening sessions. However, the time periods mentioned here are purely indicative and would vary for each technique or chosen path.

A number of techniques suggest the practice of yogic postures, physical and breathing exercises, besides a purely meditative technique. This, according to them, enhances the benefits and efficacy of meditation.

3. If I meditate more than the prescribed limit, can I get enlightened faster?

There are two opinions in this context, Yes and No.

Let us first look at arguments that favour No.

Many people are of the opinion that meditating more than the prescribed limit will not lead to faster enlightenment.

Meditation can be understood as a mechanism for providing deep rest to the mind and body. *"Rest* and *Activity,"* according to Maharishi Mahesh Yogi, "are the steps to progress". This can further be explained by the fact that rest followed by activity, followed again by rest is what leads to spiritual progress. *"Rest"* can be construed as relaxation or de-stressing derived from meditation, while *"Activity"* as carrying on with our daily jobs, duties, and tasks, thus gathering stress in the process.

Some seers have compared meditation to the old process of dyeing a cloth. In order for the colour of the dye to be strong, the first round of colouring is faded away by drying the cloth in the hot sun. After many such rounds of colouring and fading after every dip, the colour becomes strong and permanent. In a similar way, for personal evolution to take place through the experience of meditation, one must return to physical, mental, and emotional activities after meditation. The meditative effect must thus be "faded away" through contact with the material world, activities, and diversions. This must be repeated many times over. Then, the experience of pure consciousness through meditation becomes more permanent.

Now, let us examine the arguments in favour of Yes.

Some people argue that enlightenment can be reached faster with more meditation. This may be true for certain types of paths, but it does not appeal to a person who is living in society and working to earn his living. Practicing meditation all day long or for a sizeable portion of the 24-hour day may not be the most feasible approach. Sixty to 90 minutes per day seems a good enough investment and commitment. One may argue that there are people who are willing to sacrifice anything and everything to progress fast and that they would progress much faster if they meditated constantly. A counter argument is that while a deeper thirst for spiritual salvation would help, merely spending more hours meditating will work only to a limited extent. In doing so, the seeker might reach a saturation point and the law of diminishing returns may start applying to meditation as well. There is also the fear that meditation without commensurate activity can make a person dull.

As far as cutting down the time to reach enlightenment is concerned, we know that any seed needs the required amount of time to germinate. By providing proper nourishment, one can hope that it will germinate at an optimum pace and with greater surety. However, one cannot drastically cut down the time that its nature requires by overdoing resources like water, air, sunlight, or mineral-rich soil.

SUMMARY

Meditation holds the key to one's spiritual development. While a number of techniques specify a certain regimen or code of conduct, a number of techniques just emphasize regular practice and advise us to let the rest happen on its own accord. However, a balanced lifestyle is certainly an aid to spiritual growth.

The key to spiritual progress lies in selecting the right path and then following all its precepts. The rest will follow.

"Whose happiness is within, whose relaxation is within, whose light is within, that Yogi alone, becoming Brahman, gains absolute freedom."

(Bhagwad Gita: Ch. V/24)

# RE-LOOK AT THE KEY CONCEPTS

The spiritual journey is about establishing contact with our true Being, which is the source of all of the creativity, intelligence, energy, and joy that lies within us. The true Being is known by several names, such as pure consciousness, atman, soul, or the field of the Absolute.

But how can contact be established? By finding a technique that can help us experience a state of consciousness that "transcends" or goes beyond the three normally experienced states of consciousness – waking, sleeping, and dreaming. The technique is usually referred to as meditation.

Is the mere contact with this field enough? As one establishes contact with this field of the Absolute, over a period of time, this state of consciousness tends to permeate through the other three state of consciousness. So even while one is sleeping, dreaming, or awake, this field of the Absolute becomes permanently embedded. But this happens at a rather advanced stage of evolution, when one is closer to attaining or has attained enlightenment.

What can one attain by undertaking the spiritual journey? The ultimate stage of the spiritual journey is to attain self-realization or enlightenment. It is a state in which one permanently experiences pure consciousness, and therefore, one is constantly in the state of sat, chit, and ananda, or existence, consciousness, and bliss. This is the field of the Absolute and of permanent bliss. Someone who is established in this state is able to fathom the true reality of existence – from knowing oneself to knowing the entire creation.

However, it is generally believed that to know this state, one has to become one with it. How does one become one with this state? By simply expanding one's consciousness and thus evolving, so that one becomes capable of knowing the reality.

For such a person, there is also complete freedom from his or her past, present, and future karma. Since his mind is saturated with the happiness after which the mind always hankers, his cravings are also completely fulfilled. Such a person thus experiences complete contentment and peace.

But how can one learn this technique that will help establish contact with pure consciousness in the first place? There are several known techniques that can lead one to the spiritual journey. Each technique has its own principles, process, regimen, and merits. One has to choose the technique that best suits oneself. A suggested approach to technique selection is discussed in this book. Having chosen a technique, one should continue its practice without being judgmental too early. Over a period of time, one's experiences and instincts will be one's best guide.

Is learning a technique enough? Learning and practicing the technique as taught is one of the basic ingredients of the spiritual journey. The rest is known to follow naturally. Other aids along the path include reading, introspecting, observing, interacting with others on the path, and listening to talks by masters.

Is the spiritual journey one that ensures progressively higher levels of happiness? The spiritual journey enables progression towards a higher level of happiness. But along the journey, one's past karma need to be worked out before one can deserve that state of bliss. The process of working out one's karma gets accelerated by pursuing the spiritual path. This happens as one progressively becomes free from one's past karma and from attachment to one's future karma. Since this is a big thing to achieve, one must pay a price for it. This can happen in the form of trials, tribulations, and even suffering that may befall a person as he is working out his karma at a fast pace.

The one thing that the spiritual journey ensures is that the suffering, if any, will be bearable, that the grace of divinity will be on one's side, and that one will be ultimately saved.

Is it okay for me to pursue the spiritual path, if I am not interested in enlightenment or going through the suffering, but only wish to enhance my level happiness and fulfilment? A lot of techniques provide deep relaxation and rest, which in turn leads to the release of stresses and negativities embedded in our consciousness. As this negativity is released, one experiences more clarity in the mind, a sense of relaxation and lightness. This feeling enhances with practice. Also, spiritual progress enriches and nourishes all aspects of our lives thus allowing us to live fuller lives, but it may not be feasible to experience only happiness at each milestone along the journey.

As one begins to evolve spiritually, some of the past karma starts to dissolve at a fast pace. Therefore, some kind of pain or suffering may be in store, but it all depends on the stock and type of one's past karma.

Hence it is not necessary that everyone go through some kind of travails. The important thing is not to start with the worry that one will suffer pain or that any extra or undeserved suffering will be inflicted. Whatever comes will be matched with strength and grace and one will progressively feel a greater sense of fulfilment.

- In fact, a large majority of people progress to higher and higher levels of peace, happiness, and gratefulness along the journey. They feel grateful that they took the initiative to get onto this path. The prize, in the form of their changed lives and their new way of thinking, is simply priceless.

So while it is okay to come to this path driven purely by the desire to be happier, the spiritual evolution will inevitably follow as an integral part of the package. Even if a price has to be paid for attempting to reach the ultimate, one should not be afraid and should tread forth fearlessly, guided by divine force and grace.

Is a guru necessary? The guru can be a guide through one's spiritual journey and quest. Gurus are known to have held the seekers hand through the arduous journey, especially as the latter evolved to a higher level of consciousness and went through the trials and tribulations that came along the way.

In any case, one needs to learn a technique in order to progress, and the technique will invariably have been taught by a master. While many techniques suggest "connecting" with the guru as an important element in the progress, others do not require any such connection or any obeisance or surrender. They simply expect that the precepts and the steps of the path are properly followed by seekers.

How do I find a guru? Where do I look for one? Is it necessary? They say you get a guru by the guru's Grace. How does one solicit this grace? Who is the right guru for me?

There is no prescription for finding a guru. It is sometimes believed that grace is an important aid in finding a guru, but obtaining this grace is not within one's control. However, if one's quest is earnest, the doors shall open and one shall find the path to the guru. One wonders, however, whether one should sit and wait until this happens. Instead of waiting for grace or inspiration, one should try to gather information on available techniques, systems, and institutions set up by enlightened masters through friends, references, self-study, attending introductory talks, readings, and by talking to people who are practicing any of the techniques. One should decide on the technique as per one's own criteria and method. Grace may happen at any time before or even after one selects a technique. On the other hand, one may never experience or realize it. In fact, many techniques do not insist on any surrender or servility to the guru or even on any hero-worship.

But is a guru really required? There are many enlightened masters who constantly express gratitude to their guru while dealing with their own followers. There are others who state that they had no specific guru. Many are silent on the subject. The bottom line is that we need to find the most effective way to learn the technique, irrespective of whether or not it requires or results in surrender.

Is it not true that one who has attained enlightenment may have no motivation to act, to do, or to achieve anything? Would that not be a rather dull state of mind?

One who has attained divinity (enlightenment) is in a constant state of bliss. Even while doing no active karma, he is doing everything, and while doing everything, he is doing nothing. Although such a person is completely fulfilled and craves nothing, he or she is still motivated to do karma by principle of lok-kalyan, or service to mankind, and also to set the right example for others to emulate.

Enlightenment is not a dull state of mind. The enlightened one is a giver and he himself shares, his aura, his energy, and his grace with others. Since he is so sated, he feels the need to give and share; and others benefit from his presence.

How do I know for sure that I am making progress? Maybe I am getting nowhere. Is there a yardstick? How can I be sure?

The best guide is one's own experience, intuition, and instinct. Unfortunately, there are no formulae, tests, or quantifiable measurements available to measure spiritual progress. Hence, one has to trust one's inner self for answers. Patience and perseverance are needed, just as they are for any worthwhile mission.

One must try to assess one's progress from time to time, if not quantifiably, then qualitatively, through one's own experiences. It is not desirable to adopt a path based purely on blind belief. However, one must learn to give enough time to any technique or chosen path before expecting results or making a judgment on its efficacy.

IN THIS CONTEXT, THE FOLLOWING MAY BE PERTINENT

On a wall in the room next to **Mother Teresa's** tomb in Kolkata hangs a small, inconspicuous quotation from her that reads:

"We must not attempt to control God's actions. We must not count the stages in the journey he would have us make. We must not desire a clear perception of our advance along the road, nor know precisely where we are on the way to Holiness."

The above quote does not suggest that one should refrain from monitoring one's progress. A periodic review is certainly helpful as discussed in Part III. The lessons that one can possibly draw are that:

- A clear, tangible, quantifiable realization of the progress made may not be feasible, though we can try

- Expecting instant transformation or being in a hurry to know how much we have evolved may not be of much consequence.

CAN SPIRITUALITY, THEN, BE YOUR CUP OF TEA?

In this chapter, we will take another look at some of the reactions to the word spirituality that were discussed in Chapter 1 in light of what has been discussed in the preceding chapters.

1. It is too esoteric for a common man like me.

If we break the elements of spirituality down and look at just two of them – the theory of karma and the process of meditation – the principles are not as complex as they might seem at first. The essence of spirituality is in the actual experience and not merely in the acquisition of mental or intellectual knowledge. Therefore, as one gathers experience by treading the spiritual path, personal evolution ensures that understanding the principles of spirituality becomes an integral part of one's being and this removes all doubt.

2. I am an educated and rational person, therefore I do not believe in all this spiritual chatter.

While scientifically proven evidence of the various spiritual paths may not be available, some of the techniques have proven to be effective and positive on the basis of experimental research data.

Such data or validation may not be available for many techniques, but that does not take away their merit.

One's own experience along the spiritual path is the greatest test of the validity of any technique. Demanding proof of the method before taking the plunge may not be the best way to experience spirituality. As one goes through the experience, the disbelief should disappear by itself and scientific proof should no longer be required. In order to fathom spirituality, technical validation may neither suffice nor be possible. One's own being needs to evolve in order to comprehend and assimilate the elements and the essence of this track.

3. I want to make a success of life but spirituality advocates renouncing worldly pleasures.

We learned, in an earlier chapter, that an important prerequisite to spiritual progress is performing activities while being established in 'yoga' (Chapter II/48 of the Bhagwad Gita). *"Doing activity"* is just as critical as *"doing yoga"*. The theory of karma tells us that even if we want to forsake karma, it is never possible to actually be without it. So the question of renouncing the world does not arise. Several spiritual paths today unequivocally advocate that it is not necessary to renounce one's profession, family, friends, or society in order to develop spiritually. A 'karmayogi' can find the ultimate truth without having to become a 'sanyasi'.

4. Most spiritual people I have met appear abnormal

That depends purely on what kind of people one has had the chance to meet. For every 'abnormal type' of spiritually inclined person, there will be several 'positive types' who lead balanced lives full of strength and passion. Just as students graduating from an institute differ in their mindsets, habits, intellectual potential, and achievements, so, too, do spiritual persons differ from one another. It is difficult to generalize and typify what a 'normal' or 'ideal' spiritual person is like. The kind of person that one is depends on one's values, beliefs, and habits. Spirituality is not a quick-fix solution or mechanism that transforms you the moment you enter its realm. It is a process of slow and gradual evolution.

Therefore, to generalize that spiritual people are abnormal based on one's encounters with a few spiritually inclined people who may appear to be so is not a fair or valid conclusion.

With regards to losing one's mental balance, it can be said that:

- It may not have anything to do with the spiritual journey. Some such individuals may have explored spirituality, but it may not have contributed to the imbalance in any way.

- It can't happen immediately after one takes the plunge into the realm of spirituality. If at all, it would be a slow process of deterioration (assuming, hypothetically, that it could happen). Hence, spirituality cannot be squarely blamed for any semblance of insane behaviour.

If one follows the appropriate approach to selecting a technique and then utilizes the forums available to discuss one's experiences, one can eliminate the possibility of the spiritual path causing mental disturbances.

"In this there is no waste of unfinished attempt, nor is there production of contrary results. Even very little of this dharma protects from great terror."

(Bhagwad Gita: Ch. II/ 40)

With respect to the impression that many spiritual seekers get nowhere, we need to realize that each person charts his or her own unique journey. How far one has actually progressed cannot be objectively measured. It also depends on where the person began his spiritual journey, i.e. what level of spiritual evolution existed prior to his taking the plunge. The second determinant is the extent to which he or she has accurately followed all the tenets of the chosen path. Depending on these factors, different people reach different landmarks or milestones in their spiritual evolution.

The issues of rigidity and rituals associated with spirituality are, again, purely a function of what path one has chosen and what people one has had the chance to meet with. The spiritual path, as such, does not mandate ritual and superstition. In the words of Swami Vivekananda, "Superstition is a great enemy of man. Bigotry is even worse." With regard to idol worship, he says that these may be necessary for the human mind because not everyone can fathom a formless, Supreme Power, especially in the early stages of spiritual development. However, as one progresses along the path of the Divine, these may no longer be necessary.

Hence, it is not right to treat dogmas, rituals, and superstitions as being synonymous with spiritual quest.

5. Many godmen are frauds, sometimes even criminals

Frauds, criminals, and cheats can be found in all walks of life, from the most revered to the most ignoble professions and fraternities. However, that does not make the entire profession or fraternity untrustworthy.

Not everyone may find the right kind of guru, but that holds true for searching for the right expert in any other field. Doing a proper search and evaluation, and searching with an open and rational mind can increase the chances of finding the right guide.

6. I can't bow to a human being who claims to be god

Having a guru has its own merits. A guru can not only be an aid, but also a guide through one's spiritual journey. Whether or not one feels the need from within to surrender to a guru is purely a matter of personal choice. The absence of this feeling may not necessarily be an impediment in one's spiritual journey.

In fact, many masters do not expect this from their seekers. The seekers, driven by their own feelings, attitudes, and beliefs may do so on their own. Most masters say that the only way to please them and to connect with them is through the regular practice of the technique taught by them.

PART-II

SELECTING A TECHNIQUE

(An overview of some of the meditation techniques and spiritual paths, and suggested methodologies for selecting a suitable one)

WHY ALL THE FUSS ABOUT THE 'RIGHT METHOD' WHEN ALL METHODS ARE BOUND TO LEAD US TO THE SAME GOAL?

"All paths lead us to the goal, to the almighty," they say. So it does not matter which particular path you take as long as your heart and intention is pure. Even in the Gita, the Lord says that any steps taken or efforts made towards Me are never a waste. Even if you do not reach the goal or destination in this lifetime, you will have a good head start in your next life.

The above is likely to lead us to believe that the method or path we take is not so critical. But if we look at the high dropout rate in terms of ratio of people who learn a technique and who continue to practice it, we will see that people usually drop out on account of the following factors:

- Choosing a method that was not best suited to their needs
- Entering into a method with the wrong expectations, e.g. quick, tangible progress; that there would be an immediate end to any future suffering; that spirituality is the panacea.
- Not getting support in terms of the satisfactory resolution of doubts and queries when one was going through a period of inner turmoil after beginning the practice.

There are so many methods, teachers, paths, and systems that masters are mushrooming, driven by the demand for 'mental peace'. There are degrees, qualifications, requirements, or regulatory frameworks required to become a proponent of an enlightenment or stress-release method. There are no third party audits, quality or process checks, or expert opinions. No magazines that publish a comparative features, or benefits analyses. Why? Because that would be sacrilege. You are questioning God (and godmen!)? So one has to rely on gut, intuition, or limited information to help us distinguish between right or wrong, good or bad. Can we treat meditation as just another "add-on" into our lives, so that even if it does not work, at least we gave it a try? We can do this if we do not have much awareness of what meditation can do. But if the realm of meditation involves the mind and psyche, which are extremely complex and sensitive, can we, then, leave it to chance? The stakes of going wrong are too high. What are the chances of selecting an unsuitable method, anyway? If we are going to a reputed hospital or law firm that hires qualified people with merit, experience, and a formidable success rate, the chances of going wrong are smaller. In not-so-tightly-regulated fields such as naturopathy and alternative medicine, there are so many self-proclaimed physicians. The chances of finding the right cure or expert are even smaller. But many of us are casual in that too. We add on such treatments to existing ones, especially if the allopath has no cure for it. We do it on a trial basis because there are no side effects or down-sides. However, in mediation methods, with so much demand on our mind already, not getting to the method right the first time is precarious. Either we will loose faith in spirituality and quit the pursuit for good, or we may become even more distressed.

Hence, choosing the right technique and then ensuring we practice it in the right way, with regular follow ups with a master or his expert teachers is crucial.

In this part we will look at some of the popular methods and their key features. We will then move on to suggesting tools that can help us select the method that is most suitable for us.

OVERVIEW OF SOME MEDITATION PATHS & TECHNIQUES

Typical Elements of Various Techniques or Paths

Broadly, the elements of the various techniques can be classified as follows:

• Physical exercises, yogic postures	• To tone up body • To set mind-body equanimity • To remain physically fit : which in turn results in extraction of better results from meditation, japa, yoga, pranayam
• Self control (lifestyle, diet, self-restraint and reducing indulgences)	• To conserve energy • To become more conducive to experiencing higher states of consciousness
• Mantra Jaap (recitation of key word, mantra or phrase)	• Simulates feelings of bhakti, self-discipline, pursuit of righteous path, even surrender.
• Breathing Exercises	• Directly affect physiology • Rejuvenate body cells
• Meditation	• Helps to de-stress. • To go into the deeper states of consciousness
• Seva	• Builds compassion. Instils feelings of warmth and bonding in the heart. • Makes one humble. Lessens false ego. • Can even help in buidling self esteem if one is able to contribute something significant to others.
• Guru's Grace	• Resilience - strength to continue on the path despite doubts and difficulties. • Provides a buffer against the blows of suffering • Moral support and reassurance along the path

In this chapter, we take a look at some meditation techniques and systems that are popular in the world today. The techniques included in this section are based on:

- The author's own experiences with these techniques
- Interactions with people who have been practicing these techniques. The persons chosen were those who
  - Were successful in their professional and personal lives.
  - Were ambitious and rational on the one hand, while warm and compassionate on the other.
  - Had spent a sizeable amount of time and effort in selecting a technique, practicing it, and persisting with it, despite the challenges along the way.
  - Had zeroed in on the technique and were convinced that it could lead them to their goal.

The list is in no way comprehensive. There are obviously many more techniques and methods not covered here that are considered highly effective. Thus, while searching for a technique that is most suitable for oneself, the reader is encouraged to look beyond the list of techniques covered in this chapter.

While making a final selection, the reader could take cues from the approach and illustrative examples included in the next chapter. The shortlist could consist of techniques covered in this chapter, as well as any other methods. The tools and rigour used to select the desired technique should be applied to all short-listed techniques.

Disclaimer

The descriptions in this chapter are based on:

- *Information available from published literature and websites.*
- *The experiences of a few people who have practiced the technique.*[1]
- *The author's own views and interpretations. Most masters insist on the purity of their teaching and the dissemination of their message solely through trained teachers and through the use of precise words approved by*

them. Hence, for accurate information on the techniques, it is recommended that the reader visit the official website of the technique, read the official publications, or get in touch with the organization's offices.

- *Verbatim statements from the Official Description section of the particular path's website or publications, included with permission from the respective organizations.*

A brief introduction to the techniques follows:

I. TRANSCENDENTAL MEDITATION (TAUGHT BY HIS HOLINESS MAHARISHI MAHESH YOGI)

a. Description of technique:

- It is a simple, natural, spontaneous, and effortless technique.
- It is based on thought, whereby one tries to reach the source of the thought by naturally progressing towards the experience of the deeper states of consciousness. Ultimately, one experiences pure consciousness.
- A simple mantra, which is unique to each individual, is given to the student by the teacher. The mantra has to be kept a secret. By itself, the mantra may not have any religious meaning or connotation attached to it. It is simply a tool that, when properly deployed with all other instructions of the Transcendental Meditation Technique, helps one experience deeper states of consciousness.
- It is not based on contemplation, concentration, breath control, or breathing techniques.

II. ART OF LIVING (TAUGHT BY SRI SRI RAVI SHANKAR):

a. Description of technique:

- This is a simple technique based on one's breath, or life-force, or life-energy. Many people refer to it as 'rhythmic breathing'.

  (At times, the phrase, 'rhythmic breathing' raises concern in the minds of some people who would prefer to stay with their normal, natural breathing pattern rather than impose a prescribed rhythm on it. **In fact, the AOL technique does not require any conscious regulation of the breath or modification of its rhythm.**)

- There are various courses offered for various age groups, as well as for further progression on the path. Some of these are:

    i. The Basic Course (which has different programs for children, teenagers, and adults).

    ii. The Advanced course

    iii. The Sahaj Samadhi Meditation

    iv. Various courses to become an authorized or trained teacher.

The Basic Course consists of:

- A set of basic exercises

- The main AOL technique, consisting of various breathing techniques, culminating in the "Sudarshan Kriya"

(b) The Official Description

Source: www.artofliving.org

The AOL Course

Everyone wants more happiness, love, and peace of mind. What keeps us from increasing these qualities in our lives is stress. Often we don't realize the degree to which stress clouds our natural enthusiasm, saps our energy, interferes in our relationships, and affects our health.

The Art of Living Course releases layers of stress without effort, thus helping to unleash the energy and joy that are our birthright.

Ancient and Modern

The course integrates modern methods with an ancient spiritual heritage to bring you in touch with the silent core of your Being.

You will discover the hidden laws that govern the mind, as well as skills for dealing effectively with negative emotions. In addition, you will enjoy the ancient practices of yoga, meditation and rhythmic breathing, as these are combined in new ways to nourish all levels of the body, mind, and spirit.

The Art of Living Course offers practical wisdom on how to live gracefully in a stressful world, and also the deep spiritual experience necessary to put that knowledge into action.

Sudarshan Kriya

Sudarshan Kriya is one of the main techniques taught in the Basic Art of Living Course. This powerful practice has a profound effect on the mind, body, and spirit. Attention to the rhythm of the breath and its effect on the health is part of the ancient knowledge of the art of living. Developed by Sri Sri Ravi Shankar, founder of the Art of Living, the Sudarshan Kriya® is a special breathing technique that triggers the mind and body to release stress.

The key to understanding the enormous health implications of the Sudarshan Kriya and related breathing practices lies in understanding the relationship between the breath, the mind, the emotions, and the body. The breath is the key link between the mind, body, and emotions. By learning a special pattern of breathing, one can rid the system of accumulated stress and toxins as well as release negative emotions and rejuvenate the body.

"We need to do a cleansing process within ourselves. In sleep, we get rid of fatigue but the deeper stresses remain in our body. Sudarshan Kriya cleanses the system from the inside. The breath has a great secret to offer."

— Sri Sri Ravi Shankar

Recent medical studies have confirmed the beneficial effects of the Sudarshan Kriya and its related practices, taught in the Art of Living courses.

— Sahaj Samadhi Meditation

We gain so much from our efforts in life and yet there are some things that effort cannot accomplish. Meditating is the delicate art of doing nothing. Of letting go of everything and being who you are. It provides the mind with a much-needed, deep rest.

Sahaj Samadhi Meditation is a natural and graceful system of effortless meditation. The Sahaj Samadhi Meditation technique allows the conscious mind to settle deeply into itself so that it lets go of all tension and stress and centres itself in the present moment. It is only in the present moment that we find true happiness and are free from regrets about the past or anxiety about the future. Sahaj means natural. Samadhi means enlightenment. Without any effort, our inner nature is available.

Everyone has experienced this meditative state in certain moments of deep joy and happiness, perhaps on a vacation, or when we are completely engrossed in an activity. For just a moment, the mind becomes light and at ease. We have such moments and want to repeat them, but don't know how to. Learning the Sahaj Samadhi Meditation technique gives us the ability to recreate this feeling of ease and calm alertness in the midst of our busy daily life.

In just 3 sessions of one or two hours each, you will learn to tap into the depths of your own nature. Regular practice just twice a day can totally transform the quality of your life. The Sahaj Samadhi Meditation is a powerful technique and a very enjoyable one.

III. VIPASSANA

(a) Description of technique:

- This is one of the most ancient meditation techniques, taught by the Buddha.

- As compared to TM and AOL, as well as many other popular techniques today, Vipassana requires a far greater commitment in terms of learning and sustaining its practice. It is certainly a powerful technique.

- The technique is a combination of:

    – Certain dos and don'ts, or guidelines on actions applicable

during the residential program for learning the technique
and for follow-up.

– Breathing techniques that focus on the breath.

– Meditations through self-observation.

(b) The official description of Vipassana

Sources:

i. www.vri.dhamma.org

ii. www.dhamma.org

iii. Other published material from the Vipassana International
Academy, Igatpuri, Pin-422 403, Dist Nasik, Maharashtra,
India.

1. The Historical Background:

The technique of Vipassana is a simple, practical way to achieve
peace of mind and to lead a happy and useful life. Vipassana
means "to see things as they really are". It is a logical process of
mental purification through self-observation.

Vipassana enables us to experience peace and harmony. It purifies
the mind, freeing it from suffering and deep-seated causes of
suffering. The practice leads, step by step, to the highest spiritual
goal of full liberation from mental defilements.

2. Introduction of Vipassana

It is necessary to know one's true self – this is the advice every
person has been given. One must know oneself, not just at the
intellectual level of ideas and theories, or the emotional and
devotional level by simply blindly accepting what one has heard or
read. Such knowledge is not enough. One must know reality at the
actual level of a mental and physical phenomenon. This alone is
what will help us to escape defilements and suffering.

This direct experience of one's own reality through this technique
of self-observation, is what is called 'Vipassana meditation.'

Vipassana meditation leads to the total purification of the mind. It is the highest form of awareness and the total perception of the mind-matter phenomena in its true nature. It is the observation of things as they are.

Vipassana is the meditation that the Buddha discovered after trying all other forms of bodily mortification and mind control and finding them inadequate to free him from the seemingly endless cycle of birth and death, pain and sorrow. It is a technique so valuable that it was preserved in its pristine purity in Myanmar for more than 2,200 years.

Vipassana meditation has nothing to do with the development of supernormal, mystical, or special powers. Even though an individual may be awakened, nothing magical happens to them. The process of purification that occurs is simply an elimination of negativities and complex knots and habits that have clouded pure consciousness and blocked the flow of mankind's highest qualities – those of selfless love, compassion, sympathetic joy, and equanimity. There is no mysticism in Vipassana.

IV. THE MEDITATION TECHNIQUES TAUGHT BY OSHO

(a) Introduction:

Osho is undoubtedly one of the greatest mystics and enlightened masters of our time. He can be credited for revolutionizing the concept of teaching spirituality or *inner science,* as he calls it. He broke the conventional mindset by bringing this science from obscure places to the doorstep of the common man.

He was among the first masters to challenge the concepts of renunciation, self-control, and repression. He did not believe in sticking to any rules, so much so that he did not prescribe any one particular meditation technique. Though meditation is an integral part of the path shown by Osho, he allows seekers to experiment with a wide array of techniques before deciding which one to stay with. Seekers are not asked to sacrifice or give up any of the duties or desires of the material world.

"Religiousness is something that is absolutely scientific. I propose scientific methods to my people. I don't give them any belief system, I just give them methods of meditation which need no beliefs, no God, no heaven, no hell, no reincarnation — simply a method how to make your mind more and more silent. An atheist can do it, a communist can do it, and a theist can do it. It doesn't matter what you believe or disbelieve."

"The method is absolutely scientific. It has nothing to do with your beliefs. You just do the method and you discover your own godliness. You will not find any God sitting there, but you will find a fragrance that is only expressible in the word godliness. No other word can express it"

— Osho
The Last Testament Vol. 3 Chapter 30

(c) The Techniques:

Among the many techniques Osho has taught, some have been mentioned in this section:

Osho Active Meditations

- Osho Dynamic Meditation
- Osho Kundalini Meditation

These meditations involve body, breath and voice. With the practice of these, the silent meditative techniques become easier.

Osho Meditative Therapies

- Osho Mystic Rose
- Osho No mind
- Gibberish

Other Methods

- Osho Nataraj Meditation
- Osho Whirling Meditation
- Vipassana

(d) Where does one learn the methods?

Online at www.osho.com or at any of the Osho Centres in the world. In places where no centres exist, meditation camps and classes are held from time to time.

V. ISKCON

ISKCON stands for International Society for Krishna Consciousness. Founded by his Divine Grace A.C. Bhaktivedanta Swami Prabhupada, "Hare Krishna" has become a household word across the world.

(a) Description

The chanting of the mantra lies at the heart of all of the ISKCON teachings.

Hare Krishna, Hare Krishna, Krishna Krishna, Hare Hare;
Hare Ram, Hare Ram, Ram Ram, Hare Hare.

Along with the chanting of the mantra, a certain code of conduct in life is also recommended.

How does one chant?

There are no hard and fast rules. One can chant at any time and anywhere – at work, in the car, in public transport, or at home. However, the best time for chanting is in the early morning, just before and after sunrise. Setting aside a certain fixed time is beneficial for chanting.

Types of chanting

- Personal or individual, which are done with beads that can be purchased from any Hare Krishna temple.
- Kirtana, which is done in a group and is usually accompanied by musical instruments and clapping.

According to the book, *Chant and Be Happy*, published by the A.C. Bhaktivedanta Trust, "One may hold a kirtana at home with family and friends, with one person leading the chanting and the others responding. Kirtana is more of a supercharged meditation process, where in addition to hearing oneself chant, one also benefits by hearing the chanting of others. Musical instruments are nice, but not necessary. One may sing the mantra to any melody and clap his or her hands. (Especially recommended are the traditional melodies). If you have children, they can sing along as well and make spiritual advancement. You can get the whole family together every evening for chanting."

Both forms of chanting are recommended and beneficial.

VI. KRIYA YOGA – AS TAUGHT BY THE YOGODA SATSANGA SOCIETY, FOUNDED BY SRI PARAMAHANSA YOGANANDA

Note: The material in this section has been taken from

- Autobiography of a Yogi *by Paramahansa Yogananda*
- Website: www.yogananda-srf.org
- Inputs received from YSS, Ranchi

(a) Introduction

One of the most famous books on spirituality, which, in fact, serves as a guide to innumerable seekers, is the *Autobiography of a Yogi,* by Sri Paramahansa Yogananda. This book, with its familiar cover displaying a picture of Paramahansaji (a young, vibrant yogi with long, flowing hair) is an all-time masterpiece and is widely available – from pavement stalls to the best bookshops in any town.

Paramahansaji learned, practiced, and imparted knowledge about the ancient and sacred technique of Kriya Yoga. There are many Kriya Yogis worldwide, and the Yogoda Satsanga Society (YSS) and the Self-Realization Fellowship (SRF) are organizations established by Paramahansa Yogananda in 1917 and 1920 respectively to disseminate Kriya Yoga to sincere seekers. The headquarters are located in Ranchi and Los Angeles, but they also have centres and temples in other cities. Sri Daya Mata, a direct disciple of Paramahansa Yogananda since the 1930s, is currently the spiritual head of YSS/SRF.

Kriya Yoga is a systematic approach of attaining oneness with Brahman through life force control.

Kundalini Jagran is one of the things that happens during the practice of Kriya Yoga.

The aim of Kriya Yoga is to feel the unity between the individual and the all-embracing consciousness, and finally to merge with the Divine Consciousness.

(b) The Tradition & Science of Kriya Yoga

The tradition of Kriya Yoga was passed on to Paramahansaji by his guru Swami Sri Yukteswar, who was bestowed this sacred technique by Lahiri Mahasaya. Lahiri Mahasaya had received it from his master Saint Mahavatar Babaji.

Quoting from Paramahansaji's *Autobiography of a Yogi*, Chapter 26, *The Science of Kriya Yoga*:

- *"Kriya is an ancient science. Lahiri Mahasaya received it from his great guru Babaji, who rediscovered and clarified the technique after it had been lost in the Dark Ages. Babaji renamed it, simply, Kriya Yoga."*

- *"The Kriya Yoga that I am giving to the world through you in this nineteenth century,"* Babaji told Lahiri Mahasaya, *"is a revival of the same science that Krishna gave millenniums ago to Arjuna and that was later known to Patanjali and Christ and to St. John, St. Paul and other disciples."*

- *"Kriya Yoga is an instrument through which human evolution can be quickened,"* Sri Yukteswar explained to his students. *"The ancient yogis discovered that the secret of cosmic consciousness is intimately linked with breath mastery. This is India's unique and timeless contribution to the world's treasury of knowledge. The life force, which is ordinarily absorbed in maintaining the heart action, must be freed for higher activities by a method of calming the ceaseless demands of breath."*

- *"Kriya Yoga is a simple psycho-physiological method by which human blood is de-carbonized and recharged with oxygen. The atoms of this extra oxygen are transmuted into the current of life to rejuvenate the brain and spinal centres."*

- *"Kriya Yoga has nothing in common with the unscientific breathing exercises taught by a number of misguided zealots. Attempts to forcibly hold the breath in the lungs is unnatural and decidedly unpleasant. Kriya practice, on the other hand, is accompanied from the very beginning by feelings of peace and by the soothing sensation of the regenerative effect in the spine."*

VII. SAHAJ YOGA (AS TAUGHT BY SHRI MATAJI NIRMALA DEVI)

The contents in this sub-section have been taken based on information published on the website, www.sahajayoga.org, as well as in interactions with some of the practitioners of the technique)

Sahaj means spontaneous. It also means natural and without too much exertion. Hence, Sahaj Yoga is a technique that is simple and spontaneous. This method was discovered by Shri. Mataji Nirmala Devi in 1970.

(a) Introduction

The essence of the Sahaj Yoga method can be explained based on the following precepts that lie at its very core:

When a child is born, a lot of energy is blocked or lies dormant at the base of the spine in the sacrum bone. This energy is supposedly "coiled" into three and a half loops and is called the kundalini. Kundalini is the power of "pure desire" within us.

The kundalini instrument consists of:

- Kundalini
- Three Nadis
- Three Chakras

The 3 Nadis are channels of energy and are components of our sympathetic nervous system.

The Chakra is a subtle energy centre corresponding to the autonomic nerve plexuses. These centres are meant for our physical, mental, emotional, and spiritual requirements and well-being.

The essence of Sahaj Yoga lies in awakening the kundalini from the base of the spine (sacrum bone), through the central channel, piercing through the six chakras (which are our energy centres in the spinal cord). It finally reaches the seventh chakra – on top of the head (the fontanel bone area). The rising of the kundalini to the seventh chakra at the top of the head leads to self realization.

According to Shri Mataji, *"Kundalini cures you, she improves you, she bestows all the blissful things upon you. She takes you away from the worries at the gross level. She nourishes and revitalizes the centres (chakras)"*.

Among the causes of suffering are our lack of knowledge regarding ourselves and the block of energy through the Chakras. Hence, the Nadis and Chakras are imbalanced. Due to this imbalance, we tend to get detached from Mother Nature, who relentlessly takes care of us.

Therefore, Sahaj Yoga helps us attain three objectives:

- To balance the Nadis
- To raise the energy from the *Mooldhara* Chakra
- To connect ourselves with Mother Nature – the ever loving "Param-Chaitanya"

It does this by helping us purify ourselves, release negatives, and correct imbalances.

(b) What is the practice like?

The practice is quite simple. One has to sit, preferably on the floor with legs crossed, as in *sukhaasan*. Our *Mooldhara Chakra* thus touches the ground. This is recommended, as the earth and sky have the ability to take away a lot of negativity from within us.

There is also a very simple posture that can be done along with affirmations and visualizations. The affirmations are for removing the negative stresses, energy, and prarabhdha from our system, aided by Mother Nature.

They also aid in making us:

- Slowly realize our true nature
- Experience our true spirit
- Imbibe positive feelings of compassion and forgiveness
- Become our own master

SUMMARY

This chapter discusses the basics of the following 7 techniques, including their core beliefs, the key aspects of the methodology, and how to learn them.

1. Transcendental Meditation
2. Art of Living
3. Vipassana
4. Techniques taught by OSHO
5. ISKON
6. Kriya Yoga
7. Sahaj Yoga

3 SELECTING THE MOST SUITABLE PATH

The four key elements of selecting the right path are

1. Search the right sources

2. Do an objective evaluation

3. Do reference checks

4. Practice, experience, and review periodically

The factors that one can look at are:

- Pedigree, tradition, source of the technique

- Background, legitimacy, objectives/motivations, experience, skill, competence, understanding of the teacher's motive

- Process e.g. transparency, objectivity

- Methodology or type of technique e.g. concentration or self-observation

- Types of seekers

- Any credible researches, audits

- Credible testimonials, recommendations from those who practiced for long enough

- Follow-up support available after learning the technique

Let us assume that after the initial search for techniques through various methods and references, one arrives at a shortlist of 4 or 5 techniques out of which the final one is to be selected. A comparative rating as per the factors and weights can be done, as shown in the sample table given below.

The short-listed techniques are shown as Technique A, B, C, and D in the attached chart.

Sr. No.	Aspect for Factor	Weight (Total 100)	Technique A	
			Score (1 to 5)	Wtd Score
1.	Ease of Learning	5	5	25
2.	Ease of Doing/ Continuing Practice	20	5	100
3.	Physical Access to the living Master	5	4	20
4.	Systems/Network/ Infrastructure for resolving doubts	10	4	40
5.	Availability of teachers whom one can relate with	20	5	100
6.	Availability of brand ambassadors whom one can relate with or be inspired by	10	4	40
7.	Scientific Validation: recording of experiences, experiments, and research	5	2	10
8.	Tangibility of Progress	15	5	75
9.	Rate of Spiritual Progress	10	3	30
	Total Weighted Score			**440**

Technique B		Technique C		Technique D	
Score (1 to 5)	Wtd Score	Score (1 to 5)	Wtd Score	Score (1 to 5)	Wtd Score
5	25	1	5	3	15
4	80	2	40	4	80
1	5	3	15	4	20
2	20	3	30	3	30
3	60	4	80	2	40
2	20	3	30	2	20
5	25	4	20	1	5
2	30	4	60	3	45
3	30	4	40	3	30
	295		**320**		**285**

Notes to the Rating Chart

1. The second column, Factors, lists the factors based on which any seeker may select the most suitable path. The factors may vary from seeker to seeker.

2. The third column, Weights, is for deciding the relative importance of the above factors. Thus, a total weight of 100 is distributed among various factors based on importance. The seeker may assign more or less weight to any factor based on what is more important to him.

3. In the fourth column, the seeker scores each technique out of 5 against each factor; the minimum score is 1 and the maximum score is 5. The score is based on the best available information and inferences that could be gathered on the technique.

4. The weighted score is a simple multiplication of weight with score. For example, Technique B has a weighted score of 80 in the factor 'Ease of continuing practice', which is arrived at by multiplying the weight of this factor (20), with the score.

5. Availability of brand ambassadors refers to people practicing the technique with whom one can relate and interact e.g. successful professionals, businessmen, executives, intellectuals, and the like.

Sr. No	Technique	Advantages/USPs	Possible Concerns
1.	TM	• Stress release, feeling of relaxation, tangible benefits towards hypertension and lack of deep sleep even in the early stages (first few months). • Lots of scientific data available on positive effects of TM	• Initially may seem too simple to be effective. With practice and actual experiences, however, this will be addressed.

Sr. No	Technique	Technique	Possible Concerns
2.	AOL	• Experience of positivity, getting recharged, re-energized even in the initial stages (first few months) • Many brand ambassadors and role models. • Ability to relate with others - intellectuals, young professionals successful people.	• One should not stop at only the basic course. One must add on Sahaj Samadhi Meditation or any other meditation technique approved by the teacher.
3.	Vipassana	• A very intense technique. • One can tangibly feel progress or inner change.	• A tough regimen which needs a fair amount of commitment.
4.	Osho	• Ability to penetrate deep within and see oneself in all "ugliness, nakedness" & reality. Helps a lot in realizing one's core. • Well-experimented techniques practiced by innumerable people.	• Onus of deciding the specific technique is on oneself. Adequate guidance and support, however, is available to facilitate this.
		• Lineage established through innumerable people across the world who have adopted this system, benefited from it and were motivated to give up everything including their jobs to dedicate themselves full time.	• For people who come with expectations of learning a formal meditation technique, may find the whole approach somewhat different. However, as they tread it for a while they will discover how their lives can be transformed within a shorttime.

Sr. No	Technique	Technique	Possible Concerns
5.	ISKCON	• Well educated Indians as well as foreigners can be seen with shaven heads who have committed their lives to this path & pursuit. Others, who continue with their jobs but are associated with it, swear by what they have gained.	• Those who come with expectations of an elaborate meditation technique may find the approach too simplistic The path, however is powerful & effective.
6.	Kriya Yoga	• Lineage of the technique. • Examples of masters who have lived and practiced the technique and attained enlightenment. • A sound theoretical basis for the techniques is available in Paramahansaji's book, "An Autobiography of a Yogi", as well as in the lessons that one receives from Yogoda Satsang Society for those who enrol.	• Patience is required. Most of the techniques can be learnt soon after one has made up one's mind to pursue a particular path. This is often done through sessions lasting a couple of hours over 3 to 5 days. • In the case of Kriya Yoga, the pupil has to first go through the lessons and become ready to receive initiation. • Even for subsequent stages of dissemination of advanced techniques, one has to wait till one is ready to move ahead and is thus imparted the same progressively.

Sr. No	Technique	Technique	Possible Concerns
7.	Sahaj Yoga	• Very simple to learn and practice. Requires less time for practice • Direct, tangible experience even in the very initial stages • De-stressing and removal of negativities is likely within weeks of practice.	• A basic level of connect with the master, Shri Mataji is required to get full benefits. However this is not really a pre-requisite. The connect can happen slowly after one starts practice. • The theoretical explanation of method with talk of nadis, chakras and kundalini can be perplexing, to some. However, in actual practice the technique is really simple and does not involve any rigorous mental effort etc. to raise the kundalini. There is nothing that may deter the seeker.

SUMMARY

No one path, or set of paths, is "most suited" for everyone. Each of us must make our choices based on factors that matter most to us – those that will give us the comfort and motivation to continue forging ahead. A good approach is to list the parameters, assign weights to them, and then rate the short-listed techniques against each parameter. Reference checking from practitioners with whom one can relate is also useful.

In the author's experience:

• Good results are obtained if the chosen path has the following

3 elements:

- – Yogic postures or asanas or physical exercises
- – Breathing exercises or pranayama
- – Meditation or dhyana

- Techniques that force thought control, thought removal, or intensive concentration on any object may be evaluated with more caution as they have a sizeable and direct impact on the mind.

- Techniques that are gentler and seemingly too easy may be perceived to be ineffective by seekers who come with expectations of learning something heavy and deep. On the contrary, a method that is simple, gentle, subtle, and easy is usually quite effective, provided it meets the other criteria and passes the rigour of selection discussed in this chapter.

In short, we need to guard against our simpleton biases. A village doctor who spends a lot of time asking questions about the ailment while in clinical examinations and then dispenses several different coloured tablets and capsules along with a strict diet is perceived to be good. On the other hand, a capable doctor who quickly completes the diagnosis, prescribes nothing, or just one tablet and leaves you free to eat what you like is seen as being superficial.

PART - III  CHALLENGES ALONG THE WAY

- This part is relevant for those who have practiced some meditation technique in the past or are still practicing

- Readers who have no experience with meditation can skip the Chapters of this part, ***Challenges along the way***. They may come back to this part after 8-12 weeks of continuous practice of the chosen method.

STARTED MEDITATING, BUT STILL FEELING LOW....?

Getting liberation from depression, sadness, or gloom is often a key motivator for many seekers' seeking refuge in spirituality. The process of overcoming these may be slow and arduous. It is important to objectively assess one's progress along the journey so that one neither quits a chosen path prematurely, nor remains stuck with a path that was not going to bring in any brightness or cheer into one's life.

Spiritual gurus promise bliss and ecstasy. Hence, a seeker is not only attracted to this realm, but even enters with high expectations of attaining peace and contentment fairly quickly. Thus, if, after a few weeks or months of practice, a seeker does not find tangible or substantial joy, he is likely to drop the selected method, or, in many cases, the spiritual quest as a whole. He may become a disbeliever as his experience taught him that it does not work. This is bad news, as the motivation to take up a second method will be very low. In all likelihood, if the seeker achieves no tangible feeling of joy after the initial weeks or months of practice, he can be classified as a non-retrievable drop-out.

Is it wrong to enter into it with expectations of overcoming emptiness and low feelings? Was it merely a sales pitch or a grand promise to allure unsuspecting seekers whose dejected state of mind made them gullible and vulnerable enough to join anything that held promises to heal them?

While there may be methods that are incapable of leading you to the goal, in 9 out of 10 cases, the drop-out may occur because the seeker had compromised and not followed each step exactly as prescribed. Thus, he may not be practicing the method accurately; he may not be practicing for the specified duration or frequency per day; he may be irregular; he may be mixing other factors or pursuits simultaneously. As a result, either the ability to pinpoint a method was ineffective, or these "other factors" were responsible.

It is critical that a seeker regularly validate his method by a trained teacher of the path, who has been authorized by the master to disseminate the teachings and the method. Regular practice of the technique exactly as it was taught is critical. If, after doing this for several months, one still does not feel any transformation, one can consider engaging in another method, but only after discussing this with the master (where possible), trained teachers, and other seasoned seekers of that particular path.

A person may thus experience different types of emotions ranging from ecstasy to depression, before, during, and after pursuing a given path. These two extreme states are discussed briefly in this chapter to help one assess:

- Whether or not one is on the right track in terms of the spiritual path.

- What one needs to do.

At which part of the psychological cycle are you?

The chart below shows the state of mind and typical characteristics of individuals at their peak (zenith) and trough (nadir).

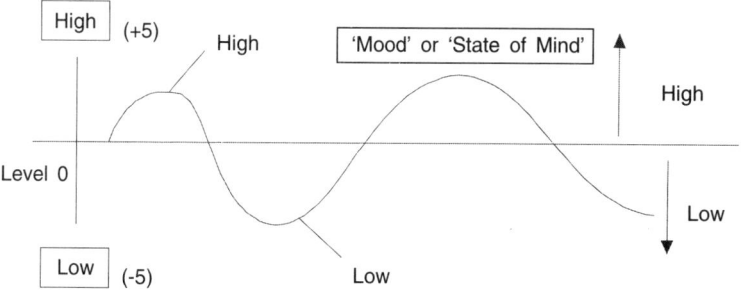

Typical Characteristics of feeling Low (-5)

- Unhappy
- Anxious
- Depressed
- Nothing seems to give joy
- Constant feeling of emptiness & hollowness
- Exhaustion and lack of energy
- Wondering what's good about life
- Not finding anything funny
- Not enjoying gatherings
- Being unable to understand why other people are enjoying themselves

Needs serious interventions including:

- Medical Advice.
- Counseling from close friends
- Change in environment at home or work, including change of job/ workplace.
- Change in profession.
- Spiritual technique review-with expert teachers of the path and other experienced practitioners

Typical characteristics of feeling High(+5)

- Humor
- Love
- Laughter
- Energy, Liveliness
- Looking forward to each day
- Waking up with hope
- Thinking that the day is too short —there's so mich to do.
- Being occupied with thoughts & things to do.
- Looking forward to reaching one's place of work.
- Looking forward to evenings or after office time.
- Enjoying chatting, gossiping, mixing around & sharing jokes.
- Looking forward to parties; unihibited behavior and spontainiety at parties.
- Feeling energetic
- Working hard and yet participating in several other activities.

On the right track

How are you feeling with the addition of the spiritual technique in your life?

Another good way to track one's psychological graph is to assess oneself on a scale of −5 to +5, where −5 and +5 denote the extreme states, depressed and ecstatic respectively, described earlier. Different people may fluctuate between the various levels at different points in time along their journey. This is not a matter of occasional mood swings. It is a matter of one's psychological makeup. *How one feels in general or most of the time (in a 24-hour day, or on most days in a week).* For example, Person A may feel rather low before beginning meditation, shown by level -3, while he progressively moves to a level of +1 after 6 months. This can be an indicator that even though the individual may still not be too happy, he is progressing in the right direction.

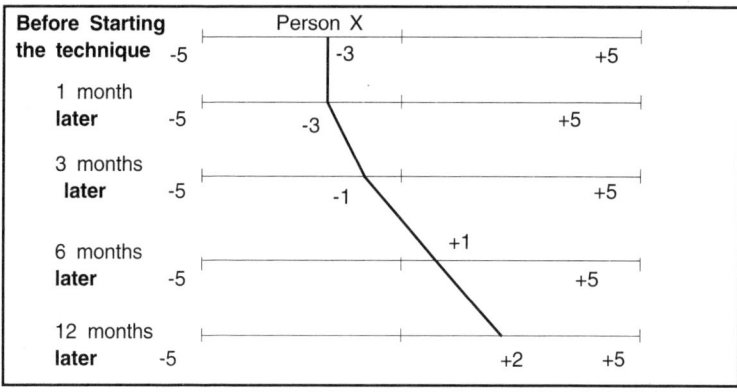

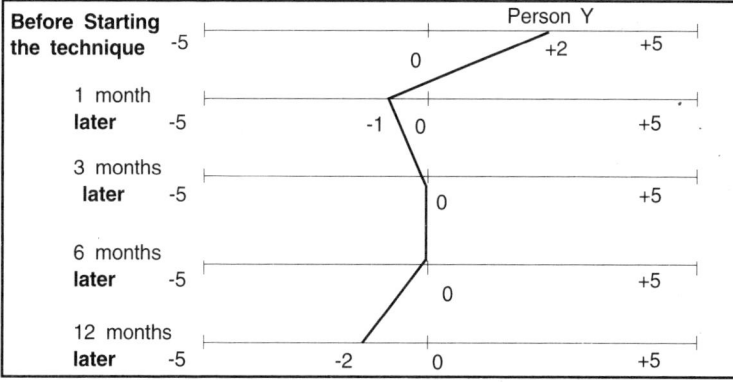

In this way, one can get an idea of where one is headed. However, one must remember some of the ground rules stated earlier:

- Give the technique enough time before passing a final judgement on whether to follow it or quit.

- Keep getting the technique checked by an expert teacher as frequently as advised when selecting the chosen path. Having the technique checked often entails meditating in the presence of the teacher. Most teachers invite people for group meditation sessions and may provide opportunities for one-on-one interaction during these sessions. If there are any discomforts or doubts, even in the initial stages, the seeker must share them with the teacher.

- One must have realistic expectations. One should not expect certain types of results to happen in a certain time frame. It is okay to have a tightly defined schedule and accountability for tangible milestones in one's work or profession. However, on this path, one cannot predefine an achievement schedule. Each individual must take his or her own course depending on the previous storehouse of karma, the current level of spiritual evolution, the impressions in the mind-body-soul, and the earnestness and honesty with which efforts have been made.

- One must not expect **only** *ananda*, ecstasy, or joy. It is important to remember that a price may have to be paid. The guru can 'subsidise' the price to be paid by making the path easier and adding buffers. But in order to *gain,* one may inevitably have to go through some *pain.*

- If, however, the pain and suffering becomes unbearable, it must be addressed and examined. The extreme reaction is to quit the path because one failed to achieve bliss even after months of practice, or because one experienced too much pain. The other extreme is to continue suffering the pain silently for a long time without seeking the help or support of the teacher, master, or other seekers who are at a more advanced stage in the same technique. Both extremes are unavoidable.

In our example, Person B, who, even after a year of practice, was feeling worse than when he had started out, may need to get a serious review done. This should include:

- Whether he or she was practising the technique correctly as per the proper process.

- A discussion of the special external circumstances that might be causing the continual low feelings.

WHEN SHOULD ONE OPT FOR A DIFFERENT TEACHER OR TECHNIQUE?

How meditation should ideally work on one's psyche:

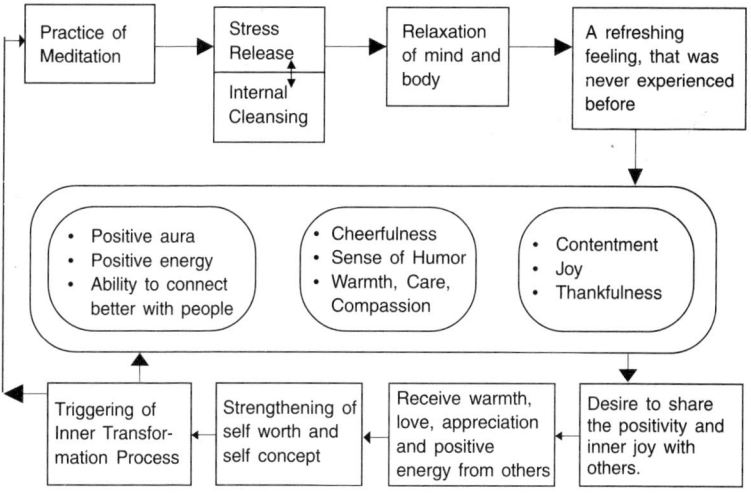

Will meditation help me overcome my gloom? If yes, how soon?

- Sadness and pain can cause a tremendous inner transformation. According to Osho, "Sadness is a very deep thing." Through sadness and pain, we realize the importance of being happy. However, the mere realization that we must be happy may not make us cheerful. If we are in pain, we obviously want to get out of it. However, will positive thinking or imagining the pain is not there actually help remove it? We may want to be happy, but merely wanting it does not make it happen.

- We all go through phases of gloom. These phases change something within us. We begin to realize how not to take good times for granted. We become humble and reckon that there are powers beyond us. We make an effort to remove our sadness and pain and may seek succour through spirituality. However, spirituality may take its own course and time to provide this. We may not be able to demand results overnight, or within a specified time frame.

- Spirituality can be likened to a homeopathic or ayurvedic treatment. It surely cures, but slowly. We know that a single homeopathic or ayurvedic treatment acts on many symptoms because it works on the root causes. When one is in acute pain and needs emergency treatment, such as a life-saving drug, a strong painkiller, surgical intervention or a highly potent antibiotic, will one opt for homeopathic or ayurvedic treatment instead? Will one wait for the results from such interventions? The situation is similar to the expectations of results from meditation. If one is feeling really depressed and anxious, to the extent that he or she has physical symptoms, then meditation can surely help, but it will take its own time and course. If the distress is too much, one should augment the meditation with other interventions, such as medication, advice from friends, counselling, or a change in job or work environment. The medication chosen may also be allopathic, ayurvedic, homeopathic or any other that the seeker trusts.

Meditation may not be able to change events that cause suffering, but can certainly make the pain much more bearable.

How do meditation and medication help us more effectively face and overcome challenges and failures without breaking down:

Each one of us has a tolerance threshold. If one is to take an arbitrary scale of 0 to 100, one person's tolerance threshold may be 30 (person A), while another person's may be 80 (person B).

Suppose both individuals have various problems – financial, health, or job-related. Let us say A's problems add up to reach the potency level of 40 (on the same scale), whereas B's problems are more severe and add up to a level of 60. In such a case, even though the absolute potency of A's problems is far less than that of B, A will not be able to cope and may start experiencing problems like anxiety and depression. Person B, on the other hand, with a greater set of problems would be able to cope well without any major distress or psychosomatic symptoms. This is because in the case of A, the intensity of the problems is more than the threshold tolerance level, whereas in the case of B, even though the absolute intensity of the problems is greater, the tolerance threshold is higher. Meditation and medication help us increase our tolerance and forbearance threshold. Meditation may take longer, but the cure will also be deeper. In the above example, A is unable to cope with problems that add up to a potency of 40. If the potency of troubles increases even further to 50 or 60, A might just have a nervous breakdown. Hence, in order to prevent that from happening, it may be a good idea for A to quickly increase his threshold of tolerance from the current level of 30. A can only do this by supplementing his meditation (which may take a couple of months to provide tangible relief) with medication, which may start showing effects within a few weeks. Hence, a decision needs to be taken on a case-by-case basis, depending on the severity and the duration of what one is going through.

What should I do if I am neither too happy nor too unhappy?

A large majority of people feel somewhere 'in-between'. They are neither too happy nor too unhappy, and in this state, they do not know whether any action is really mandated besides the simple pursuit of the path. This refers to scores ranging typically from +3 to −3. While it is difficult to set a cut-off criterion by which one can judge whether any specific action is needed, if one experiences one or more of the symptoms mentioned below, one should seek the interventions mentioned earlier in this chapter, namely an expert opinion, medical advice, counsel from very close friends, a change of workplace or job, or a change in home.

Symptoms indicating that intervention other than meditation alone may be required if meditation does not lead to any major improvement even after 6-8 weeks of practice:

- *Feelings while waking up in the morning.*
    - 'Oh, yet another day!'
    - 'I would rather sleep than step out into the world.'
    - Deep hollowness or emptiness
    - Lack of hope
    - Nothing to look forward to
    - Palpitation

- *Thoughts while going to work*
    - 'I wish I could go back home.'
    - No thoughts about the important tasks at hand.
    - 'What a boring life.'

- *State during the course of the day*
    - Very low energy level
    - Low enthusiasm level
    - Dullness and lethargy

- *Feelings and thoughts while returning from work*
    - 'Yet another day passed by without my learning or contributing much.'
    - 'Did I really earn my salary today? Do I deserve to call it a day and leave for home?
    - 'Yet another day of wasted time and energy.'
    - 'Was I worthy today?'

- *Feelings while going to bed*
    - Sadness, gloom, and melancholy
    - Palpitation (due to anxiety, fear, insecurity, worry for next day, nervousness)

- Inability to fall asleep quickly
- Lack of deep sleep
- Feelings of concern like, 'How will I handle tomorrow?'
- Speaking distressfully, or screaming in sleep

Other symptoms that can occur at any time are tension headaches, a strong aversion to sounds/noise, impatience, irritation, feeling of loss of life in limbs, and the like. These can vary based on severity of the psychological distress.

It is important to get out of the above state of mind as soon as possible. A temporary onset of such feelings due to the nervousness when starting the practice of any meditation technique is normal. The important thing is to not let the gloom establish its stronghold on the mind. One should be able to bounce back before the feeling settles in.

Another crucial thing to realize is that the intensity of the pain we feel may be severe based on the nature of the events that caused it and our tolerance threshold, or resilience. If, at a given point in time, even after months of meditation, one did not feel significantly better, it may be a good idea to look at other *additional interventions* rather than dropping spirituality or the chosen path by concluding it is useless. These additional interventions can be:

- Counselling by a qualified expert
- Consultation with a neuro-psychiatrst. If need be, he may consider a course of antidepressants, or anti-anxiety medications.
- Alternative medicines: nerve soothing and strengthening ayurvedic/herbal medicines or supplements (brahmi, ashwagandha, shankpushpi); panchkarma treatment (e.g. shirodhara)

For any chronic problems that are not too severe, we look at alternative systems of medicines knowing fully well that they may take time, but the cure will occur at the root level. If one's ailment was severe, for example, acute pain, very high or very low blood sugar or blood pressure levels, very high fever, throwing up, low count of platelets, or a severe asthmatic attack, one would require immediate intervention, such as hospitalisation, intravenous or intra muscular injections, or drips in order to stabilize the patient. Then, once the individual was treated, he could return to using the alternative medicine.

The alternative interventions suggested above are in between the two:

Increasing severity of mental distress

↑
- Hospitalisation
- Additional intervention (counselling, physician advice)
- Additional intervention (herbal/ ayurvedic medicines, panchkarma)
- Meditation

It is important that we allow ourselves at least 8 to 12 weeks before moving on to the next level of intervention. It is critical that we not discard any intervention as ineffective without providing enough time for it to take effect, as well as allowing the person being treated the adequate opportunity to make modifications and adjust to it. Otherwise, we will never allow any useful intervention to have its full effect.

That said, however, one should not operate from the following two extremes:

- Complete submission to the master: Even if no positive results are experienced, neither the method nor the master is reviewed. The individual does not even want to share doubts regarding discomforts with the post-meditative phase.
- The attitude that "No godman can show me the way".

We need to guard against both distrust and blind surrender. We have discussed this in Part I where we covered the question: "Do I need a Guru", and why people are averse to adopting a "Particular Method or Meditation Technique". This is being reiterated with the earlier examples of medical treatment.

Distrust: Suppose a doctor has prescribed us medicines that taste bitter and are expensive. Moreover, he mandates a diet regimen and a cumbersome list of dos and don'ts. Will we follow the doctor's advice if we have no faith in him? Will we not resist his advice, especially the difficult and inconvenient aspects, if we distrust him? In the same way, whichever technique we choose, we must have a minimum level of faith to pursue it with regularity and entirety, i.e. following all prescribed aspects religiously. We may be tempted to drop some of the doctor's recommendations based on our judgement that these were not critical in the treatment and therefore not worth the effort. Then, when the treatment does not work, we will blame the doctor.

Partial Trust: What if our faith in the chosen doctor is partial and we know of another doctor whom we also partially trust? If we believe that our knowledge of medicine is fair, we could mix the prescriptions of both. For example, we may opt to take the antibiotic prescribed by the first doctor and the vitamins and painkillers suggested by the second doctor. If the second doctor says that we can eat according to our regular diet, we would love to ignore the strict diet regimen specified by the first doctor. How will this work? What if the treatment does not work? What will you tell the first doctor about what you did and did not follow? What will you tell the second doctor? How will you know which one was more reliable of the two? You may even go for a consultation with a third doctor whereas both the first and second were well-equipped to treat you fully, if you had not used your knowledge, judgement, and distrust.

In the same way, one should avoid mixing techniques or aspects of two methods/paths/masters. We cannot judge which particular aspects worked and which did not work, and we are depriving even the doctor from the ability to change his earlier prescription because he is assuming you followed all aspects exactly as prescribed. If you tell him you picked and chose your treatment, if he is a self-respecting doctor, he may kick you out!

Blind Trust: Suppose we follow all the aspects of the treatment prescribed by our chosen doctor with regularity and still do not respond to the treatment. What should we do? The first thing is to inform the doctor of all the symptoms pre- and post-treatment and give him a chance to make modifications. What if still we are not recovering? Should we persist with same doctor? A more logical thing to do would be to get a second medical opinion and decide if the line of treatment should be changed. There will, however, be seekers who will blame the lack of progress on themselves, believing a guru or doctor can never be wrong. It is true that diseases often flare up before being cured, but it is important to be sure that it does not keep worsening so that it becomes incurable or leads to death. Blind trust should not mean:

- Not sharing discomforts
- Not checking if one was on right path or was improving (e.g. diagnostic tests as treatment progressed)
- Considering a second opinion as sacrilege

In smaller towns, when a trusted family physician treats a sick person, even if the condition keeps deteriorating, the person will often refrain from consulting another doctor. The physician would be offended if they did. The physician might keep asking for trust and patience until the patient is no more!

Surrender: Trying to force oneself to surrender is not required. Over a period of time, if surrender happens due to one's own mental processes and experiences, it is alright. If it does not, one should still continue with the technique by relying on one's experience of how the technique was helping in one's evolution. An individual would need to trust one doctor at a time and take the medicines exactly as prescribed in order to benefit from them or even to judge the suitability of his treatment. That, however, does not imply blind surrender to the doctor, because if one is not satisfied after a reasonable amount of time, one can go for a second medical opinion and, if required, change the doctor or treatment completely. But it may be only appropriate to do so after having granted a minimum amount of time for the medicine to take effect.

In the same way, after dedicating a minimum amount of time to a given technique, one can:

- Talk to the master or the teacher about one's experiences, problems, or discomforts. (This may be done as frequently as suggested by the teacher under normal circumstances, or even more frequently if one is not satisfied. Typically, one should interact with the teacher within one week of beginning the practice and then once in two weeks for the first 1-2 months).

- Talk to other people practicing the same path (after a few weeks of practice, say 8 weeks, but only if permitted and vetted by the teacher/master)

- Talk to other people following other paths (if not satisfied after 3-4 months of practice and interaction with the teachers or practitioners of the current technique)

- As a consequence of the above, consider learning another technique.

It is important to realize that, based on complex permutations and combinations of our prarabdha, residues in the nervous system, stress levels, current evolution level, suitability of the method, accuracy of learning, and regularity of practice, different people among us may have different types of experiences. The teacher or master may need to tweak the way you are practising based on your experiences in the first few days and weeks. In cases of high or low BP/sugar level, it may take a few trials before the doctor is able to decide the most optimal drug, both in terms of choice of drug and quantity to be administered. In fact, once stabilized, it may again need to be reviewed from time to time. Many times, the doctor may not change anything in the follow-up visits, but that does not that mean that follow-up visits are useless.

By their very nature, the half-life of different medicines, or in other words, the time required for them to take full effect, varies. An antibiotic may start showing its effect only on the third or fourth day, depending upon the severity of the infection. An antidepressant may take 3 to 4 weeks to show some tangible effects. Thus, it may not be fair to doubt the doctor or the treatment and switch to another too early. If one has been irregular, this is all the more reason not to be too anxious to switch. Changing treatments without giving the first a fair chance is hazardous and may lead to the rejection of a line of treatments that may have been good. In fact, before switching to another doctor, we know that it might be better to give him feedback so that he has a chance to adapt or tweak the prescription or line of treatment. At the same time, one does not need to surrender blindly to a given doctor and believe that his first prescription is gospel.

SUMMARY

Feeling low, gloomy, stressed, or anxious often drives a person to seek solace in spirituality. It is important to understand that, depending on the severity of one's mental and emotional turmoil, meditation may need to be supplemented with other interventions, such as counselling or medical attention. Depending solely on spirituality may not be advisable if the severity is high and significant recuperation is not seen after 6-12 weeks of meditation. Eventually, these additional interventions may be unnecessary and meditation may suffice. But if an individual is feeling miserable, he should certainly entertain alternate therapies until he is stable and in fairly good spirits. A periodic assessment of how you are fairing along the path is critical. Even if the pace is slow, you should be progressing in the right direction.

2   I WAS PROMISED ANANDA, THEN WHERE DOES SUFFERING COME FROM?

The spiritual path has been called the 'razor's edge' by a number of people who have tread upon it – cuts and wounds seem inevitable.

A poet has compared the spiritual path to the painstaking search for one's beloved. His rendition in Hindi goes as follows:

Kathin bahut hai prem dagariya
Door bahut hai pee ki nagariya
Tujhe kaanto par chalna hoga
Tujhe aag me jalna hoga
Tu man hi man prem barsaaye ja
Tu gaaye ja, pee kahan, pee kahan

(The path of love is very difficult. The place of the beloved is rather far. One has to walk through the treacherous path. One has to pass through perilous fires. But the seeker (lover) must keep letting the energy of love flow through his heart and soul. He must keep trudging the path while wailing and singing along, O' beloved, where are you?)

In finding one's love, or beloved, one often has to go through trials, tribulations, and pain. So does the seeker of spiritual enlightenment. Earlier we had said that spirituality is the path to bliss, to *ananda*. In fact, that seems to be the bottom line of all spiritual teachings. One may wonder why, suffering should be associated with spiritual path at all, when it is the desire to put an end to one's suffering that attracts many people to spirituality in the first place.

Based on the experience of several people who have gone through this path, it is fairly certain that bliss is to be found. However, prior to that, one often has to go through a process of self-evolution in order to deserve that bliss. For evolution, change is a must, and change is often accompanied by pain.

The spiritual path is like an internal cleansing. When our clothes are washed, the dirt is driven out from the hidden pores by the detergent. Before enough water has flowed to wash off the detergent and the dirt, the clothes seem to be in worse condition, and even more un-wearable. It is only when the cleansing process is complete that they come out looking better than what they did before they had gone in to be cleaned.

A spiritual journey can be compared with the above example. When meditation begins to dig out the deep-rooted stresses, or *prarabdha*, for the purpose of cleaning them, one may feel worse than before he or she had started meditating. This feeling of uneasiness can be looked at as suffering. In fact, some other forms of suffering can occur during this cleansing process through events or psychological changes. This state is like the interim state when clothes are being scrubbed with the detergent. The deep rooted stresses and karma are culled out, unfolded, and brought to the surface. Hence, one often feels the distress in the first few weeks of starting the meditation process or of setting out on an active spiritual journey. This state can last for a while until 'more meditation' washes off the stressful thoughts that have manifested themselves, just like water does in the case of clothes.

One may ask

- But why this suffering and distress at all?
- Can't it be bypassed?
- Can't bliss emerge directly?

We shall view these questions from different perspectives:

The presence or absence of suffering or the extent of it depends upon several factors, **one of them being one's own *prarabdha*, or the stock of past karma, both quantitative as well as qualitative.**

The following are plausible explanations for suffering, if and the extent to which it occurs, as one advances on the spiritual journey:

(a) We saw in Part I that there is no mechanism to offset the bad karma by the good. The results of the good as well as the bad karma have to be suffered in order to work out the karma. In that chapter, we also learned that meditation accelerates the process of working out the past karma. Because of the above two factors, the past karma starts getting worked out at a faster rate. This happens for all types of karma, including the negative ones for which we need to suffer.

(b) The second type of suffering occurs due to an interim phase through which we may pass wherein, by becoming inward-directed, the attachment and zeal for external objects and sensory gratifications begin to abate. We may no longer derive the same sense of delight from indulgence, sensual stimulation, or material gratification. Things that mattered so much until yesterday begin to lose their charm. Even though we learned that this detachment is purely due to the experience of a better source of joy within, there can be a mismatch in the quantity or quality of *material pleasure* substituted with *pure joy* at a given point of time. That is, the loss of joy from material pleasures may not be fully compensated by a commensurate amount of joy flowing from within at a particular point of time in our lives. Why does this happen? Let us try to explain through an analogy even though, in reality, the process may be far more complex:

> We may have had glimpses of the inner source of pure joy in flashes. These glimpses make the pleasures of the material world look small and insignificant and we therefore lose interest in them. However, a constant flow of the nectar from the inner source within us may not yet have become a reality. We may thus go through a unique dilemma: the mundane life is no longer exciting, but spiritual bliss is not yet a reality. This can cause strange feelings in the interim, including unhappiness, uneasiness, and even depression.

(c) A third way of looking at suffering is to consider the fact that we have to pay a price or make a sacrifice to acquire even ordinary objects in life, so why should we be afraid of paying a price for becoming one with the ultimate? A price has to be paid only so that one's being and consciousness evolves to an extent that one can absorb it and deserve it.

In the words of Swami Vivekananda:

"The heart has to be cut and the bleeding heart placed on the altar of sacrifice. Only then great things are done."

But what kind of sacrifice are we talking about? Giving up sensual gratifications by exerting physical pressure or control? Or giving up certain type of foods, a lifestyle, habits, or addictions? As discussed earlier, some techniques do require a certain rigor and discipline to be followed.

However, other priorities may prevent us from devoting the time meant to be committed to this pursuit (e.g. for meditation). Work and household commitments, time pressures, not receiving any positive feedback or not experiencing positive repercussions leads many seekers to quit because of inadequate motivation or reassurance/reinforcement.

However, the suffering in question is something more subtle and intangible that cannot be directly attributed to the path. As an example, this could include the difficulties that befall a person through a change of circumstances or external situations after he starts treading upon this path. These circumstances, situations, or events may cause one to suffer. The only conscious sacrifice expected is to persist and, even while suffering, continue treading the path rather than quitting it.

There are always exceptions to this. Those whose accumulated karma in the past are not so negative and do not suffer as much as those who have a huge pile-up of negative karma. The spiritual path will only accelerate the working out of one's past karma. It will not determine the consequences one will have to undergo, as that will depend on what one has sown in the past.

The next question that may arise is: "Am I not better off working out my karma at my own pace? That way, at least I will not risk having to suddenly face an overdose of suffering due to an accelerated karma redemption process."

Two responses can be given to the above dilemma.

In Part I, in the chapter on Karma and its principles, we learned that apart from accelerating the rate of working out one's past karma, the spiritual path decelerates the accumulation of present and future karma. It does so by causing less attachment to new karma and therefore lessening the bondage to the fruits thereof.

While we could possibly avoid the accelerated suffering by not following the spiritual path (due to working out a large stock of past karma in a shorter time span), we would still continue to accumulate new karma. The new karma would also need to be suffered; and thus we could never possibly come out of this vicious circle.

By following the spiritual path, one is, in a way, trying to reach the Ultimate Truth. By thus offering ourselves into the hands of the Divine, we should trust Divinity to decide how much suffering is bearable as well as the optimum route to work out our karma.

"If even a very wicked person worships Me, with devotion to none else, he should be regarded as good, for he has rightly resolved."

(Bhagwad Gita: Ch. IX/30)

"Soon does he become righteous, and attain eternal Peace, O son of Kunti; boldly canst thou proclaim, that my devotee is never destroyed."

(Bhagwad Gita: Ch. IX/31)

Then, there is the aspect of Grace. Grace provides the inner strength to bear suffering and acts as a buffer to disillusionment. In the next chapter, we will discuss a story on how grace flows.

SUMMARY:

The path of spirituality holds promises of bliss, of *ananda*. However, there often comes an interim phase in the path of many seekers where they may experience some trials and tribulations. This is often the period when the grip of worldly pleasures has loosened, but the flow of nectar from the spiritual realm has not yet begun.

By pursuing the spiritual path, one goes through a process of evolution and internal cleansing. Any process of change involves pain; hence, one may face certain difficulties. However, one should continue on with determination and go through the process in its entirety. The resulting self-purification is a prerequisite to fathoming the Absolute Reality. It is like a price to be paid. But Divine nature may make it less painful for the deserving.

3   YOU MAY HAVE LEARNT THE METHOD, BUT PERSISTENCE IS THE KEY

There are impediments to persisting on the path with faith and motivation. These impediments are discussed in this chapter so that a seeker is better prepared to deal with them.

1. Inaccessibility of the guru

It may not be possible to meet, touch, or talk with the guru or master of the technique short-listed by the seeker. One needs to evaluate how important this is to oneself. If the master is not available, can the bona fide teachers of the path make up for this?

It may be noted that a number of masters have institutionalized their techniques and teachings to such an extent that it can reach the masses in a pure and undiluted form, even without their presence or direct supervision.

2. Finding Inspiring Teachers

One of the critical elements in most techniques is to find a suitable teacher with whom one can relate and who can satisfy one's doubts. The other important aspect is finding brand ambassadors

a. Who have practiced the technique for long enough (at least two or more years) and will vouch for its efficacy

b. With whom one can relate intellectually.

c. Who can empathize with what a new learner may be going through and can provide useful suggestions.

Note: It may be mentioned here, that most paths may dissuade an individual from sharing specific experiences with anyone other than the trained teacher. This is because each person's experiences are generally different and sharing can lead to a bias among other seekers. Hence, it is important to let the teacher know about any other persons with whom the seeker intends to share his or her experiences.

3. Tangibility of results

Some people do experience tangible results with the practice of a technique. For example, this may include relief from

- High blood pressure
- Disturbed sleep
- Paranoia
- Stressed nerves

At the same time, there may be others who do not feel that they have achieved anything worthwhile, even after months of practice. This may be viewed as follows:

a. It is virtually impossible to objectively measure spiritual growth, irrespective of the path chosen. Hence, the feeling that they have not progressed may not be a true representation of reality. It should not lead an individual to automatically abandon the technique.

b. Each person's experience may be different depending on the chosen path. We know that different medical approaches take different time periods to have an effect, e.g. homeopathy vs. allopathy vs. ayurveda.

c. It may also be a function of the individual's current level of evolution. Even within the same approach (e.g. allopathy), it may take different lengths of time for relief to be felt, depending on the nature and severity of the ailment.

   - An ache may subside within hours.
   - A cold or fever may take few days to recede.
   - An antidepressant may take a few weeks before it shows any perceivable results.

- A patient with a chronic condition may only feel any tangible relief after a few months.

Hence, the important thing is to be able to decipher what one needs to do in order to address one's current situation or predicament. One needs to choose from the following possible measures:

1. Share the predicament/feedback with a trained teacher, and seek advice and intervention.

2. Listen to feedback and seek counsel from known and trusted people who have been pursuing the same path or any other spiritual technique.

3. Review the chosen path.

The simpler and easier techniques may be more prone to doubt, as we do not easily believe anything that is simple. We may expect something complex and intricate, just as we tend to trust the doctor who shows off his degrees or prescribes a number of medicines or dispenses a number of tablets or capsules of varied colours and sizes!

One should thus not be biased against the potential efficacy or potency of a seemingly simple technique.

4. Feeling worse – especially dull and lethargic

This may be due to:

- The body's longstanding need for deep rest, which had been repressed or ignored for years and is finally being manifested.
- The internal cleansing process
- Incorrectly following the instructions of the technique
- The technique not being in sync with one's being
- The technique itself being suspect

If this is not quickly overcome, one may suffer due to self-doubt. The dropout rate is often high in such cases. Hence, one must take suitable counter-measures that are well-considered and based on facts.

5. Aversion to Satsang, Kirtan, or Bhajan

A large number of popular techniques today may not have any of these elements. If the chosen technique does emphasize these and one is not comfortable with them, one has the option of simply ignoring this part. This should not alter the effectiveness of the technique if this is not an integral part of the technique.

6. Supplication to the guru

Many fellow seekers may be so enchanted with the master that they cannot stop expressing their love and obeisance to him or her. Rationalists who are just beginning to explore this particular technique may feel a little out of place with this, as they may not feel this way about the guru. In such a case, the seeker should realize that there are always several seekers on any path who are progressing forward without expressing such reverence to the master.

In most of the paths, one is likely to realize, with closer observation, that the path itself or the master himself may not be seeking this. The master may simply be accepting whatever the seekers are showering on him, without either encouraging or rejecting it.

7. Residential Programs

Many techniques require or strongly recommend residential programs to reinforce the technique. These programs could be between 2 and 10 days long and be held every year. This can be a challenge for busy, overworked professionals who are barely able to manage a few days' break in a year with family.

8. Finding the Time

An hour or so a day for spiritual practice may seem doable and undemanding. But this needs to be put into perspective with regards to the time pressure people face nowadays.

• The morning walk or workout that one may need because of

one's health and weight problems is often ignored because one wants to get that extra bit of sleep. An individual may rationalize this by telling himself that since he works so hard and so late, any compromise on his sleep would make him dull and worn out throughout the day.

Would it be easy for such a person to wake up a bit earlier to practice meditation before leaving for work?

Those who work late in office tend to:

— Eat dinner soon after arriving home, or

— Eat dinner at the office

However, most techniques require a minimum of three hours of fasting before meditation. If one is returning late, say after 9 PM, what option does one have? Meditating before dinner will mean eating after 10 PM, which is bad for the health and will meet with resistance from the family. In the 10-12 odd hours that one is at home on working days, one has to allocate time for sleep, watching TV, unwinding, taking care of the kids, chatting with one's spouse, and reading, among other things. Therefore, deciding what of these one should sacrifice in order to incorporate meditation into one's life becomes a challenge.

Hence, one needs to be:

1. Determined,

2. Able to prioritize activities, and

3. Able to seek and receive the support of all stakeholders in one's life in order to ensure that one can actually take out the time to practice the spiritual technique.

SUMMARY

While finding the right path is a definite challenge, continuing practice is often not so easy due to several doubts and practical difficulties that a person may face. The doubts can include: "Am I on the right track? How do I know for sure? I cannot really feel anything dramatic?" Another impediment is finding the time to practice in the morning and evening, amidst so many pressures, commitments, and activities. Knowing this up front, and also realizing that many others go through this predicament, is helpful in being prepared to handle it..

PART-IV.

WE NEED MORE THAN JUST SPIRITUALITY TO FIND FULFILMENT

(This section covers other aspects that help us find fulfilment)

IS SPIRITUALITY THE MEANS AS WELL AS THE END?

There are teachers who will tell you, "Just Meditation is enough. Nothing else is required. It will take care of all your physical ailments as well." While this may be true in a certain sense, a seeker is better off not leaving every solution of life to meditation and spirituality. In other words, spirituality is an aid, but may not be the panacea for all our ills.

Some of the ailments might actually recede due to the practice of meditation, as meditation can help to:

- Repair and heal one's mind, body, and soul.
- Nurture all the dimensions of one's life
- Help in the fulfilment of physical and emotional needs

However, simply stating that meditation and spirituality are the panacea for all the ills in life is not easy for a seeker to accept. Many teachers will ask:

- Are you experiencing pain? Are you anxious? Are you depressed? Meditate and all will become well.
- Have you been separated from a loved one? Are you feeling lonely? Meditate, do Satsang and Japa and you will feel fulfilled.
- Has someone hurt you? Has your ego or self-esteem been undermined? That is only because you don't yet have humility. You need to progress on the spiritual path and be humbled by spiritual evolution. Hence, you need to practice more intensely what has been taught to you.

They may even go beyond this and say:

- If you are not actively following a spiritual path or a technique, you are missing a lot. You are incomplete. Your life, efforts, and achievements are of little worth, and you have no purpose in life. You are like a rudderless ship on the sea. The ultimate purpose should be to attain God, to attain enlightenment and to be free from this cycle of birth-death-rebirth.

Many will tell you that the very purpose of human birth is to attain enlightenment. One of the theories in India is that after being born 84 lakh (10 lakh = 1 million) times in various species, one is given the human form, and that only the human form has the capacity to attain God.

This is further expounded by the fact that only the human form/species has been endowed with the capacity to break away from the karmic cycle and attain enlightenment/liberation.

Summarizing what has just has been said, the two key messages of many spiritual tracks are:

- *Follow an active spiritual path. That is the ultimate and only remedy and recourse.*
- *If you are not following it, your life and existence have little meaning or purpose.*

This seems incredible for someone who is just beginning their spiritual path and is trying to figure out if it makes sense, to what extent, and how much time to commit to it. But what one is being told is to make it the very aim of one's existence. This becomes too assuming, demanding, and difficult, and creates doubts in the minds of seekers.

Is there any rationale to stating that spirituality is the only way? Or is it simply a pure attempt to sell spirituality?

Let us view this from the four dimensions in which one lives, as mentioned in the previous chapter, juxtaposed against Maslow's hierarchy of needs.

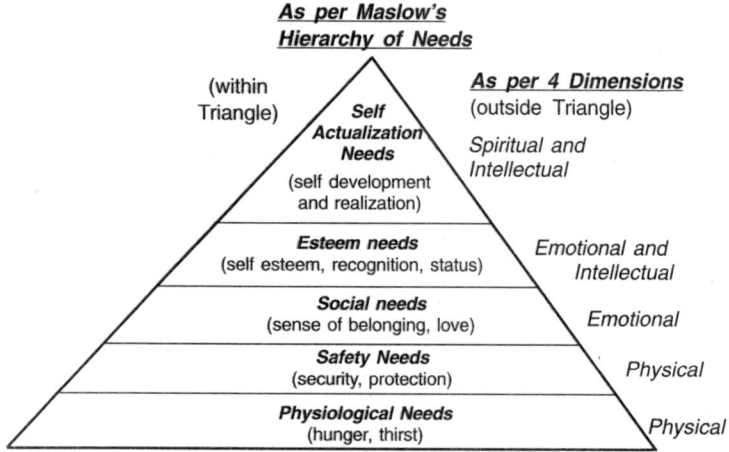

According to this theory, human needs are arranged in a hierarchy, from the most to the least pressing. A person will try to satisfy the most important (or pressing) needs first. When a person succeeds in satisfying an important need, it will cease to be a motivator and the person will try to satisfy the next most important need.

In fact, if we look at the top of the grid, i.e. at self-actualization, we can perhaps further divide this into two parts, upper and lower:

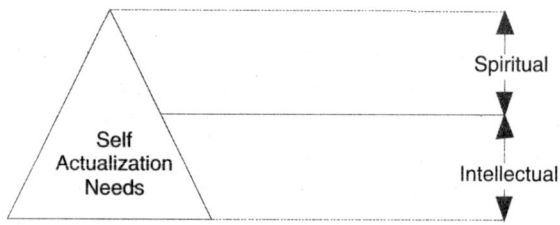

Spiritual needs are placed in the upper half of this grid, while intellectual needs are a notch below, in the same grid.

Following the hierarchy of needs, one can reckon that one only reaches this top grid (Spiritual + Intellectual) after one's lower needs, i.e. physical, emotional, and, to some extent, intellectual, are fulfilled.

In the same vein, a person will seek the fulfilment of his spiritual needs only when the other three (physical, emotional, and intellectual) have been taken care of.

"You can't teach philosophy to a hungry man," said Swami Vivekananda.

However, following the strict, unidirectional approach to the hierarchy of needs might lead us to some disconnect. One could argue that if one still feels the need for more physical comforts, financial security, emotional bonding, and intellectual stimulation (which most of us probably do):

* *One is not ready for the spiritual journey. So why should one attempt it at all at this stage?*

* *If one has all the three needs – physical, emotional, and intellectual – does that mean that he or she has not progressed upwards beyond the first grid of physical needs on the hierarchy of needs?*

Let us tackle the second disconnect first. Our own experience shows that the hierarchy of needs is not really a **"water-tight grid"** with a **"unidirectional movement"**. Even a person thirsting for the fulfilment of spiritual needs may feel insecure, and look for protection, love, and belonging at times. Maslow's theory helps us understand our own behaviours and motivations, especially with respect to certain specific decisions that we might take in a given context or situation. However, the theory does not say that once we arrive at a higher need level (e.g. the need for spiritual fulfilment), we will never act or exhibit a lower need in any given situation.

Now, the first disconnect. The experience of one's yearning for intellectual, emotional, or physical needs does not mean that one is not eligible for the spiritual quest or journey. As mentioned above, one can thirst for spiritual knowledge even while one's desires in the other three lower dimensions are not completely satiated. Hence, feeling any of the lower needs is not a sign that one is not yet ready to undertake an active spiritual journey.

Now, let us look at the question that we raised at the beginning of this chapter: Is there a logic or method in stating that spirituality is the only way?

In order to understand why such a statement exists, one may look at Maslow's grid, inverted.

- **When viewed this way, the grid implies that the fulfilment**

Maslow Hierarchy's Inverted

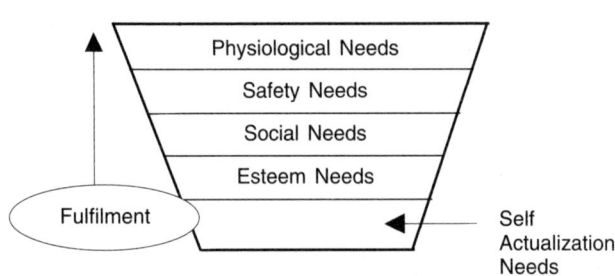

of one's spiritual needs can lead to the fulfilment of all other needs.** Many spiritual teachers and methods tell us that treading the right spiritual path helps one nourish and nurture all aspects of one's existence. As Maharishi Mahesh Yogi explains: The experience of the pure state of consciousness can be compared to the sap, which plants draw from the ground. The sap is colourless, odourless, and pure, but the same sap helps to make the leaves green, the flowers red, and the fruit of another colour and taste. It acts as nourishment, providing life and energy.

- Thus, the idea that spirituality takes care of many problems is not purely a selling point. In fact, even in the very early stages of the spiritual journey, a number of paths enable the seeker to experience more fulfilment in various other dimensions of their existence.

SUMMARY

Many teachers and spiritual organizations claim that spirituality is a panacea for the many ills that a person suffers. The method or logic is based on the fact that the spiritual journey helps to nourish and vitalize the other three dimensions of one's life – the physical, the emotional, and the mental.

Many people claim that spirituality is the most important purpose in a person's life. There is no need to internalize this all-powerful view of spirituality just to begin pursuing the path. One can simply add spirituality to life without submitting or surrendering any other dimension. Nor should one take the complete satiation of all other needs – physical, emotional, or mental – either as (a) the yardstick of spiritual progress, or (b) the readiness to undertake the journey. Such a fulfilled/gratified state is not a prerequisite for treading the path in full earnest; rather, it is a goal.

A modern, ambitious person who is *first* seeking fulfilment in *this life,* and then in the *after life* would be advised to consciously work as much on the other three dimensions (physical, mental, and emotional) as on the spiritual one. Thus, the shift from ignoring and doubting spirituality to making it the primary pursuit need not be sudden. The good news is that irrespective of the goals that one was seeking to fulfil through spirituality, any path would serve the purpose, provided it is right and capable. What this means is that if Person A is looking at spirituality to reduce stress, Person B for cosmic knowledge, and Person C for enlightenment, they need not adopt different paths that vary in intensity. The same path can help these three different individuals achieve their respective goals. However, this does not mean that just any path will do. The path has to be chosen carefully, and the selection criteria need not be intensity, objective, or goal because even a person seeking out a release from stress would progress towards path of enlightenment, while one who is not bothered by stress but is seeking supreme consciousness will receive relief to soothe the nerves.

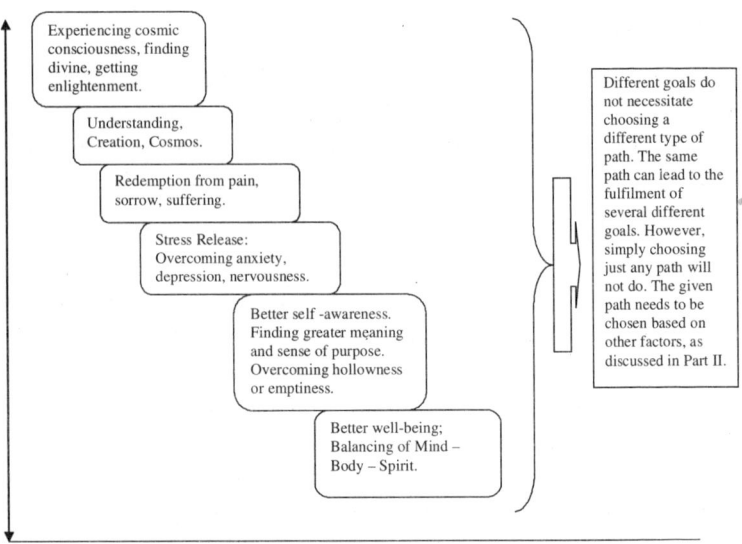

A beginner just starting out on an exploration of the spiritual realm and still having a number of doubts, queries, and concerns should look at spirituality as an add-on in their lives. There is no need to be in a hurry to believe or trust it completely, to surrender to it; or to make it their ultimate goal of life.

Modern science is increasingly pointing to the fact that the physical, intellectual, mental, and emotional dimensions are not mutually exclusive. Rather, they are constantly interacting with each other.

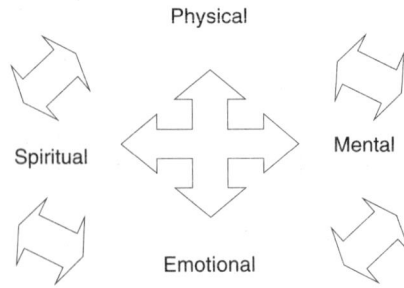

SUMMARY

Among the 4 dimensions, spirituality is often the least understood and the most ignored. We are often led to believe that this path, shrouded in mystique, would mean compromising one's rationality. However, the important thing is to pursue the path in an unbiased way – neither surrendering to it nor distrusting it. Give the chosen path enough time before passing judgment on it or rejecting it. Seekers often quit because they do not receive satisfactory answers to their questions. Most importantly, one must learn to be patient with one's doubts and misgivings. One should be prepared to wait to get all the answers, as immediate resolutions may often not be forthcoming.

Should one, then, focus only on the spiritual life hoping that it will take care of all other aspects or dimensions of living? A safer and far more logical approach would be to consciously maximize living in all four dimensions, rather than focusing on only one and neglecting the others.

Thus, knowing that (a) each dimension is interlinked, i.e. good physical health may also mean sound mental health, and (b) the spiritual dimension can nurture all the other dimensions, **it is recommended that one actively and consciously focus upon all four dimensions** – physical, intellectual, emotional, and spiritual.

ALL OTHER DIMENSIONS ARE JUST AS CRITICAL AS SPIRITUALITY

THE PHYSICAL DIMENSION

Vivekananda often said: "First make your biceps and forceps stronger. Then you will understand the Gita better!"

To live life well in the physical dimension, one must:

- Incorporate regular physical exercise into one's lifestyle
- Take care of one's diet
- Get an adequate amount of sleep and rest
- Lead a balanced lifestyle

One may react to this and say, "What's new in this? One hears this all the time."

That may be so, but the important thing is to actually implement these into one's life. A simple thing as regular exercise, or even a daily brisk walk, can make a lot of difference in the quality of one's existence. The important thing is not to say "I know", but to actually do it. Inertia is inevitable and it makes one resist the effort to undertake such activities, but that little extra resolve to overcome the inertia is critical. This is so because once one experiences the benefits of taking care of one's diet, exercise, lifestyle, and sleep firsthand, one will realize that the difference is significant. And that would provide the motivation to continue.

"Should I be a vegetarian? Should I follow a diet consisting mostly of fruit, like many yogis and saints?"

The choice of being a vegetarian or a non-vegetarian is a purely personal one. While many spiritual paths do encourage vegetarianism, it is difficult to prescribe the right thing to do. An advisable thing would be to start the active pursuit of whichever path one has chosen and follow its precepts. As most masters will tell you, as you progress along the path, the things that should stay with you shall stay, and those that should not will slip away of their own accord. In other words, if being a vegetarian is good for you, then through your natural evolution along the path, you will instinctively leave non-vegetarian food without force, self-control, or sacrifice.

As far as putting yourself mainly on a fruit and milk diet, not only depends on the dietary recommendations of the chosen path, but also its relevance and practicality, as well as the state of one's health. Most paths may not suggest this on an ongoing basis. In a nutshell, one should look at the situation with a practical viewpoint based on what is desirable and necessary.

THE MENTAL/INTELLECTUAL DIMENSION

Many psychologists have said: "The mind needs to be fed continuously. It is always churning. If it does not find any input, it starts feeding on itself."

What does this mean? It simply means that the old adages, such as "an empty mind is a devil's workshop" and "more people have died of idleness than overwork", are perhaps true.

All of us have experienced our mental condition when we are unwell, indisposed, and locked up at home. Things that we had longed for, such as sleeping as long as we would like, not going to work, or watching movies at home seem like a joy for the first few days. However, depending on our individual thresholds, just a *"few" days,* is the limit. After that, we feel desperate to be up on our feet and on the move. We pray to get well so that we may resume our work and get back to our normal schedule. Why does that happen? It happens because the mind is no longer being stimulated through external inputs and the work that one was used to.

Our mind and intellect constantly hunger for more knowledge and stimulation. The level of need, however, may vary from one individual to another. Even the nature of things that can provide a similar level of satisfaction or mental stimulation may be different for different people. The important thing is to understand '*the nature of*' and '*the quantum of*' the '*intellectual diet*' that one needs in order to be happy.

A psychologist once said:

"The tools of the mind become an unbearable burden when the environment that made them necessary no longer exists".

This simply means that if our mind is accustomed to churning and running at a certain rate, we should not try to hold it back. We should continue to facilitate the utilization of the tools, capabilities, and energy of the mind.

Many people find that they are unhappy simply because they feel they are not contributing enough. They tell themselves: "I don't seem to be adding much value."

To whom and to what do they want to add value? To the task at hand? To their immediate environment? To the lives of people they work, live, and associate with? To themselves?

This dilemma typically applies to an under-utilized employee who thinks he can do much more, but is not being given the opportunity. A dominated and inconspicuous housewife, whose mother-in-law does all the noticeable work, such as cooking special dishes on important occasions is another example. Both of them want to do more.

But what do they really want to do? We will examine this by looking at the nature and quest of the mind.

By its very nature, the mind can also be visualized as a perpetual processing machine, for as long as it is alive. It works on whatever inputs it receives, processes them and the creates the output.

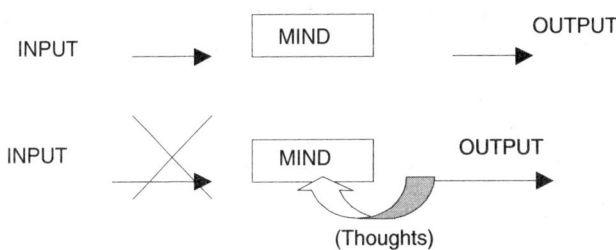

If one stops the inputs from coming in, the mind still continues to work, process, and churn. In the absence of any inputs, it churns on what it already has, which are the various thoughts already in the mind. These thoughts may be enjoyable for some time, but may soon lead to boredom. One will then want to get out of this state by undertaking some external activity, which may be as simple as a chat with a friend or even a stranger.

It is easy to say that in times of slow external activity, one must learn to accept and live with oneself, to be content in the self, and to experience the peace within. However, most people cannot bear this state for long because external silence, quietude, and inactivity can often wreak havoc in the mind after some time.

What does the mind really want? It wants a quality input that satisfies and that preferably leads to a quality output. By generating such an output, the mind knows that it has contributed and added value to itself. And that serves as a significant reward and reinforcement for the mind.

The awareness and recognition that one's mind has contributed or added value can come from:

(a) The mind's own intelligence, assessment, and auto-feedback system.

(b) Receiving appreciation and praise from others.

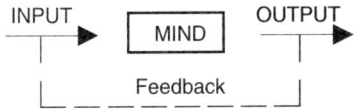

In the same way, if one obtains feedback that one's output or contribution is useless, then one may feel a loss of self-worth.

In many situations, one may feel that even negative feedback creates a better state for the mind than the unhappiness that it experiences due to the void created when inputs are blocked.

What inputs or stimulations are we talking about?

In our example of the under-utilized employee, the employee may seek a higher level of responsibility or more challenging work because he thinks he can handle it. His mind (and his *being*) know intuitively that by doing so, his level of output will be higher. In turn, he believes this will lead to more positive feedback and recognition from others and thus an increased sense of self-esteem.

In the case of the bored housewife, she may want to do something concrete and tangible; everyday household chores may simply not satisfy her. The nature, capability, and energy level of her mind may be compelling her to seek more out of her life. Many may enjoy cooking food. They may get satisfaction from providing it to the family and receiving appreciation for it, but for others, cooking may not be such a gratifying activity. "Even a paid cook can do it," they might say. Or their satisfaction may come from doing up their homes in different ways by utilizing and expressing their artistic talents. For others, it may be the pursuit of fine arts, music, painting, or dance, while for some, teaching, social work, or entrepreneurship may provide fulfilment..

Let us take another example: A person is in a profession that he or she does not like. He may work hard at it and yet still feel a sense of emptiness. He gets little satisfaction from what he is doing. How does one explain this? Here again, the principles are the same. Even while his energy was being expended in whatever work he was doing, the, mind driven by its nature and capability, may be dissatisfied. The mind wants something else, but it may be unable to pinpoint what that is. It may simply continue to suffer with the feeling that "something is amiss".

For people who experience such a state of mind, the way out would be to form an understanding of their deep desires and motivations. It may not be easy, and simple introspection may not help. They may need external help through advice from experts, close friends, and family members who understand them deeply. Intensive interactions with them may help provide broad directions as well as specific insights into their nature and their drives, strengths, weaknesses, and latent talents.

The above can be augmented by deep introspection and self-analysis. This may include an *assessment of how and why they acted in certain ways and what events of their lives could have influenced this.*

- What have been my happiest moments? What have been my saddest moments? In daily life, what gives me joy? What excites me? What books, magazines, and articles interest me? What TV programs do I like? What movies have I liked, and why? Who are my role models? Who are the people I admire? Who are the people I hate, and why? What attracts me? What turns me off? What am I generally seeking? What are those small and big things that give me goose bumps? What brings tears to my eyes?

- What is my idea of unwinding? What re-energises me? What gets my adrenaline pumping?

- What am I really looking for in life?

Working on the following, often-quoted thought-triggers (which have become clichés) may be useful:

- What do I want my epitaph to read? How do I want to be remembered when I am no more?

- If I had only one month left to live, what would I do?

- If I were to relive my life from the beginning, what would I do and not do?

The above analysis may need to be done over a period of time. It may be a good idea to jot down whatever comes to one's mind in relation to the above questions. It may make no sense initially and very few conclusions or inferences may seem to evolve. However, over a period of time, depending on the depth of the above analysis, one might be able to paint a full memoir of how one's psyche, emotions, intellect, and spirit work.

How are these insights different from the ones obtained through self-observation or meditative techniques, such as Vipassana? There may be subtle differences, as described below:

  i. *The process of seeking insights*: In Vipassana, the focus is not so much on intellectual analysis, but on the observation of thoughts and mind-body sensations. In the process of the intellectual self-assessment discussed above, the focus is on mental *analysis*, remembering or recalling events, dwelling upon them, and introspecting on how we behaved in a certain way or in certain situations. Also of great benefit would be deep introspection on what constitutes our joys, sorrows, victories, and defeats.

 ii. *The outcome of each process:* While Vipassana will also lead to spiritual progress and transformation, the self-analysis might only lead to a better awareness and sensitisation about oneself.

After one has gained insight through either method, what should one do? It's simple. **Give to the mind-intellect the food that it needs.** One will need to figure out how to do so, but below are a few examples of activities one may add into one's schedule:

(a) Seriously pursuing a hobby of one's taste (e.g. photography, painting, music, dance, sports)

(b) Acquiring knowledge over a period of time so as to earn the status of being an "expert" on any chosen area or subject of interest. This may include things as erudite as Greek mythology or metaphysics; mundane things such as wines, horses, or cars; or mass appeal things such as career counselling, futurology, gemmology, astrology, or feng shui.

(c) Doing something inventive or creative based on one's passion or skill. (e.g. devising a software program or building a machine.)

(d) Joining a club, association, or forum of like-minded people who meet and interact at regular intervals.

(e) Sharing one's skill, knowledge, and competence. This can start out in an humble way through one's immediate local fraternity/society/network/club, which may have been formed through the workplace or community. This sharing and recognition can serve as fuel for further pursuits and greater achievements.

How will the above help in satiating the hunger of the mind? Such activities will result in an enhanced quality and quantity of input to and output of the mind. The involvement of the mind in things it likes will trigger more creativity. This may lead to recognition and even accolades. The natural outcomes would be a higher sense of self-esteem and a positively engaged mind. This utilization of the mind, feeding it with what it yearns for will cause it to work harder, process the inputs, and yield an output. Leaving aside the output, the functioning of the mind will, in itself, be a reward that one can feel and be grateful for. This occurs whenever the mind is made to move away from a state of under-utilization to "being on its toes". However, the output itself will be meaningful and will lead to a sense of achievement. This will lead to a sense of fulfilment that will nurture the emotional dimension.

THE EMOTIONAL DIMENSION

One may ask: "How does one work towards emotional fulfilment? By developing a love for all living things including fellowmen, colleagues, and neighbours? But how can I do this?"

One may further observe: "After all, love can't be forced. If I don't have any feelings for certain types of people, how can I forcibly nurture them? What is being suggested to me? Should I smile at or hug every person I meet? Should I have compassion for every animal or tree that I see? I am not yet a Buddha. Please don't force me to live in an illusory world!"

The above reactions are not unnatural. Many of us react this way when we hear sermons on "loving everyone". What, then, do we mean by living fully and nurturing the emotional dimension?

Since a majority of us live, feel, enjoy, and suffer at the *emotional level* for a substantial part of our existence, it is important to explore how to improve this dimension.

Let us look at the **emotional dimension** from the following perspectives or challenges. They are being referred to as challenges because we are unable to practice or implement the mandates of most spiritual teachings on these subjects or aspects.

Thankfulness:

If we can achieve this one thing called thankfulness, we would be rid of so many ills such as jealousy, frustration, or the feeling of being cheated. We would thus be charged with so much positivity. Even though thankfulness sounds so simple, it is, in fact, one of the most difficult things to come by. Let us explore why we do not feel thankful, *even though practically all teachings, across so many religions and spiritual masters, tell us to be grateful*. Many of us may have gone through some of the following thoughts in this context:

a. Even though I have feet to walk with and I know that many don't, I still can't feel grateful all the time for having them.

b. Even though I have a decent house, family, job, and friends, I am still not satisfied or thankful. I find myself yearning for more.

c. Even though I have enough food to eat, it is difficult for me to feel thrilled about it all the time.

Upon deeper introspection, we might even say:

"I will be shattered if any one of the above is taken away from me. I need each and every one of these gifts from God. I even know many who are not as lucky as I am to have these things. However, I still don't feel grateful or content."

In fact, we don't even wonder why we are not grateful unless we are made to think about it.

The genesis of this may lie in the fact that we constantly tell ourselves, consciously or unconsciously, any of the following statements:

- "Even if I do have all of the above, so do my friends, family, and acquaintances. After all, I should compare myself with people with whom I have lived, studied, and grown up. They have all the same things as me, and perhaps more. There are many people who are better looking, live in bigger homes, drive better cars, and are more popular with the opposite sex. Though we may have graduated from the same college together, many of my friends earn twice as much as me, and some of them have created a name for themselves in the industry, whereas I am practically a non-entity. I feel out of place, even with some of my classmates, because they have made it much bigger in life than I have. They are in a far better 'class' or 'league' than me. Of course, if I compare myself with the poor children living on the streets, I am certainly better off, but is that a fair comparison? Should I not compare myself with my equals? I may be better off than some of my acquaintances and distant relatives, but I can count many more who are better off than me."

- "I am told to enjoy the chirping of birds in the morning, the sunrise, the fresh air, the greenery, but how can I feel excited about things that I see on a daily basis? Would that not be abnormal and hypocritical?"

Intuitively, we take these things, which are critical to our survival, for granted. Hence, we do not see the merit or feasibility in constantly reminding ourselves about these.

Now let us look at situations when we are, in fact, thankful.

- When a loved one goes through a critical illness or undergoes a surgery and the doctors say that he or she is in "serious" condition. We pray, cry, and take vows, saying, "Just cure him, Lord, and I will..." And miraculously, the prayers are heard and we can't stop our tears of thankfulness.

- When we have been suffering from acute pain for a long time and no treatment seems to be working. Life becomes unbearable, and we are willing to do anything to get rid of the pain, but we do not succeed. Then, somehow, the pain disappears. We can't believe it, and fear its recurrence, but are thankful nevertheless

- When we win a prize, award, recognition, or honour that we did not expect.
- When the results of an exam are far better than our expectations.
- When we are living an average life and we suddenly find its quality dramatically improved. We compare what we have now with what we had earlier and we rejoice.

Many people may even go through such bad times that retaining their possessions becomes threatened. Some may suffer a setback and drop down to a lower level of satisfaction. If this drop is temporary and they recoup fairly quickly, their mind will discard it as an aberration. However, if living life at a lower level (say at level 5, when they were already dissatisfied at level 8.5) continues for a long enough period of time, they might slowly become convinced that they may actually have to accept living their life at this lower level. More events may occur that may even threaten their ability to sustain themselves at this level.

Suppose that, after the above phase, the wheels of fortune slowly start to change and the person rises back to the level of 8.5, where he had previously been unhappy. How would he react to this reinstated level? Would he now not be grateful for bouncing back to level 8.5? In fact, he would likely pray to be sustained at this level, without ever again experiencing the fall to a lower level. Why does this happen?

Because:

(a) Earlier, one expected much more out of life, and thus, past achievements seemed inadequate and inconsequential.

(b) Having experienced that one can't take anything for granted (even an existence at level 5), one realizes the value of what one possessed earlier and also of what he has been able to regain (i.e. an existence at level 8.5).

The above also explains the value of pain and suffering. Either we learn to be thankful with what we have, or we go through pain that teaches us to be thankful and not to take things for granted. If neither happens, we may continue through our life with complaints, envy, and despair.

The *auto-suggestion* that suffering might come to us any time or that we may lose everything we have may not be good enough, because deep within, we are always telling ourselves that "it will never happen to me". We may hear, for example, real stories of young people in their 30s or 40s who have become paralyzed and cannot get up from their bed for the rest of their life. This might have been caused by a brain fever, a small injury, the dysfunction of some nerve in the spine, or perhaps a sudden spurt in blood pressure, without any forewarning or symptoms in the past.

Yet do we feel thankful that we are able to stand on our feet and walk and run? Do we feel ecstatic about the fact that we are able to go out, play, watch movies, visit friends, go shopping, and go to work? Do we ever think how miserable life would be if we were confined to our room and bed and needed a wheelchair to move around?

The acute suffering of others who may be of a similar profile or reference group may affect us for some time, but deep within, **we believe their pain is far removed from our lives and that we will never be touched by it.** We may justify such situations as freak incidents, or try to infer that perhaps the individual's past karma was responsible. Life continues as usual for us, and we continue to live with complaints, emptiness, and a lack of enthusiasm for what we have.

Different people operate from different levels of fear and insecurity, which in turn influences how they think about the likelihood of good or bad events occurring in their lives. This is shown in the chart below:

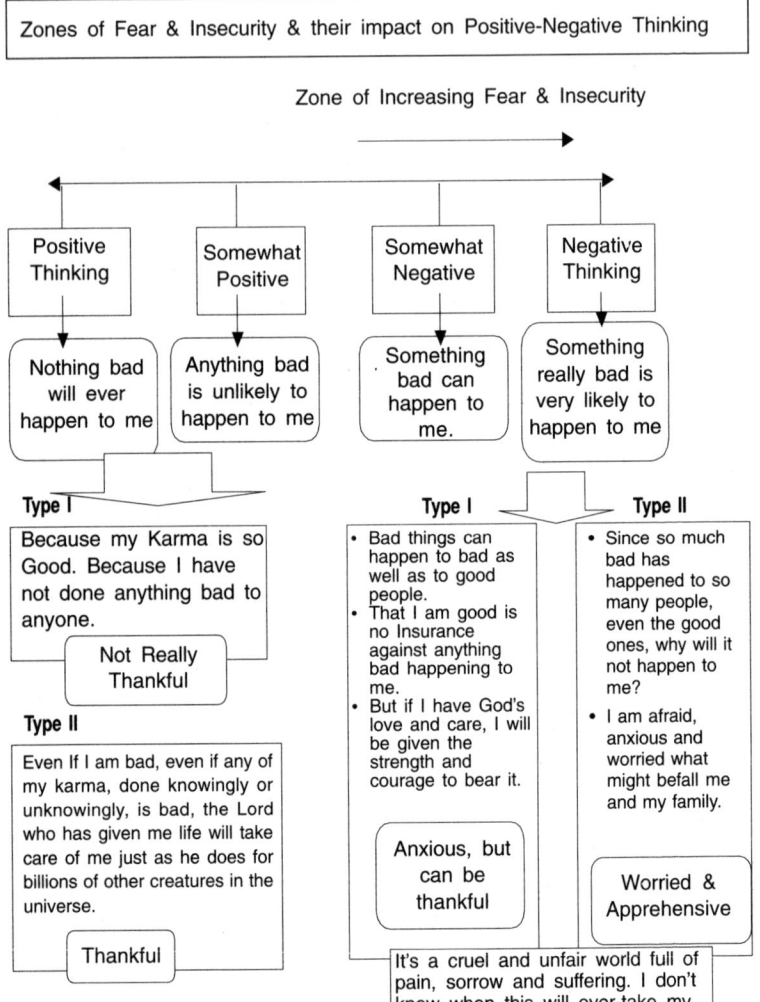

Zones of Fear & Insecurity & their impact on Positive-Negative Thinking

Zone of Increasing Fear & Insecurity

| Positive Thinking | Somewhat Positive | Somewhat Negative | Negative Thinking |

| Nothing bad will ever happen to me | Anything bad is unlikely to happen to me | Something bad can happen to me. | Something really bad is very likely to happen to me |

Type I

Because my Karma is so Good. Because I have not done anything bad to anyone.

Not Really Thankful

Type II

Even If I am bad, even if any of my karma, done knowingly or unknowingly, is bad, the Lord who has given me life will take care of me just as he does for billions of other creatures in the universe.

Thankful

Type I

- Bad things can happen to bad as well as to good people.
- That I am good is no Insurance against anything bad happening to me.
- But if I have God's love and care, I will be given the strength and courage to bear it.

Anxious, but can be thankful

Type II

- Since so much bad has happened to so many people, even the good ones, why will it not happen to me?
- I am afraid, anxious and worried what might befall me and my family.

Worried & Apprehensive

It's a cruel and unfair world full of pain, sorrow and suffering. I don't know when this will over-take my life

As we can see from the chart, there are two types of *Positive/Somewhat Positive* thinkers:

- The first type are generally not thankful because they always expect only good things to happen to them, and when good things do happen, they do not consider it to be a big deal.

* The second type are generally thankful because of faith.

There are also two types of **Negative/Somewhat Negative** thinkers:

* The first have their feet firmly on the ground and know that bad things can happen to anyone. Though they may be anxious, they are grateful for whatever positivity they have in their lives.

* The second type consists of those who are too worried, apprehensive, and anxious to be grateful.

SIGNIFICANCE OF PAIN

"What is the use of pain?" we may wonder. "Why did God create pain at all?"

If God really wanted to teach us how to be strong in life, He could have found an easier way than subjecting us to pain and grief. While we might want to protest against all the suffering that God has created, we must also objectively take into account the value of painful times or phases in our lives.

* They are humble experiences that help to crush our inflated egos.

* They make us realize that *it* (bad things) can happen to us and hence help us to be aware of what (good things) we have. This can often be a big aid in nurturing thankfulness within us.

These experiences can be transformative. They can:

* Build sensitivity in us towards the pain and misery of others.

* Implant seeds of compassion in us.

* Increase our emotional quotient.

* Make us gentler and more caring.

* Make us better human beings.

* Grant us more maturity.

But is there no flipside? There surely is. If one's tolerance to pain is low and the severity of the pain is very high, many might just succumb to it or be overwhelmed by it. Nervous breakdowns, depression, and other psychosomatic diseases may occur. This is more likely if severity is combined with a longer duration of pain and suffering. An **acute pain** for a **short duration** may also cause damage, such as instilling in us an obsessive fear of pain and faintheartedness. Long, drawn-out pain, however, can be far more damaging to one's psyche.

We can compare the pain in our lives to salt in a dish. If there is too much or too little, it is bad. Since **we** do not decide how much pain is right, or how much we should go through, we need to find ways to cope with the "too much" or "too little" that may be given to us by life's circumstances:

- *Too much:* We can enhance our capacity or threshold to bear pain. Following a spiritual path can be of help in this. In the physical plane, it can help strengthen our nerves and raise our tolerance levels by reducing our accumulated stress. In the spiritual plane, by establishing the "connection", we might be able to ensure that Nature, or the Almighty, will be considerate enough to administer only the right proportion of pain to us at the right time. Also, we shall receive the required forbearance, strength, and grace to cope better.

- *Too little:* It would help those who have been smooth-sailing through life remain connected with the sorrow and affliction of others. We can be mindful of the sick, the poor, and the lonely, and extend a helping hand to them. Thus, even if we do not have much pain in our life, remaining aware of this whole aspect can help.

A conversation between two seekers went as follows:

Person A: I am really surprised at your attitude. On the one hand, you believe in God, bow to him, and visit temples, while on the other hand, you have so much anxiety and fear about the future. Do you have a split personality? If you trust him, then just relax; otherwise, don't trust him. Don't be a hypocrite.

Person B: Well, I do believe in God and I know he does come to the rescue of people who trust him, but I have been through hell in the past. My agony has been unbearable so many times, but my faith in him is still as strong. Since the unbearable pain lasted so long in the past, I fear that it could happen to me again in the future. I simply dread going through a similar phase in my life again.

Yes, I admit that ultimately I was saved, but I wonder: What if things had worsened? What if such things were to befall me again?

Person A: Your pain was unbearable simply because your faith faltered.

Person B: No, that is not true. I did have trust.

Person A: While suffering, were you not more worried with questions such as, "Why am I being punished? Will the pain end? Will it get worse? Will I survive it? Will I be saved?"

Person B: Yes, I did have these thoughts and worries, but isn't that natural when the pain is so intense?

Person A: It is natural for a doubting mind to worry like this and it is also natural to have some doubts in one's mind until one attains self-realization. However, it depends on the degree of your faith versus the degree of your doubt. A strong intensity of faith could have made the pain more bearable because it would lead one to think, "Just hold on, it's only a passing phase and is bound to end. God won't forsake me. I know he will see me through this bad phase. My debt of bad karma is being worked out and I can feel his presence through all this agony and suffering, even though He may be at a distance."

Person B: But what more should I do to enhance my degree of faith? I pray and I trust as much as I can. What can I do to overcome this fear and insecurity?

Person A: His grace is there even while we are in agony. We may feel that we are suffering because he no longer cares for us or because we have annoyed Him. While the latter may be true in some instances, He will not forsake us if we have genuinely sought Him. Thus, our reaction to times of distress depends on our faith in Him and our understanding of his inexplicable ways. For example, grace and forbearance often come when all seems lost and one can handle no more – when one is hopeless, when one least expects it, or when one has completely exhausted all patience. But it does come.

Person B: How do I get such faith? How should I understand His ways?

Person A: Just follow the path that will bring you closer to Him. Prayer is a very powerful thing, but if you are unable to penetrate deep enough by simple prayer, you can augment it by the active pursuit of a path. The precepts of a chosen path – e.g. meditation – can help make your heart and mind purer, your doubts weaker, and your experience of Truth more vivid and clear.

Look at times in the past. Were you saved? You may have gone through agonizing pain, but did relief not come? What if such grief or sorrow were to come again? There is no use seeking insurance against such events. The conviction that the strength to bear such pain will come can diminish your fear.

NURTURING THE SELF THROUGH COMPASSION

Seva is of utmost importance in spiritual development. It is very helpful to make concrete efforts towards alleviating the misery and anguish of those who do not have the same luxuries as us. Often, those who have the means and willingness to help, do not know how and what to do. Some simple things that they could do are:

i.   Provide one square meal for someone:

This can be done by creating a facility at any spot in the town or locality – e.g. a corner in the marketplace or in the courtyard of a place of worship – where anyone can come and eat a meal free of cost within specified hours. If the costs become too high, other donors can be invited or a limit can be fixed. For example, the first one hundred people will get the meal every day, starting at the given time.

ii. Rehabilitation for the disabled:

We still find handicapped people begging at traffic signals, and outside temples and churches, despite so many organizations working on this cause. One may argue that these people don't want to work or be rehabilitated. However, is this really true? Do these people have the choice to go somewhere where they can feed themselves and live and die with dignity?

iii. Medical Aid:

We see advertisements in the papers of young people whose kidneys have failed and whose family cannot afford dialysis or a transplant. Many times, the inflicted person is the single or main earner of the family. Renal disease, incidentally, is one of the most expensive treatments. A single afflicted person can cause all the resources and savings of a middle-class family to be completely consumed.

Just a visit to any government hospital or the general out-patient department of any private hospital will show how people:

– Wait for hours to be consulted by a physician.

– Wait for days for diagnostic tests to be done.

– Cannot afford the expenses for the treatment or surgery, even if the room and doctors' fees are not charged by the hospital. They simply have to stop all treatment once their money and all sources of borrowing have been exhausted. Their family members have no choice but to see them suffer in pain and agony, and eventually die.

– Are bed-ridden for the rest of their lives due to delayed or improper medical treatment.

iv. Nursing:

Many old and young persons suffer from ailments that make them immobile – e.g. paralysis or back problems. They cannot stand, walk, or even go to the restroom on their own. Their loved ones serve them with compassion for some time, but after a while, their patience gets exhausted. Their love and feelings towards serving a suffering person weaken slowly, as the stress and discomfort of nursing them increases. Mentally ill patients also may require such constant care.

Rich families, who take care of such patients in their homes, sometimes hire full-time nurses so that they or their spouse/ children do not have to help them. However, only a small percentage of households can afford this.

One way to help families who take care of such patients may be to create facilities or a network or infrastructure wherein a nursing aid can be provided at subsidized rates. The nursing aid could be for domiciliary treatment or even at economic hospitals created for this purpose. This can help provide relief and dignity to patients as well as to the families who had been nursing them. On the other hand, it can provide a source of livelihood to the destitute and needy.

v.   Source of income:

In India, a lower middle class family of 4 needs a minimum amount of money, say Rs. 4000 - 5000/- per month, apart from rent, just to exist with the bare minimum – to be able to cover food, electricity, education, and medical expenses. Innumerable families exist in India whose chief earner is unable to earn this level of income, in spite of the willingness to put in 12 hours or more of work every day. Some typical examples may be:

–   White/blue collar employees in their 40s or early 50s having lost their jobs and are unable to find alternative employment as they possess no specialized skills.

–   Non-graduates whose business has failed. They have debts on top of having to continue paying for their bills and household expenses. They go into deeper debt and they cannot find a job, even considering their age, work experience, and skills. They are under constant pressure to pay the rent or be thrown out of their house.

- The only earning member in the family has become ill and is unable to work.

What do they do? Commit suicide? The obvious suggestion might be to send the kids or spouse to work. Even though this seems logical, it may not be feasible because:

- The children may be too young or in their early teens. Even if they try, they may not find a suitable job. Perhaps they can work as an assistant in a factory or office, but there, they may barely be able to earn Rs. 1000 - Rs. 1500/- per month working 12-14 hours a day after school. Innumerable such families can be found in all towns and cities in our country.

- The spouse may not be very well-educated and may not even be a graduate. Hence, getting any respectable job that would generate a decent income may be difficult.

- In extreme and really desperate cases, kids, mainly female children, are sold off for small amounts of money. The thought of how these girls are treated after they have been bought is horrific.

- Even after reading stories such as these in the morning newspaper, most people will feel no compunction in spending the same amount of money eating out that evening for which a child may have been sold off!

What can we do for such people? Let us see after the next point on idleness.

vi. Idleness:

Many people who have lost their jobs, have taken voluntary retirement, or have failed in their business and are unable to find an alternative job or source of income do suffer from the following:

- Within the above, there may also be those who are financially better off due to alternative sources of income (interest earnings on savings, having another earning member in the family), but they, too, may suffer from idleness as they do not have a job or vocation to keep them occupied.

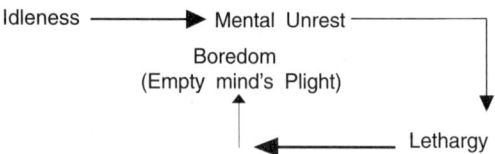

These people desperately need a place where they can work, and win back their dignity, honour, self-esteem, and self-confidence. Getting paid for such work may be a secondary consideration for many of them.

vii. Counselling/Psychological support:

Counsellors, psychiatrists, and neurologists usually have a flourishing business all over the world. This applies to India as well. While many have started doing well in recent times, the general tendency among people is to continue to suffer anxiety, depression, and self–pity, rather than visit a counsellor or medical practitioner.

They believe that these feelings can be overcome and it is as simple as modifying the way one thinks. They think that going to a counsellor would be akin to admitting they might be losing their sanity. Consulting a psychiatrist is a step further, almost a confirmation that there is something seriously wrong with them. Hence, most people continue to suffer from psychosomatic diseases without seeking expert help.

This is another area where a service could be rendered. A forum could be set up where individuals could come and share their problems, concerns, and distresses. The forum could also include expert doctors or counsellors. It could provide necessary help or advice, such as counselling, yoga, meditation, or medication.

The beneficiaries need not only be the poor, but even those who are well off and who do not know how to cope, or were hesitant to seek out a formal solution or remedy.

viii. Help Line:

Today we have help lines for every product or service being sold. However, suppose one finds a poor, hungry child being beaten because his begging was irritating someone. Where does one call for help? What if one finds an accident victim battling for life, but does not have the wherewithal to help him? What if a limping stray dog was howling in pain because it had been run over by a car? Where are the equivalents of large corporations, MNCs, and foreign banks with a 24 x 7 helpline number in the social service field that can be called to help those who are poor, sick, hungry, lonely, or in severe pain?

Social service must be done with humility. One of the important aims of *seva,* or service, should be to restore the dignity of suffering individuals. Whenever any problem becomes insurmountable, self-confidence is one of the first thing a person loses. This may further deteriorate into withdrawal or self-pity. This state of mind and spirit makes one even more vulnerable to the problems that one may be facing. The will power weakens further, and so does the fighting spirit. One succumbs to problems, which then become insurmountable.

How does one actively engage in service?

A lot of people want to render service to others, but they simply do not know what to do and how to go about doing it. They wonder:

- How will I know what help to give?
- How can I identify people who need help?
- Is it worth the effort?
- When should I start?
- What should I do?

Once an individual starts taking active steps in this area, he would automatically find the answers and the direction in which to contribute.

How does one identify the people?

One does not need to go far and wide searching for people who need help and succour. The more sensitive an individual is, the greater are his chances of naturally coming across those in need.

Is seva important? How important is it?

One may wonder whether *seva* is worth the effort, time, and energy one will be putting into it. One may ask oneself: "Is it worth my getting into it? Am I not better off focusing entirely on my job and family? Do I really need to do all of this for my spiritual development? Is meditation not enough? After all, meditation consumes enough of my time, and now I have to devote another portion of my time to *seva* as well!"

A large number of spiritual paths actually focus strongly on *seva*, or service to mankind. They regard it as important for spiritual growth, equivalent to the practice of the chosen meditation technique. Remaining connected to the suffering of others and actually trying to assuage it is most definitely an aid to one's spiritual progress.

This is because service, as discussed in the previous chapter, begets:

- **Compassion**
- **Sensitivity**
- **Self-esteem** (through granting it to others)
- **Thankfulness** (When one receives gratitude from the one being helped, one might say "Thank God I could help").
- **Humility:** Serving others can sometimes result in pride and conceit, especially if one believes he is being magnanimous by helping. However, if done in conjunction with the practice of a spiritual technique, and with the right understanding, it can lead to humility. One might begin to think, "I, too, could have been in this situation. I might be in such a situation at any time in the future. There is nothing great in my doing this. I am only performing my duty as a human being." One may gradually understand that giving was contingent upon those who had received.
- **Sense of purpose:** By doing *seva*, one begins to realize that, unlike most other people who work only for the survival and benefit of their family and themselves, they begin to see and feel a deeper meaning and purpose in their otherwise *'normal'* and *'ordinary'* life.

When should I start? This may seem a strange question, but some people might say, "Well, I do have an urge to help, but it is not strong enough to make me spring into action yet. Maybe I need to develop some more compassion before I can really start. So let me meditate and wait until I feel motivated enough."

Initially, the motivation to help may not be very strong due to inertia or lethargy. It is thus better to "intellectually" convince oneself that it is good to start right away rather than wait, because no one knows when he will be ready. One must therefore avoid the chicken and egg trap of which comes first – doing service or developing compassion – because service itself will cultivate compassion.

Often, the rich and famous may be heard saying, "I have more than I deserve, and I am grateful for it." If they indeed feel that way, they would do well to share a part of the 'extra', which is even beyond what they need to maintain their future financial security. Perhaps one of the best ways of expressing thankfulness for what one has is by helping out those in need. The type of giving in question is not merely done by adopting a popular cause and showing up in some meetings; the focus should be on the extent and impact of actions taken for those in need.

A large number of corporations have Foundations and Trusts for social and community work. Several leading industrialists, corporate founders, CEOs, and celebrities and/or their spouses are already pursuing several noble causes to help the poor or needy. Some have taken up causes such as education, the environment, caring for the aged, rehabilitation, and animal care. Celebrities and film personalities are no exception. Nana Patekar is known to donate a sizeable part of his earnings to charities. Jackie Shroff is supposed to have given his cell phone number to the children who polish shoes in Mumbai, and is known to have said, "They can call me if they are hungry any time. I will try to reach food to them. I am also planning to give some of them cell phones so that they do not have to search for a local call booth or spend a rupee in order to call me."

A disaster like the Tsunami shook the whole country and brought several celebrities and businesses together. This only goes to show that the desire to alleviate others' suffering is inherent to our nature. We simply do not know how, where, or what to contribute, and do so in such a manner that it reaches the needy, rather than getting wasted somewhere in the process.

The compassion and desire for service that rests in the hearts of so many people does not translate into active, concrete action. It remains at the level of intent or desire, rather than an active or dedicated pursuit.

The effort should be to move up from the level of *Intention* to the level of *Active Service*.

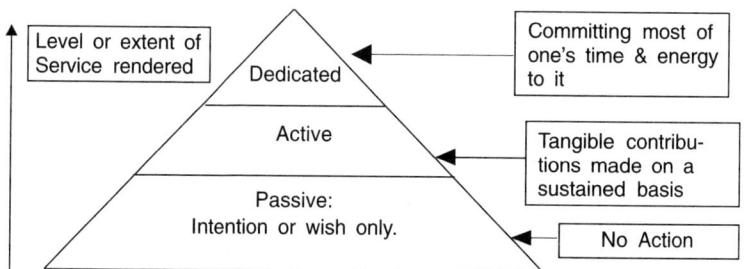

Many people who find they lack a sense of purpose in their lives and feel guilty and empty can benefit from actively pursuing activities that can bring succour to others. It will also help them build a sense of meaning that their existence involved more than fulfilling the needs of their family.

Many wealthy people are fond of giving expensive presents to their spouse and children on special occasions. It gives them a great sense of satisfaction and helps them "score points" with them. Some of the gifts are so expensive that the interest on that amount is large enough to enable a poor household of 4-6 members to survive.

The price of a dress that so many individuals casually purchase can procure the monthly ration for a household that may be going hungry. What people spend on a holiday can be enough to help a dying youngster pay for, and therefore survive, a critical surgery.

Does that mean we should renounce or feel guilty for eating out, giving expensive gifts, buying good clothes, or enjoying a holiday?

No. For many, it gives us the required motivation and the passion to strive for more and earn more. Renouncing or abstaining from these external stimuli and not deriving a sense of joy from them can render one's life dull and, boring, devoid of excitement, passion, or charm. However, it wouldn't hurt to become conscious of the fact that the amount of money we are capable of splurging without thinking is often large enough to help someone else in a very dramatic way.

This realisation will slowly drive us to use a small part of that "extra" that we have to reach out to others. For example, once in two months, this could involve putting aside the amount (of time, money, energy) we would normally spend on a weekend dinner with our friends and family and using it to feed someone really hungry, or help someone in agony. They don't need to be large sacrifices. A happy occasion or achievement could also be a time to commit a small portion to others, out of the thankfulness that we might be feeling.

SUMMARY

Serving others and alleviating their suffering is a catalyst to spiritual growth and development. It has a tremendous impact on one's entire being. The gratitude received from those helped can actually cause a transformation. It can instil pure compassion. That is why Osho says: "Be thankful to someone who accepts any kind gesture from you, because you don't know what he has given you."

Different people have different capacities and capabilities to help depending on their personal struggles, achievements, resources, and liabilities. Nonetheless, within one's means, one should do his or her best to provide succour and support to the needy, and possibly find a form of unique self-expression in the process.

The only way to receive is by giving.

"A generous heart, kind speech, and a life of service and compassion are the things which renew humanity."

— Buddha

LIVING THE FOUR DIMENSIONS

The sketch on the following page shows how living life fully, on all four dimensions, leads to a better sense of self-esteem and self-worth.

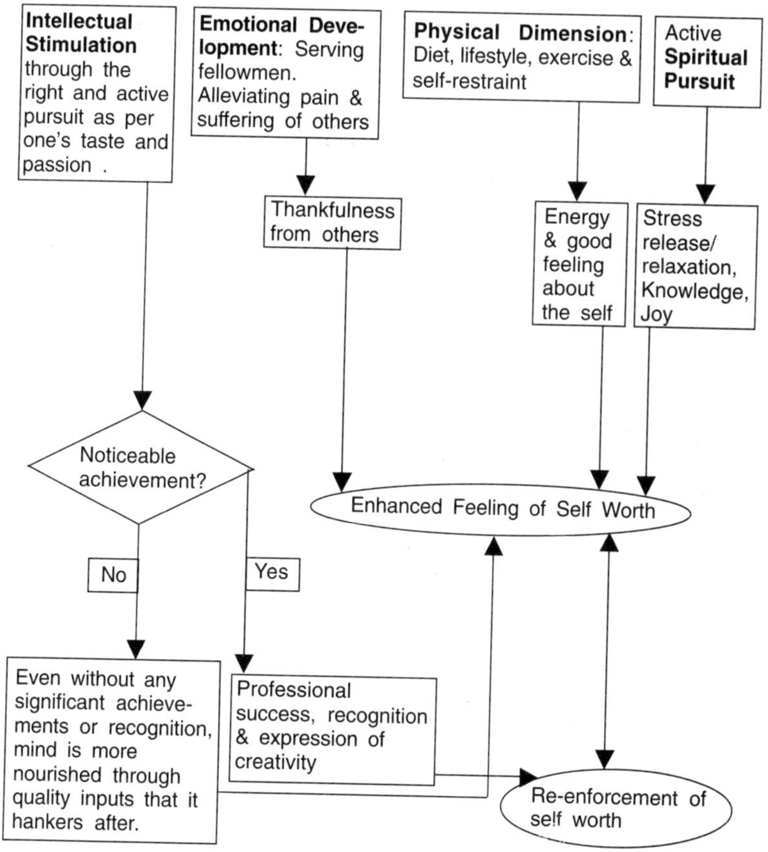

Intellectual Stimulation through the right and active pursuit as per one's taste and passion .	**Emotional Development**: Serving fellowmen. Alleviating pain & suffering of others	**Physical Dimension**: Diet, lifestyle, exercise & self-restraint	Active **Spiritual Pursuit**

Thankfulness from others

Energy & good feeling about the self

Stress release/ relaxation, Knowledge, Joy

Noticeable achievement?

No — Yes

Enhanced Feeling of Self Worth

Even without any significant achievements or recognition, mind is more nourished through quality inputs that it hankers after.

Professional success, recognition & expression of creativity

Re-enforcement of self worth

SUMMARY

It is important to understand:

(a) That each of the dimensions of our lives needs nurturing

(b) How to accomplish the above in a satisfactory way.

One need not forsake material pursuits, passions, goals, aspirations, relationships, or achievements through intellectual suppression or sacrifice. The significance of these material achievements in our lives may fade over time as we evolve and develop on the spiritual plane. The importance of these may not go out in a flash, though it has happened as such for many masters in the past. However, until one has reached enlightenment, one cannot starve the needs or hunger of the mind, intellect, physical body, or emotions. They need to be nourished in order to build self-esteem and self-acceptance.

The attachment to and yearning for material goals will recede in a natural, spontaneous way, but the prerequisite for such an unrestrained way of living is to pursue the chosen path through to the last detail and to follow the prescribed regimen. If one is committed to pursuing the path as advised, the rest will fall into place.

Hence, we should avoid falling into the 'denial trap' due to the misinterpretation of spirituality. When we are not successful and are feeling dejected, the suggestion that all material pursuits are useless gives us solace: "So I am not a loser after all, as it is immaterial whether I succeed or not."

However, one should not use spirituality merely to justify one's inability to do one's work conscientiously, or to rationalise failure. If someone tells us to exercise self-restraint towards indulgence, it may still be acceptable as it has a rational basis in health. But if anyone tells us to withdraw from action or achievement, that person should be handled with caution.

PART-V CONTRADICTIONS & INTELLECTUAL BOTTLENECKS

IMPORTANT NOTES FOR THE READERS:

- Readers may choose to go through each of the seeming contradictions discussed in this chapter.

- Alternatively, they can read the ones that are a cause of concern to them right now and skip the rest. They can be referred to in future.

- **Those who are not really concerned with any of these or eager to quickly know the Dos & Dont's and key lessons from the book may proceed directly to part VI.**

1 SPIRITUALITY IS ANTI-MATERIALISTIC

The world is an illusion. All ambitions and achievements are futile. The renunciation of wealth, possessions, relationships, and cravings is necessary for spiritual growth.

It is assumed by many that spirituality makes you dull by dissuading aggression, passion, and ambition. Spirituality states that the world is a myth or illusion; that whatever we experience through our senses is not reality. In a way, it implies that whatever we do, achieve, or enjoy in this world is inconsequential. Material pursuits are futile and have no ultimate value. In fact, some schools of thought advocate the idea that too much wealth is detrimental to one's spiritual growth. As a result, this can make an individual feel guilty for having acquired material success. Many spiritual sermons tell us that material possessions will not lead us anywhere, and this thought can create a dilemma. One wants to have assets and possessions that will be envied, admired, or even loved; but the spiritual path might say that such desires are a manifestation of an inflated ego, which is a sure recipe for decline.

That the world may be worth denying or renouncing is reinforced by the fact that most enlightened masters and luminaries that we know of had, in fact, given up everything – Swami Vivekanada, Ramakrishna Paramhansa, Buddha, Swami Ramana Maharishi, and Yogananda Paramhansa, among others.

Many of the masters of recent times, including Osho, Maharishi Mahesh Yogi, Sri Sri Ravi Shankar, and Asaramji Bapu tell us that we need **not** give up our jobs, possessions, or families in order to seek spiritual growth. They encourage us to fulfil all our duties and obligations to ourselves, our family, our friends, and society. However, if we look at each of them, they, too, have given their 100% to this path.

Many of us are aware of the rigorous penance and self-sacrifice of a Jain Muni. We know how much self-denial they practice, including:

- Fasting for days.
- Eating once a day, and only if certain pre-conditions are coincidentally met. For example, many of them decide that they will eat only if they happen to see a certain thing, or only if a particular type of person feeds them.
- Walking barefoot for miles.
- Forsaking clothes.
- Plucking out all the hair on their heads.
- Practicing total celibacy.
- Maintaining a vow of complete silence for days.

Intuitively, we know that all this cannot be without a commensurate purpose and gain. This makes us doubt whether an easier way can, in fact, be effective in leading us to the Truth.

What about the intelligent and enthusiastic youth dedicated to ISCKON who have shaven their heads, adorned saffron clothing, and have left their families and jobs? Is their commitment and sacrifice of no consequence?

It may be difficult to resolve this disconnect. On the one hand, we have spiritual paths that tell us to continue our full-time job and take care of our family and social obligations, and on the other hand, all the traditional teachings on spirituality have taught us for years that the world is a myth and that sensual gratifications or indulgences are a sure recipe for moral downfall. We also have examples of enlightened souls who have come up the hard way, through sacrifice and years of penance. One way may be to admit to oneself that *perhaps* those who were completely focussed on spirituality and had committed their life to it stood a better chance of progressing faster as compared to those concurrently pursuing material success. But then, are we willing to commit ourselves to spirituality on a full-time basis? Many of us even doubt whether spirituality truly exists and whether there is another world at all, whether there is a fourth or fifth state of consciousness.

While we are willing to pursue and discover the path, many of us would be wary of leaving everything for it without first experiencing it to be True and Ultimate. Renunciation is obviously not the route for those of us who feel this way. This is because those individuals with such a mind frame are willing to make some sacrifices here and there to seek the Truth, but may not be comfortable with forsaking everything. Rather, we should try to figure out whether we can actually make any meaningful progress if we adopt a spiritual technique and practice it in right earnest while continuing to pursue our worldly aspirations and activities. The answer to this seems to be yes. We need not bother ourselves with trying to prove wrong the theory of renunciation or complete commitment. That, too, is a path, just as any other. It may be a faster one, but it may simply not be for people like us – ambitious, rational, with the desire to achieve a great deal in our life.

There is a notion that *since spirituality dissuades you from pursuing your ambitions and material goals, it makes you dull*. There is hope for those who want to pursue both the spiritual as well as the worldly path. There are logical reasons and convincing arguments to this effect.

We have discussed earlier that activity (action) is as important as rest (meditation). Engaging solely in meditation can make a person dull and ineffective. Osho also believed that the silence of a recluse seeker who has run away to the mountains is dull and not as vibrant as that of a seeker who is living amidst all the noise, distractions, and social pressures.

Maharishi Mahesh Yogi, for example, says that *rest* and *activity* are steps to *progress*; (the term 'progress' is referring to spiritual progress).

- By *rest*, Maharishiji means deep and regular meditation
- By *activity*, he means undertaking worldly pursuits, actions, tasks, and duties.

In our pursuit of Activity, however, we may gather stresses and karmic bindings once again, thus dissipating what was gained during the Rest period. This is satisfactory as long as we rest again by plunging into meditation after a period of activity. Hence, notably, Activity is not only *permitted* by Maharishiji but deemed as an important step in one's journey. We can thus pursue all types of actions and tasks in the physical and material world without guilt or remorse.

While the idea of adding spirituality without forsaking anything else seems to be a win-win situation, different paths may ask for different levels of sacrifices. For example, some paths such as the ISKON might suggest that you become a vegetarian, while others may suggest a more balanced lifestyle so that the meditation is deeper and less energy is consumed in sorting out the stresses gained from an unhealthy lifestyle.

Thus, even though there may not seem to be much motivation and convincing logic for us to quit everything for the sake of spirituality, some sacrifices or commitments inevitably need to be made in order to find time to even practice the chosen technique, say, twice a day for 20-45 minutes. The entire cycle consisting of yoga postures, physical exercises, breathing exercises, *pranayama,* meditation, japa, or prayer may take that kind of time.

Finding the time in the evenings may be especially difficult since many ambitious people work late and face the following challenges as a result:

- By the time they get home, they might be very hungry. However, most meditation techniques need to be practiced before meals and this means dinner would be delayed further, which can be unhealthy.
- One may end up having a late dinner after the practice of the technique. Thus, catching up on sleep because one slept late

may become difficult. As a result, mornings may also become rushed as one would ideally like to squeeze in time for exercise and the morning cycle of meditation before leaving for work.

Thus, simply organizing oneself into a routine wherein one can regularly practice the techniques despite work pressures, social obligations, business dinners, and travel poses such a formidable challenge that many people simply quit. They are simply unable to manage it is a regular practice. Finding the time for regular practice in a hectic schedule is a real challenge, but is mandatory for spiritual progress.

Renunciation does not necessarily mean sacrificing one's family, job, talents, or dreams. It does mean that one needs to take time out for this path, which, in turn, might mean re-prioritising some other things, such as:

- Time spent with family or friends
- Leisure or spare time
- Pleasures or indulgences
- Daily Schedule, i.e. working late in the office, hectic travel schedules

SELF-CONTROL AND REPRESSION ARE CRITICAL TO SPIRITUAL GROWTH

Self-control basically refers to the control of the senses and the avoidance of indulgences. This has been advocated from time immemorial by several schools of spirituality and religion.

Q: *According to these teachings, how is one supposed to practice self-control?*

Ans: Through the intellect.

Q: *How do they suggest the intellect be used?*

Ans: By being conscious that indulgences and sensual pleasures are not good and using one's free will to exercise discretion, avoidance, and control. The intellect is supposed to act like the charioteer, controlling the reins of the senses, which, like horses, are capable of running fast and going astray in any direction.

A more severe form of self control is repression and self-denial.

At the other extreme, we have schools of thought that encourage us to indulge as much as we can. The key tenets are:

- Do not form judgments about what is good or bad. Just do as you feel, but follow a path that will give you a sense of spontaneous judgment between good and bad.

- Do not feel guilty. Guilt is a bottleneck in spiritual growth. Guilt and fear of retribution for our acts only demonstrate that our concept of God is as an accountant who keeps track of who is doing what, and distributing punishment or rewards accordingly.

- You are born to be free. Trust in God. Forgiveness is available to humankind. The kind Lord shall forgive and forget, but you need to trust and open your heart to him.

- Do not repress any desires or cravings. By repressing them, you are only pushing them down, and they might erupt with a high-intensity vengeance one day, like a volcano.

- When you have attained or enjoyed the objects you were craving, you will outgrow the need for them over a period of time. This outgrowth can happen due to any of the following factors:

  — Having had enough

  — Fatigue

  — Having developed other interests, needs, and priorities

  — Having evolved spiritually so that one no longer yearns for these things

These are two extreme forms of thinking. On one extreme is *self-control,* which has been taught by a large majority of masters. On the other extreme are the schools of thought dissuading repression. Then, there is the philosophy in between these extremes, which says, "Exercise control, but do not be harsh on yourself. Don't be too forceful in exercising self control either. However, restraint, rather than indulgence, will do you good."

So the spectrum ranges as follows:

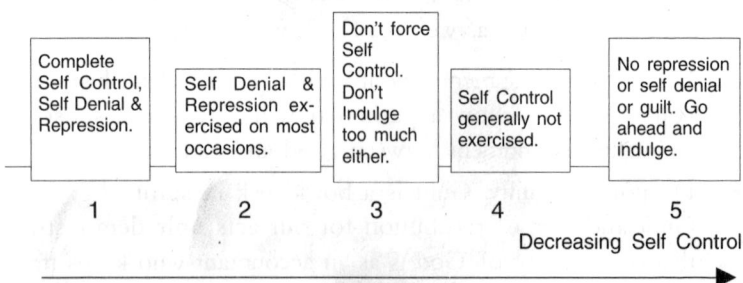

Let us rate the levels of self-control from 1 to 5 as shown in the figure above, where 1 is complete self-control, while 5 is unrestrained behaviour. Most of us are in the 2 to 4 range of the above figure. What's wrong with that? Where should one be?

The recommended approach would be as follows:

- Follow the precepts and teachings of the chosen path and master. It may be anywhere in the spectrum of 1 to 5 shown above.

- However, a general, common-sense approach may be to predispose oneself towards 2 rather than towards 4. Why? Because spiritual evolution to such an extent that all undesired behaviours drop off naturally might take some time. Before getting there indulging too much without restraint, poses the following risks:

  - Sizeable damage may occur to our mind, body, and soul in this phase.
  - Some things may become entrenched habits that may become difficult to overcome, even with the force of spiritual evolution.

Repression and self-restraint vs. cherishing a full life:

Since I have only one life to live and enjoy, why should I follow the path of renunciation? Why should I leave my sensual pleasures when that is what adds to the charm to living? Please tell me whether I will have to control all my desires and senses and live like a saint to progress on this path.

It is true that most of us know only one world — the material or physical world. Until the time when one actually experiences a deeper, spiritual joy from within through the process of self-evolution, one enjoys satisfaction from material objects, achievements, and sensual gratifications. When one has spiritually evolved to a significant extent, the mind naturally directs itself away from the sensual and corporeal plane by turning inwards. One is not expected to physically block or repress senses or desires, as it will happen of its own accord and at its own pace, in its own shape and form. What is required is practice, and treading the path in earnest.

Osho explains this very well. He says that a person who has always drunk from a stagnant pond of water thinks that it is the best thing and enjoys it thoroughly. However, if that person were to be taken to a fresh spring, with a clean, sparkling stream of water flowing down from the pristine, melting snow of the Himalayas and asked to drink from it, would he go back and still be content with drinking from the pond? One need not give any sermons on which would be better for him, as his being would automatically know and act accordingly in the future.

On the other hand, what if one does not let him taste this fresh spring water and only tells him that his pond is not good and that a better source exists, without letting him experience it himself? He would not forsake something he has always known, lived with, and derived benefit from (i.e. the pond) for something that is merely a promise and is completely unknown to him (i.e. the Himalayan spring). This is exactly the case with material pleasures versus spiritual bliss. You have to find a way to experience the latter. Then, no one will need to tell you what is good for you and you would not need to force yourself to doing anything. All things would happen naturally.

So the important points to remember are:

- Is self-control necessary? Yes. It is important to gain control over the senses, as indulgence is known to distract a person from his path. This is also true for trying to achieve any material goal. Full commitment without distractions or diversions is often required.

- Does that mean, however, that one needs to force self-control, repress sensual desires, practice chastity, and abstain from things that provide pleasure? This is a difficult and complex question, but to answer it simply, there is no harm in exercising self-control in a kind, gentle way to oneself. At best, self-control can be at the level of action and it may not be possible to control the mind or prevent it from savouring the objects of desire. The mind may continue to dwell upon thoughts and fantasies of all things that bring it joy. Hence, as explained above, one has to provide oneself with an alternative source of joy that is real and that can be substituted with the pleasures obtained from indulgence and the gratification of the senses. Only then can one naturally outgrow the need for the latter.

Let us take the example of someone who is overweight, but is fond of sweets and high-fat foods. As per the dieticians' and doctors' advice, both sweets and high-fat foods are detrimental to his health. Now the person has two choices: either he can indulge, eating as many sweets or high-fat foods as he likes until he becomes completely sick, or he can completely deny himself sweets and fats by resolving that he will not touch them because they are akin to poison for him.

The first approach is dangerous. He might gain so much weight in the process that losing it becomes even more difficult, thus harming his health. The second extreme, where he becomes determined not to touch those foods, though good from a health point of view, has an element of sadness due to the denial of the senses. His subconscious mind might keep yearning for them. However, this is still better, as many individuals who stop eating certain foods, such as sweets, over a period of time stop craving them.

A third approach would be to follow the rating of 2, as discussed earlier – i.e. self control on most occasions, the middle path:

"I know that this food is bad for me, however I am not going to totally deny these to myself. There will be occasions when I might eat them, but let me avoid them today. Even if I feel really tempted, let me *postpone* it for another day. I have not denied them, but why not avoid them as much as possible?"

What are the advantages of this approach?

- Complete and rigid self-denial has the pitfall that one may continue to contemplate and yearn for the object deep within.

If, by chance, one's will power weakens, one might go back to the indulgence mode with a vengeance. This is somewhat equivalent of what Osho tells us: "Superficial repression is of little use. You are pushing it (desires/cravings) down deeper. They might erupt like a volcano one day." Hence, instead of engaging in "Denial" (rating 1), we follow the "Avoidance" (rating 2) approach. The difference is subtle, but important. The focus shifts *from Denial and Repression* by using the force of will power *to Self Control* by choice.

• Successfully postponing the indulgence today acts as motivation to exercise control again in the future, on another occasion. This happens as one does not want to break or undermine his record of achievement of the self-control exercised so far. The only catch is that if one gives in and indulges once, the next time, he will fall prey to temptation even faster.

The key take-away from above discussion is that there are four optional courses of action:

Sr.	Option	Characteristics	Advantages	Disadvantages	Rank
a.	Repression	Controlling indulgences by Force	Higher success rate. Since only strong and unflinching determination can help to overcome the temptation.	It has elements of sadness and regret. It has dullness - moving or escaping from the real, dynamic world into a forlorn realm. it can also lead to obsessive thoughts about repressed cravings & yearnings.	2

Sr.	Option	Characteristics	Advantages	Disadvantages	Rank
b.	Moderate Self Control, Avoidance & Self Restraint	Avoiding indulgence as far as possible.	One does not become as sad, dull, obsessive as in Forced Repression.	Temptation may get better of the self imposed restrain on many occasions.	1
c.	Living life spontaneously	Indulging in desires.	Evolution is natural. It is based purely on spiritual growth without any external input.	Seems somewhat directionless. Temptations will often win.	3
d.	Indulging to the maximum	Gratifying oneself to the maximum without any restrictions whatsoever. Similar to Living Life spontaneously as mentioned above, except that here the pandering will be even more deliberate & unrestrained.		It might be too late before one overcomes the desire. Enough damage to one's mind, body, being may have happened.	4

To sum up, some kind of self-control is perhaps better than opting for unrestrained indulgences without remorse or guilt. Self-control here means intellectually realizing the importance of restraint and utilizing one's will power to accomplish the same. However, *while intellect and will power can help in avoiding acts of indulgence, they may not be able to prevent the mind from savouring what it yearns for* - e.g. good food, a good life, material wealth, exotic holidays, physical relationships, parties, dancing, and drinking. As one progresses and evolves, only then will the desire, craving, lust, and thoughts of these melt away as one begins deriving joy from other sources.

This ability to overcome the temptation to indulge is aided through spiritual growth through the following mechanisms:

- It spontaneously and naturally provides us with wisdom regarding what is good and what is bad for us.
- It *naturally* kills the desire in us for that which is undesirable.
- It gives us strength and the ability and counterforce to overcome temptations.

This is quite different from repression, which is done by force and often out of fear. Self-restraint through intellectual conviction, will power, and spiritual growth leads to a better sense of self-esteem. One can boldly say, "Look I have the courage and strength to say no to something, based on my own free will." Repression is sad, "Oh I just can't have it." It is based on fears: "I had better not, otherwise." That is the basic difference between repression and self-restraint.

MEDITATION IS NOTHING BUT CONCENTRATION

Osho's thoughts on stopping the mind, as quoted in an earlier chapter, are as follows:

"The mind needs understanding, awareness. Don't try to stop it. If you try to stop it, in the first place you cannot succeed; in the second place, if you *can* succeed – one can succeed if one makes persevering effort for years – if you *can* succeed, you will become dull. No satori will happen out of it."

Meditation, according to a number of spiritual paths, means concentration on an object, thought, or mantra. This concentration involves the exclusion of all other thoughts. A number of meditative techniques actually teach that meditation is only successful when you go from a state of mind to no mind. The state of *no mind* is one where there is no thought. How do you get to a state of no thought? As per the concentration technique, it could be a single thought, a mantra, a word, an image, a point, a source of light, or the centre of one's forehead. However, a disconnect seems apparent here. Are we talking of No thoughts or of One thought (i.e. the object being concentrated upon)? There are two views on this:

- Principle I: Concentrating on one thought, excluding all other thoughts, will lead to the state of *No* or *Zero* thought (and thus no mind). How? Because eventually, in this process, even the one single thought on which one was concentrating will evaporate. So the process is the progression from *Many Thoughts* to *One Thought* to *No Thought*.

- Principle II: Concentrating on that one thing while excluding all other thoughts, itself, is meditation.

However, some masters have categorically said that driving other thoughts away or trying to concentrate on one thing is not meditation at all. In the words of Osho (part of which has been quoted earlier), concentration is undesirable:

"In the first place, you cannot succeed; and it is good that you cannot succeed. If you *could* succeed, if you managed to succeed, that would be very unfortunate – you would become dull; you would lose intelligence. With that speed of mind there is intelligence; with that speed there is a continuous sharpening of the sword of thinking, logic, intellect. Please don't try to stop it. I am not in favour of dullards, and I am not here to help anybody to become stupid.

"In the name of religion, many people have become stupid; they have almost become idiots – just trying to stop the mind without any understanding about why it is going with such speed... why in the first place? The mind cannot go without any reason. Without going into the reasons, in the layers, deep layers of the unconscious, they just try to stop. They *can* stop, but they will have to pay a price, and the price will be that their intelligence will be lost.

"You can go around in India, you can find thousands of sannyasins, mahatmas; look into their eyes – yes, they are good people, nice, but stupid. If you look in their eyes, there is no intelligence; you will not see any lightning. They just sit there. They are vegetating, they are not alive people. They have not helped the world in *any* way. They have not even produced a painting or a poem or a song; because even to produce a poem you need intelligence; you need certain qualities of the mind.

"I would not suggest that you stop the mind, rather, that you understand it. With understanding a miracle happens. But intelligence is not lost, because mind is not forced."

"What are you doing if you don't remove the causes by

understanding? You are driving a car, for example, and you go on pressing the accelerator and at the same time you try to press the brake. You will destroy the whole mechanism of the car. And there is every possibility you will have some accident. This cannot be done together. If you are pushing the brake, then leave the accelerator alone; don't push it any more. If you are pushing the accelerator, then don't push the brake. *Don't* do both the things together; otherwise you will destroy the whole mechanism; you are doing two contradictory things.

"You carry ambition – and you try to stop the mind? Ambition creates the speed, so you are accelerating the speed – and putting a brake on the mind. You will destroy the whole subtle mechanism of the mind, and mind is a very delicate phenomenon, the most delicate in the whole of existence. So don't be foolish about it."

— from The Tantra Experience, Chap 8

Maharishi Mahesh Yogi tells us that Transcendental Meditation is neither concentration nor contemplation. Thus, there is no need to make any efforts to drive the thoughts away.

Even Vipassana tells us not to force the thoughts out, but to observe oneself, to observe the sensitivity and the sensations. There is, of course, a small element of concentration involved – one tries to concentrate on what is happening inside one's being, but it is quite different from concentrating on a point, thought, or mantra. One is only trying to be more watchful of the sensations happening inside.

There are a large number of techniques and paths that have always, and still continue to, emphasize on concentration as being the essence of meditation. Many seekers may have found spiritual fulfilment through these techniques, so it may not be right to discard them completely.

The personal conviction of the author, however, is towards techniques that do not suggest any kind of concentration. The reasons for this are as follows:

• The concept that in order to go to one's source, one needs to expand one's consciousness rather than limit it through concentration seems logical.

- Discussions with several people who had found peace through various non-concentration-based techniques.

- Emphasis on the idea that *meditation is not concentration* by some renowned and venerable masters, such as Osho and Maharishi Mahesh Yogi.

- Consistency that meditation is not concentration among the following:
  – Sahaj Samadhi taught by AOL
  – Transcendental Meditation (TM)
  – Vipassana
     Osho's various techniques

- The author's own experience with non-concentration-based techniques.

Hence, the point being made is that meditation is not only about concentration. While concentration-based techniques abound, and they, too, might lead to enlightenment, there are many paths that dissuade concentration as an approach towards meditation. Thus, concentration and meditation are not synonymous, since many popular paths may not involve concentration at all.

SPIRITUALITY ENCOURAGES A FATALISTIC, DESTINY DRIVEN MINDSET AND NOT AGGRESSION TO CREATE ONE'S OWN DESTINY

Q *Should I pursue active karma or leave it all to my destiny, prarabdha, and past karma?*

As explained earlier in Chapter 4, the renunciation of karma is neither possible nor desirable. In fact, engaging in active karma is better than indulging in passive karma.

Then, one may ask, 'What is destiny?' Destiny is nothing but the consequences that one has to face due to all past karma. Can one change one's destiny? Let us explore.

Suppose one has done the best possible karma that one could, but still hasn't reached anywhere. In such a case, one will remember the saying: 'You will reach only as far as your destiny will take you.' However, this also implies that the karma that is done now is of little or no consequence. This is when one begins to wonder whether one should leave it all to 'kismet' or destiny, since that is supposedly far more powerful than any individual effort. This is one of the most dangerous traps an individual can fall into – the 'fatalist' trap.

Often, individuals are misguided by counsels such as: 'There is no use struggling so desperately. Whatever will be will be.' This thereby suggests that there is no use in trying too hard. By taking such advice seriously, one may, in all likelihood, fall into a passive mode. The deeper one becomes entrenched in this mode of thinking, the greater will be the inertia and reluctance to strive to do one's best. Subconsciously, one may begin to think that it is better to leave it all to fate since 'Whatever will be will be'. This may especially happen to people for whom success remains elusive despite intense struggles. One may have given 99% of one's effort to something, but to give 100% or 110% invariably requires a strong inner conviction and drive. This fatalistic attitude is bound to dampen or kill one's drive and determination. That 1% (or 10%) difference can ultimately separate success from failure.

It is also important to intellectually understand why one person may not get the desired results or triumph in spite of one's best efforts, while another may get whatever he or she wants in life without any struggle. Does it mean that the theory of karma has failed or changed its mind here? Not really. It only means that one person was unable to overcome the 'pulling down' force of his past negative karma by striving in the present. The other person was propelled forward by his past positive karma and did not need much push from his present efforts.

For example, let us assume that one was striving at an Effort Level X to achieve a desired result in one direction, but the storehouse of past karma was exerting a Counter Force Y in the opposite direction, which was far greater than X. The result would be that instead of moving forward in the direction of success, one would go in the opposite direction because of the stronger opposite force Y.

But the positive thing is that as Force X slowly but surely consumed or annihilated Force Y over time, only the residual amount of Force Y would successively come into play. This would thereby enhance the chances of Force X surmounting Force Y and, as a result, one would be more likely to progress towards one's desired goals.

Another way to look at this is that the agony and suffering that Force Y was causing by not letting the individual attain his object of desire was also concurrently helping in dissolving (or working out) some of his past karma. Over a period of time, as Force Y (or the negative force of past karma) weakened, the effort X of the present would begin to yield results. One obvious prerequisite might be to not keep strengthening Forces such as Y by adding negative karma in the present.

Why is it that those who often do not achieve success after many struggles achieve results with minimum efforts on some critical, unexpected occasions? This is because Forces X and Y may not collide head-on on many occasions. Hence, often Force X, even if it is weak, may yield results if it is the only force acting at that time. On the other hand, at other times, no matter how hard one tries, the desired result is not achieved because only Force Y may be acting at that time. What happens to the Force X created through efforts? The contribution (or energy) created by Force X is reserved somewhere and may come into play at another time.

The joys, successes, and failures that life throws at us when we least expect them are examples of the two Forces operating at different points in time, without one challenging the other.

TO SUMMARIZE

1. One should never forsake or reduce one's karma, even though karma is binding. Forsaking or easing off karma is not going to help in one's spiritual growth in any way. To get over the effects of one's previous karma, one need not consciously cool off or ease off one's karma. However, one should follow a technique that will help one exit the karmic cycle, as discussed in various chapters, particularly Chapter 4.

2. Slowing down karma has another pitfall: what if the very theory that everything is a result of past karma were faulty or untrue? At least by doing one's best now, one ensures that the lack of effort does not become the reason for one's failure. Besides, there is no merit in not striving to do one's best. By putting in one's best effort, one would build a stronger sense of self-esteem and a more peaceful inner conscience. Leaving everything to destiny is a dangerous proposition.

3. Karma is like a bank overdraft (OD) account with an unknown opening balance, (either positive or negative) and a withdrawal

cycle that is not in one's hands. Therefore, one cannot determine when to withdraw one's net earnings. The best way to create a positive balance is to keep depositing positive karma into the account so that it can be created and augmented. There will, of course, be debits because one cannot be perfect all the time. But by consciously ensuring credits through active, positive karma, one can at least be sure that at some time in the future, one will benefit from the positive reserve whenever the encashment cycle of the account happens (the timing of which, as mentioned earlier, may not be determined by the individual).

The above explanation thus implies that theoretically, one can have a net negative or positive balance in the karma OD account. By that logic, individuals should either experience only suffering or only happiness, depending on their balance. But in reality, the account does not operate so simplistically. The karma OD account maintains all debit and credit entries separately, without offsetting one by the other. This implies that a person with a high positive karma balance may still have to go through pain and suffering due to the entries in the debit side of the account.

The above also partly explains why "bad things happen to good people" and why "good things happen to bad people". Often, we may wonder why an undeserving person can get such good things in life while a gem of a person has to go through strife and suffering. This is simply because of his or her stock of past karma, and because there is no mechanism to offset the good karma with the bad.

The point thus remains that in order for good things to happen to us, we must keep investing into the positive karma side of the account through our best active efforts.

There are also strong arguments and reservations against the concept of God 'keeping karmic accounts' for every person. Many seers say that God is not an "accountant" doling out rewards and punishments according to what his account book says. He is the almighty who loves all beings equally and gives us things from his bounty. He is only seeking our union with him through compassion and devotion. He is kind and forgiving and it is not his job to act as a mechanical appraiser.

There are also theories that God balances out happy and sad times for everyone and that ultimately, there is a fair amount of parity in our joys and sorrows. But this theory is very difficult to digest because we know from experience that so many individuals are distinctly more fortunate than others in a number of ways.

Since it is difficult to accept that God is partial, or that all the fortune and agony in the world is randomly distributed, the only plausible way of explaining the disparities in the world is through the paradigm of karma, which reveals that *we* are ultimately responsible for what we go through, or what we achieve in our lives. Good luck or misfortune occurs because of the principle: "as you sow, so shall you reap", which catches up with each one of us sooner or later.

Just as pain or a fever urges one to act, the feeling of emptiness is only a symptom that may be telling us to do something more. There is also a need in most of us to create, to find self expression, to leave our mark on the planet, to be remembered, to be immortal. The ultimate culmination of spirituality is enlightenment or attaining nirvana, by which one is merged with the Supreme Being. This drive towards immortality may be due to the very essence of our nature, of our soul. While trying to achieve nirvana or enlightenment, we can concurrently try to leave our mark through something noble, laudable, and noteworthy on the physical plane with our efforts, pursuits and actions. In this way, we can also establish that the mundane and the spiritual can co-exist. Mother Teresa's enlightened soul was not against action. It was in no way withdrawn from the material world. It served the poor, the hungry, and those in pain. Gandhi did not live the life of a recluse, but led his country into the light of freedom. Vivekananda motivated the people through his words and actions. He created an altogether different image of our country in the western world. Yogananda Paramhansa wrote the most intriguing book on spirituality, which is a must read for anyone wanting to tread on the spiritual path. Tagore created unequalled prose and poetry that can transform hearts, minds, and souls. There are many examples of enlightened souls making a deep impact and contribution in the real world.

The actions of a great man are an inspiration for others. Whatever he does, becomes a standard for others to follow.

— Bhagavad Gita

SPIRITUALITY TALKS OF DISPASSION, WHILE ALL ACHIEVEMENTS AND SUCCESSES ARE BUILT THROUGH PASSION

Q.I want to make a success of my life, but spirituality teaches calmness, contentment, and dispassion. I want to work aggressively with all my zeal. Why should I slow down? Is it really good for me?

By observing ourselves and our acquaintances, we recognize only two stereotypes in one's psychological make-up. These are

- People who have the passion and the drive to go on and to do whatever it takes in order to achieve their goals.

- People who are calm and content and are not desperately longing to be a part of the rat race. They have either 'arrived' in life, or even if they have not, they are not frantically trying to make it there.

The worry that many people, particularly those who want to achieve much in life, have is that the pursuit of spirituality might extinguish their drive and zeal. This might prevent them from achieving their goals and they might have to live a life full of excuses and apologies.

However, a spiritual pursuit of the right kind does not purport to either kill one's drive or to make one dull and stagnant. It does aim to make an individual calm and relaxed, but it does so by giving rather than depriving. The calmness is vivacious and gives one the potential to achieve and do more.

Hence, even after progressing on the spiritual path, one may settle for either option a. or b. below:

a.   May want to continue to pursue his goals and ambitions. This can be:

- With the same, less, or more passion, depending on how one has been transformed from within as a consequence of the spiritual pursuit.

- With less disquiet and anxiety, and with more poise.

- With more energy and drive, since a de-stressed person can focus better and be more enthusiastic.

or

b. May no longer wish to pursue the same goals, as one's vision and needs may have undergone a metamorphosis. One's inner being or self may now be directed towards some other mission or pursuit.

Hence, spirituality is not against achievement or material success. Nor is it a path that will extinguish one's passion to succeed. It can substitute one's current goals with another set of goals through an inner transformation. It can also re-energize one's fatigued nerves and propel one to pursue one's goals with greater vigour.

6 SPIRITUALITY TALKS OF FOCUSING SOLELY ON KARMA (AND NOT RESULTS), WHEREAS PROFESSIONAL LIFE IS RESULTS-ORIENTED

Q. The Gita tells us that we have a right and control over karma only, and not over the results of karma. Does that mean that while doing karma for any task, I should not have the goal in mind, or that I should not aggressively set my focus on the goal?

Life's practical experiences and work pressures constantly emphasize that the "results" are what is important. The efforts, per se, are of not little or no consequence. Today's mantra for success at work is "Result Orientation". If any of us were to say that we did our best (karma), but were unable to achieve the desired results, would we get a pat on our back from our organization for being true to the Gita? Would we be condoned for not succeeding in a given task by expressing that our focus was on the effort rather than result?

Many even go to the extent of believing that if they intensely think that they will win or achieve success, they may in fact lose, because they are not supposed to be thinking of results, but only of doing the action. ***They are guilty of thinking about results.***

This is also a typical misunderstanding. These contradictory and skewed interpretations of karma can be quite misleading.

If we were to put the Gita or spirituality aside for the time being, it is a commonly understood phenomenon that one often does not have control over the results of a task as external forces and factors may be at play, which may be more potent than an individual's effort. However, that is not the point being made by the said shloka of the Gita. The plausible lessons from the shloka are:

- That karma must be performed with such dedication that one is oblivious of everything else, even of the fruits desired to be obtained from the karma. The perfect karma is one that is done with 100% dedication, in which case it is like a *tapasya* or *saadhna*. Rather than dwelling upon the rewards that will accrue or that one may enjoy in the end, one should focus his entire energy on doing the karma itself. ***Even the contemplation of the fruits of the karma is, in a sense, a distraction, resulting in the draining of energy that might have otherwise been utilized to do the karma.***

Most of us have experienced times when we are so deeply engrossed in some task or mission that we are unmindful of time, hunger, or fatigue. We feel a deep sense of joy and satisfaction when we are so completely absorbed in such work. Many compare this state to the deep, meditative state of Samadhi. Often, people in creative pursuits, who are passionately involved in *abhyaas* or practice, reportedly experience higher states of consciousness at such times. For many of them, the way to salvation is reliving those moments when they were completely absorbed in their pursuit as often as possible.

- The shloka was stated by Krishna himself, whose involvement with the Pandavaas and the Mahabharata shows the highest level of focus and results-orientation. In fact, some people wonder whether what Krishna did was ethical. But what was his approach? "Do the best and leave the rest," or "Do so that you achieve the goal". Hence, using this shloka as an excuse whenever one fails to achieve a goal is not right. In no way does the shloka give us the license to dilute our 'result-orientation'.

- The other aspect is how to direct one's efforts and energies towards the attainment of a specified objective or goal. The effort is not supposed to be divorced from the results being sought, not even for a moment. In fact, the effort should be fully aligned with it. Hence, if one is being "results-oriented" and doing whatever one can do, in order to achieve the desired result, one is not going against the Gita's teachings. Mahatma Gandhi, who said that the Gita had guided and impacted his life in a major way, had even said, "The man who wins is the man who thinks he can."

- The shloka also teaches one not to be too attached to results. Now, what does that mean? People often question, "How can I work so hard for something that I get fully absorbed in doing it and yet not be attached to it or concerned about its results? Would that not make me a split personality? Either I work with passion for something and give it my very best; or I work despondently, trying to do what I can and not caring much about what eventually happens."

Such doubting is natural. The Gita, however, does not tell us to consciously or intellectually be detached from the results of our hard work. That may be tough. What it says is that if one were to give his best efforts while being established in yoga, (i.e. "Yogastha Kuru Karmani"), one would be neither bound by nor attached to the results. So the emphasis is on following the path by which one can naturally attain detachment from within, rather than through conscious repression.

The fact that the results are not in one's hands should not be a refuge, or excuse in the case of failure. Neither should it be a trigger for despondency and negative thinking. One must not have a defeatist or fatalistic mindset at any given point, but should focus one's energies and efforts towards the goal.

HOW CAN I BE THANKFUL ALL THE TIME, AS THE SPIRITUALISTS SUGGEST, WHEN EVERYTHING IS ORDINARY AND I AM ASPIRING TO BE EXTRAORDINARY

Q. Often, I have been told: "Be thankful for what you have", "Live in the present moment", "Think positive"... but all of this is easier said than done.

Many teachings and sermons on spirituality revolve around this. One is repeatedly taught to enjoy each moment of one's life by living in the present moment and living life to the fullest. Spiritual masters urge us to appreciate the beauty around us, and to see divinity in everything. However, if one were to tell this to a person who is going through a painful period, or someone who is living an average life in which many of his desires remain to be fulfilled, he would be cynical about the suggestion.

He may exclaim, "How can I extract joy from these mundane things – the sunrise, the birds, and the limitless sky? I respect the fact that these gifts of creation are amazing, but how can I feel ecstatic about these everyday things?"

Happiness cannot merely be acquired by understanding that we should be happy all of the time. Mere intellectual appreciation is not enough; we know very well that it would be great if we could live each moment fully. But just saying, hearing, and wanting it doesn't make it happen.

When we ask why we can't experience this elusive joy all the time, we are told that it is because we have not been able to uncover the layers and masks of *maya,* and that these masks are the hindrance. How does one uncover this? By thinking or trying hard at an intellectual or mental level? Perhaps not. It is the actual evolution of the self through the practice and pursuit of a path that will bring fulfilment and help us really start living in the present moment with gratitude and thankfulness.

If we ask the question: "When does one feel grateful," we may come across the following answers:

- When we get what we want
- When we get more than what we had expected
- When we get more than what we think we deserved
- When we experience better times after an agonizing phase in our life

In the absence of the above, when life is going on as usual and we feel we deserve more, thankfulness may not come by auto-suggestion or intellectual goading. Hence, integrating oneself with the domain of eternal happiness may be the way.

Going back to our earlier discussions, we experience joy due to

- Wish fulfilment, which in turn leads to contact with the source of joy within us.
- An experience of a higher state of consciousness (e.g. in the state of Samadhi) through spiritual practice.

8 LIVING IN THE PRESENT MOMENT IS A VERY IMPORTANT PREREQUISITE FOR SPIRITUAL GROWTH

Some might go to the extent of saying that, "If you can't live in the present moment, you have not made any spiritual progress."

What does it mean to live in the present moment? It means enjoying each moment of one's existence and not brooding over the past. It means not worrying about the future. This sounds rather simple, but is living in the present moment with perfect contentment possible when one has so many unfulfilled goals and dreams? Is it possible to stop the mind from looking forward to them? Is it desirable? How does one stop the mind, anyway?

Thus, as we have seen and discussed many times in various chapters of the book, living in the present moment may not be feasible until one becomes connected with the source of joy, and until the consciousness becomes a living reality and permeates at all times, through all states of consciousness. As it has been mentioned earlier, the simple desire to be absorbed in the enjoyment of each moment may not be enough to make it happen. The sound of the birds in the morning, the sunrise, the trees, the fact that one has a roof over his head, or that one has enough food and clothing may not be enough to provide contentment from moment to moment.

However, the fulfilment of one wish is soon followed by the craving for another wish to be granted, and the effect of samadhi is bound to fade away in the course of the day. How, then, does one live in the present moment all the time? By making the higher state of consciousness, or *Samadhi*, permeate through the three states at all times. This may happen progressively, with more and more practice. It may even happen in a sudden, given moment, as it did with Buddha.

RITUALS, RELIGIOUS CEREMONIES, IDOLATRY ARE AN INTEGRAL PART OF SPIRITUALITY

Q. I am averse to rituals, elaborate forms of offerings, and visits to religious places. I believe in a Supreme Power, but the clamour around organized group prayers, meetings, federations, jagrans, kirtans, and karmakaand do not excite me. Do I have a chance to progress spiritually?

It is true that today, spirituality, religious practices, and rituals are often treated as identical. This, however, is not a true reflection of spirituality. As we have seen, spirituality can exist with and without these. As such, the spiritual path in its purest form does not mandate any types of rituals.

For an understanding of rituals and idolatry, let us look at an excerpt from one of the addresses of Swami Vivekanada on Hinduism at the Parliament of Religions at Chicago in September 1893 (taken from *Selected Works of Swami Vivekananda*, quoted with permission from Advaita Ashram, Kolkata, published by Advaita Ashram, 5 Dehi Entally Road, Kolkatta):

"Superstition is a great enemy of man, but bigotry is worse. Why does a Christian go to church? Why is the cross holy? Why is the face turned towards the sky in prayer? Why are there so many images in the Catholics Church? Why are there so many images in the minds of Protestants when they pray? **My brethren, we can no more think about anything without a mental image than we can live without breathing. By the law of association, the material image calls up the mental idea and vice versa. This is why the Hindu uses an external symbol when he worships.** He will tell you, it helps to keep his mind fixed on the Being to whom he prays. He knows as well as you do, that the image is not

God, is not omnipresent. After all how much does omnipresent mean to almost the whole world? It stands merely as a word, a symbol. Has God superficial area? If not, when we repeat that word "Omnipresent", we think of the extended sky or of space, that is all.

"As we find that somehow or other, by the laws of our mental constitution, we have to associate our ideas of infinity with the image of the blue sky, or of the sea, so we naturally connect our idea of holiness with the image of a church, a mosque, or a cross. The Hindus have associated the ideas of holiness, purity, truth, omnipresence, with different images and forms. While some people devote their whole lives to their idol of a church and never rise higher because with them religion means an intellectual assent to certain doctrines and doing good to their fellows. The whole religion of the Hindu is centred in realization. Man is to become divine by realizing the divine. **Idols or temples or churches or books are only the supports, the helpers, of his spiritual childhood: but on and on he must progress.**

"He must not stop anywhere. **"External worship, material worship,"** say the scriptures, **"is the lowest stage; struggling to rise high, mental prayer is the next stage but the highest stage is when the Lord has been realized."** Mark, the same earnest man who is kneeling before the idol tells you: "Him the sun cannot express, nor the moon, nor the stars, the lightning cannot express Him, nor what we speak of as fire; through Him they shine". But he does not abuse anyone's idol or call its worship sin. He recognizes in it a necessary stage of life. "The child is father of the man." Would it be right for an old man to say that childhood is a sin or youth a sin?

"If a man can realize his divine nature with the help of an image, would it be right to call that sin? Or, even when he has passed that stage, should he call it an error. To the Hindu, man is not travelling from error to truth, but from truth to truth, from lower to higher truth. To him all the religions, from the lowest fetishism to higher absolutism, mean so many attempts of the human soul to grasp and realize the infinite, each determined by the conditions of its birth and association, and each of these marks a stage of progress; and every soul is young eagle soaring higher and higher, gathering more and more strength till it reaches the Glorious Sun.

"Unity in variety is the plan of nature, and the Hindu has recognized it. Every other religion lays down certain fixed dogmas, and tries to force society to adopt them. It places before society only one coat which must fit Jack and John and Henry, all alike. If it does not fit John or Henry, he must go without a coat to cover his body. The Hindus have discovered that the absolute can only be realized or thought of, or stated, through the relative, and images, crosses, and crescents are simply so many symbols-so many pegs to hang the spiritual ideas on. It is not that it is necessary for every one, but those that do not need it have no right to say that it is wrong. Nor is it compulsory in Hinduism.

"One thing I must tell you. Idolatry in India does not mean anything horrible. It is not the mother of harlots. On the other hand, it is the attempt of undeveloped minds to grasp high spiritual truths."

From the above passage, it is clear that image worship is neither a necessary nor sufficient condition to attaining moksha. It is not something to be criticized. We can extend the same thought to other forms of associated rituals. It is evident that these are just aids. If one does not have a need for them, one neither needs to condemn them nor worry that he cannot progress without them. The idolisation, ceremonial customs, and the life should be seen as an individual affair. Associating spirituality with religion, religious practices, and rituals should not drive an individual away from its very essence. One can keep away from these and yet progress rapidly on the spiritual journey.

PART-VI WRAPPING UP AND SIGNING OFF

(This section is relevant for all seekers irrespective of which stage of the journey they are at. It Summarises Key Learnings from the book and crucial Dos and Dont's of pursuing this path.)

THE SPIRITUAL AND MATERIAL QUEST... THE YIN & YANG OF HAPPINESS

Why do we seek praise, endorsement, and recognition from others? A spiritualist may look at this craving with disdain and say:

"It is only a manifestation of how big an ego you have. That is why you want to attract the attention and envy of others. Ego is the biggest trap and hurdle on the path to spiritual progress and you constantly want to harbour and nurture it."

Seekers would then respond: "Perhaps it is the ego, but so what? The fact is that I definitely want to be the apple of other people's eyes and there is no point in superficially denying this."

The spiritualist might then say:

"Happiness lies within. Why seek it through endorsement from other mortals? Tap into the eternal source within. You will then be self-content. You will not crave eternal props, such as appreciation from others, in order to experience joy. Even in absolute silence and solitude, that joy will be experienced. More importantly, that joy will not simply come and go. It will not be sporadic. It will remain. It will be eternal. It will permeate through all your states of consciousness. Depending on others is like denying, ignoring, or belittling the divinity within. Your nature is fulfilment and you are capable of discovering this individually. By encouraging and fuelling your ego through seeking one-upmanship and praise, you may actually be straying from your path."

The above counsel of the spiritualist might be true, but a seeker might ask:

- Will I really ever reach the ultimate destination, where ananda flows from within, without any external prop or support, love or appreciation?

- When will I reach there?

- While waiting to reach there, should I be content by telling myself that even my ordinary, unnoticeable, and unremarkable existence will see the light of bliss, joy, or *ananda* one day?

- How should I be happy today? I am trying hard and meditating, but I am still not quite at the place where I can be happy from "within". I do need accolades, love, and recognition from others to be able to respect myself and feel content. Denying this is of no use. It would be an escapist and repressive approach if I were to say, "Yes, I will seek happiness only from within." Please allow me to strive for endorsement and appreciation. Please do not make me feel guilty by telling me that seeking this is wrong. I am already suffering from doubts about whether I am actually making any progress on the spiritual path I am following. When you tell me that my desire to succeed and to be noticed is detrimental, it hurts. On the other hand, my not receiving the awe and honour in the measure that I yearn for it makes me feel low. I am losing hope. Shall I just quit this spiritual quest and be my normal materialistic self, the one that is in my DNA? At least that way I will not carry the burden of guilt that I harbour today because of my actions that are contrary to all your spiritual teachings.

- But I have even tried that. By being a pure materialist and not making any tangible efforts on the spiritual plane, I suffer from another type of guilt – the guilt that I might be missing the very essence of life. After all, the Buddha and so many other noble masters cannot be wrong when they say that the whole purpose of our life is to attain enlightenment. My failure to make any strides towards that goal would cause a strange feeling of discomfort in me. Which way should I go?

The way out of this dilemma is not as difficult as it may seem. We need to understand and accept that until we reach such a state of spiritual evolution where we attain self-contentment and self-fulfilment, we would like to receive appreciation from others. We may continue to remain dependent on what others tell us or think of us in order to determine how good we feel about ourselves.

In the absence of such positive strokes, we may even suffer from *low self-esteem*. Low self esteem may also happen because of how we think when:

- We do not match up to the reference group that we have chosen and think that others are seemingly more talented, better off, and more blessed than us.
- We do not match up to our own expectations to be the best.

Our well-wishers, finding us low and depressed, may rationalize and tell us that the others in the reference group are better off, not because they are more talented, hardworking, capable, or deserving, but simply because of (i) their luck (ii) what they have inherited (iii) they adopted the wrong means. However, such a rationalization may not assuage us or enliven our spirits because we have also heard and believed that:

- In life, we get only what we deserve.
- We are responsible for our own destiny.
- If we are good, we shall receive praise, love, and admiration. We will be noticed.
- That the rising sun does not need to shout its arrival. In its silence, it compels us to see, feel, and experience its light and warmth.

And also that:

- Success is all-important.
- Nothing succeeds like success.

Hence, failure cannot be accepted as an excuse, or as justification. We should not even try to be defensive with thoughts that material success is futile, or short-lived.

The bottom line is thus to strive on the material plane with one's full capacity. Do everything to nurture every aspect of one's life. Live life fully with passion, drive, and achievement orientation. Give yourself as much stimuli as you need. Do not feel guilty if material achievements, recognition, and praise still matter a lot to you. But while doing all of this, follow the spiritual path with intensity and as per the precepts laid down by the master. Live spontaneously. Sacrificing or giving up your ambitions is not necessary at the intellectual, mental, emotional, or action level. Let it happen naturally, if at all. Our only objective is to pursue all the dimensions without bothering about how one dimension differs from the other at its core. For example, if the spiritual dimension tells us to seek only from within, it does not mean you should not seek from without. It does not mean forced withdrawal or repression.

However, besides this, there is another type of *self-doubt* that can make our lives miserable, particularly if we are living in the low self-esteem zone. This type of self doubt stems from our uncertainty about whether we are doing enough, i.e. whether we are stretching ourselves to our fullest capacity. This thought process may lead to our constantly being haunted, in our sub-conscious mind, by doubts, such as:

- Am I making enough effort?
- Am I taking enough risks that are necessary to succeed? Or am I losing out on the high road of success and achievement due to my faint-heartedness? Should I put everything at stake and take the leap of faith to sail through to the land of my dreams?
- Have I utilized all the opportunities that have come to me? Or have I been slow to react or too lazy to catch on to them or leverage them?
- What more could have I done? What have I missed? Where have I been careless, indolent, and lacking initiative?

What, then, is the way out of this type of self-doubt?

One of the simplest things to do is to maximize one's conscious efforts to live life fully and to develop and nurture one's existence on all the four planes or dimensions of life:

- Physical
- Emotional
- Mental/Intellectual
- Spiritual

How this can be done has been discussed in the preceding pages of this chapter, and will continue in the next chapter.

Any number of sermons on positive thinking and believing in oneself would be regressive if an iota of doubt creeps in regarding whether one has put in one's best effort. We should be able to confidently yell, "Yes, of course!" to all such winds of self-doubt that blow through our beings, right from the time we wake up to the time we retire each day. We should be able to decide how to best utilize our time so that we nurture ourselves in all aspects of our lives, with respect to:

- Health, lifestyle, diet, and exercise.
- Pursuing other intellectual efforts besides those related to our profession, especially if our job is not our ultimate passion and/or if our being is looking for more.
- Nurturing kindness, compassion, concern, and helpfulness
- Taking up a formal, defined path to making spiritual progress under the guidance of an expert

It is important to be able to say with 100% honesty that:

 i. I am doing the best I can.
 ii. I do have something unique (besides merely having a unique face or body!). I am pursuing my unique gifts, strengths, talents, interests, passions, and endowments.
 iii. Even if I don't have an outstanding talent worth talking about, I have a positive attitude, I have energy, I have hope, and I am trying to spread these.
 iv. I am doing my best to help others in whatever way I can.

It is important to live without guilt and regret with regards to what we could have done or can do. It is important to earn our salary or livelihood every day. It is important to feel worthy of what we have in terms of opportunities and resources, by utilizing them and creating value.

When we drive back home from work, we should feel the tiredness of having done our best, and the sense of self-worth of having earned our bread with honour. If, in the course of the day, we have also been able to extend a helping hand to someone, in whatever small or big way, it will be the icing on the cake and we will be bestowed with additional positive energy.

Pursuing spirituality alone at the cost of passionately pursuing other aspects of one's life may not be the best way to live for people who are ambitious, conscientious, and raring to go. It is important to understand that we must pursue our other goals and enhance the other dimensions and aspects of our life without feeling guilty.

Guilty? Do people really feel that way?

Well, the guilt may arise from the superficial understanding of the spiritual pursuit and the conditioning resulting from sermons such as:

- The world is mithya.

- All worldly achievements, relationships, and possessions are futile. Thus, pursuing them is a waste of precious time. Since one has been born a human being to be able to work out one's past karma after millions of births in varied species, one must never lose sight of the one and only goal of human life – that of attaining enlightenment.

- Ultimately, nothing will remain with us after we die. Hence, why should one invest time and energy seeking or pursuing material things?

- All relationships and attachments hurt, and it is therefore better to stay away and detached.

2 SOME OF THE DON'TS FOR SEEKERS

Knowing what not to do is as important as knowing what to do:

(a) ***Don't compromise on any of your material pursuits, goals, ambitions, passions, or relationships.*** Don't let go of your pursuits in any way by listening to those sermons that claim 'all these pursuits are futile, as the world is unreal'.

(b) ***Don't depend solely on spirituality to fulfil all your needs:*** Spirituality may eventually fulfil all one's needs, but that may not happen for quite a while. Hence, continue to pursue all your other needs. Spirituality is not a substitute for pursuing and achieving everything for which you have ever aspired. Pursue other goals in conjunction with the spiritual path.

(c) ***Don't be in a hurry to choose a technique:*** Do a reference check by talking to those who are practicing any technique or the ones you have short-listed. Companies do a reference check for even the most senior of management positions. This does not mean that the prospective employer doubts the credentials or statements of the prospective employee. Reference checking is an accepted norm. Hence, do not enter head first into the first one or two techniques that you find to be acceptable based on cursory exposure. Do some studying and find out their backgrounds, pedigree traditions, and the like. Is there support available after one has learned the technique? Exercise the same kind of care that one would do before buying a house or a car.

(d) ***Don't be in blind awe of any guru:*** Awe, faith, love, or surrender may take time. These are not prerequisites. They may not even develop significantly later on, but that will not affect the efficacy of the technique in most cases. What if surrender to a guru and singing his praise are a prerequisite or a norm in any method that one were seriously considering? If one does not feel comfortable with this aspect, one can either drop it, or do a relative evaluation vis-à-vis other paths that do not have these attributes.

(e) ***Don't be in a hurry to quit a technique:*** You may ask the teacher how much time it will take before you can obtain any tangible experiences. You may not get a precise answer in most cases. You can try to set a tentative time frame. For example, you may say, "I will persist for the first 4 weeks even if I have no experiences, bad experiences, or if I start feeling worse. Provided, however, that I will (a) keep having my methodology examined by the teacher, (b) practice group meditation, and (c) discuss my doubts with a trained teacher or the master. If I am not satisfied even after this, I will begin to consider other options."

(f) ***Don't quit because you do not have logical answers to all of your doubts:*** Even though you may find a disconnect between many concepts and theories, such as the karma theory (results-orientation vs. not thinking of the fruits of one's labour), the guru's grace, rituals vs. rationality, and the like, do not be in a hurry to quit the path or the quest for spirituality itself. Give it time and opportunity.

(g) ***Don't read arbitrarily:*** Read literature that is in sync with the chosen path, though it may be written by different masters. Take the example of a person who chooses a path that does not advocate "concentration" as a methodology of meditation. He begins reading a book that treats concentration the essence of meditation and expounds this with reasons and justifications. What will the result be? Confusion, anxiety, and exasperation. Hence, one needs to be careful in one's readings, studies, and the adoption of concepts. A guide or mentor can help along the way.

h) ***Don't compromise your rationality even if you do not get rational answers:*** Learn to live with unanswered doubts. Try to resolve them at the earliest, but if this is not getting done, then learn to shelf or park them. Insisting on their resolution before taking up a particular path may not be a very effective approach.

(i) ***Don't ignore physical exercise:*** Physical exercise generates chemicals that can make you feel better and that can recharge each cell of your body. This is just as important as sleeping, eating, working, or meditating.

(j) ***Don't go crazy with indulgences just because the path is not too strict on this:*** Some paths may tell you that there is no need to repress your desires and cravings and that they will be overcome, naturally, on their own, over a period of time. This should not become the reason or excuse to ignore one's conscience or one's sense of discretion. This should also not be an excuse to go overboard with indulgence and lose one's existing level of self-restraint or control.

(k) ***Don't panic if you feel low or depressed after the first few weeks of beginning meditation:*** Depression, or a low feeling where one starts finding things futile, may happen for some time after the experience of deeper states of consciousness. This may be due to the release of deep-rooted stresses. This is okay as an interim, limited phase. One need not panic. Rather, one must continue to practice. It is important, however, not to remain in this interim phase for too long. Losing interest and passion may also lead to a lack of motivation to continue pursuit of the spiritual path. The low feeling can result in increased inertia and withdrawal. One may even quit the path in this phase. Hence, it is important to exercise care and caution and be in touch with the master or teacher, especially at this phase of meditation.

EIGHTEEN IMPORTANT TIPS FOR ANY SEEKER

1. Use the mind and intellect to objectively select the method that is right for you. Do not go by blind trust or forced belief. Just as you would be careful in selecting a career path, an educational institution, or a specialist in the medical field, use your rational mind to complete the necessary due diligence before committing yourself to a path or a teacher. Make sure you do not allow yourself to become prey to a fraud. Do not go by hearsay. Use your analyses, sources of information, and reference checks before zeroing in on a method. Faith or surrender by a friend of yours to a particular guru is a good yardstick, but should not be the *only* measure you deploy. Use criteria that are best suited to you.

2. Do not let your intellect become a bottleneck such that your doubts or unanswered questions become so overwhelming that you quit the path. If you question every prescription the doctor gives you, what would the result be? You would either not follow his advice or would do so only partially. That is a sure recipe for ineffectiveness. Satisfy yourself with the credentials of the doctor (path, master, meditation technique) before taking the plunge. Having chosen one, follow it in its entirety.

3. Regular and accurate practice, exactly as taught, is critical. Else, you will end up blaming the teacher or method for your own irregularity or inaccuracy. Regular practice is a far greater challenge than either finding the right technique or learning its practice. The absence of tangible results or "good feelings" for weeks may de-motivate you. You may need to make sacrifices

to find time for meditation. You may need to reprioritise. It is difficult to find time in the morning when you barely have time to get ready. Just as you miss your breakfast, skip reading the newspaper, or miss your prayer or morning walk, so will you will skip this. In the evening, you will be too tired or too hungry. You will not find a peaceful secluded place in the middle of the hectic activities at work and home. Hence, unless you integrate spirituality or meditation into your professional, family, and personal goals, you may not have the urge to pursue it.

4. Do not let the absence of a tangible transformation in the initial stages dissuade you from regular practice.

5. Periodic checks with the teacher (ideally with the master) through group meditation or follow up sessions is critical, just as you go to the doctor for regular follow-up visits until you are fully cured. He may tweak the treatment based on your progress, or may leave it untouched. But the call is his, provided you give him the opportunity.

6. A meditation technique is not like a consumer product such as a FMCG (fast moving consumer good), which is used and consumed within a short span of time. It is rather like a lifelong and durable product that will be with you forever. It is also different from a professional degree, which you acquire once. Treat it as something that will require periodic checks, after-sales support, maintenance, refreshers, and revitalisation. Hence, the quality, availability, and infrastructure for the after-sales support are vital factors in choosing a technique.

7. In spite of good after-sales support, there will be times when you will not get any answers, or get unsatisfactory answers to your doubts and queries. Do not be in a rush to quit. As long as the chosen path is right, you will get the answers sooner or later, either by insights or through other means.

8. Learn to live with the doubts while they are unresolved. It is distressing, but you need to have patience. Practice every precept exactly as it was taught. If you quit too early, you may

come to the wrong conclusions, such as "the path was not right" or "the master was not enlightened" or "spirituality is of no use". At the same time, if the method, teacher, or master is always evasive about your doubts, examine why he is acting this way? Does he, himself, not know the answer? Does he want you to wait before giving you the answers? Does he want you to experience doubt-resolution from within? While many masters will not give you black and white answers, they may give you useful pointers. Use your doubts to progress on the path with objectivity, but let them not be a bottleneck.

9. Surrender or hero worship to a guru is not a necessary pre-requisite in all methods. Do not deprive yourself of the benefits of meditation and the spiritual quest just because you are averse to bowing to a human being whom other seekers have deified. You can make progress even without faith or surrender. A medication works irrespective of whether or not you trust it. It will do its job and show results, provided you are taking it exactly as prescribed.

10. The master who is an outstanding orator may not have the most suitable technique for you. On the other hand, a master whose talks are not too impressive may have a method that can lead to rapid transformation. Hence, do not look for perfection in all aspects – personality, communications skills, aura, charisma, method – you would be lucky if you got them all. Focus more on the process and other means to evaluate the method rather than impressive talks, a fan-base, or publicity alone.

11. An unsuitable or imperfect teacher (as per your self-created images or expectations) does not render the subject, institution, or concept of teachers ineffective. Not having the benefit of the best Maths teacher in school does not mean that maths is useless, education is no good, or the subject is impossible. Derive the maximum benefit out of the teacher. Even with his limitations, he may be able to bring you to a stage from where you are virtually on your own, when you do

not need the same level of hand-holding, where reconnecting with other seekers or the master only once in a while will be good enough. But we are always searching for a demigod to teach us, and we may not all be so lucky as to find one. That, however, should not deprive us of seeking out the path.

12. If, after 8-12 weeks of regular practice, you neither experience any positive changes nor get any rational answers, re-evaluate whether you need to reconsider the teacher or the chosen method. But do not be in a hurry to drop the teacher, technique, or master. At the same time, do not remain stuck with a path that is incapable of taking you to the goal after you have given it adequate trial and opportunity. Sticking with one method for months and getting nowhere is no good. But come to this conclusion if you have been regular, accurate, and have given the opportunity for correction. Once that is done, if you are still down and de-motivated to continue, by all means, go through a second phase of due diligence and look for an alternative method.

13. Do not depend solely on meditation or the guru's grace to get you ahead. Pursue your duties to your work, family, and to yourself with all your passion and might. On this path of self discovery, you may come across times when you feel that your professional pursuits are hollow and that you were meant for greater things. This can be a result of your connecting with your deeper levels of consciousness. But do not be in any great hurry to divert your attention away from your profession to your true calling. This is because, as you progress more and connect with your Self even more, you will find that you were associating different things as being your "true passion". Nurture both your profession and passion. Give yourself the space, time, and opportunity for silent introspection in solitude every day. You will find your true calling.

14. No spiritual path tells you to quit the material world or material pursuits. Try to do your best in your profession. Do everything to gain success, popularity, stature. Do not feel

guilty. These will not become a cause of your failure in the spiritual realm. Engaging in active karma at all times with one's full commitment is critical. Remember: material success and financial security can be an aid in this quest, as your worries on this major front would at least diminish. That way, spiritual energy and experience can work on other aspects of your being.

15. Do not seek refuge in Gita's shloka, "Karmanyeva dhikaraste mafaley shu kadachana" for not achieving results or for not being results-oriented. You have to succeed. Many of us fail as we may not have given our 100% to the task, and we then seek refuge under this shloka. This is tragic. Did Arjuna fail or remove his focus on results after hearing this shloka from Lord Krishna? We should not easily accept failure by telling ourselves that we can only do our best as the results were not in our hands. We must learn to operate with a "Do or Die" attitude.

16. Serve Others

   • It can cause inner transformation.

   • It will teach you compassion.

   • It will create cosmic benevolence for you.

   • The thankfulness received from the beneficiary will be addictive.

   • It will help build your sense of self-esteem.

17. You need to be convinced that you were doing your best, as the most difficult person to fool is yourself. Make small progresses everyday. Feel the self-development or learning acquired and the value added to the self and to others every day. That is one way to buy peace with your conscience and being.

18. Invest in relationships. Do not be a recluse. Do not decide to have only those friends who are spiritually inclined. Anyone with or without a passion for spirituality can help in your personal growth and fulfilment. Network with people who

stimulate your thinking, your compassion, your zest for life. Do not keep avoiding your critics. You may dislike them for their bitterness, but a bitter medicine is better than a sweet poison. Osho says that the meditation performed by a person living amidst the noise of society is deeper than one who has left everything for the mountains, as the latter's struggles with people, relationships, and social duties are insignificant. Learn to share your warmth with people you interact with as it will come back to you. Even the master thinks of his disciples. Mata Amritanandmayi hugs each disciple. Sai Baba of Shirdi said he was indebted to the seekers who sought him and who looked to him.

APPENDIX

DETAILED OVERVIEW OF SOME OF THE SPIRITUAL PATHS & MEDITATION TECHNIQUES

This section describes in greater detail the paths and methods introduced in part II. Each method is defined through official descriptions available from published materials from the organisations, which have been included with their permission. it also has sections containing the author's critique on each method.

The list of techniques included in this section have been randomly selected based on:

- Interactions with people who have been practicing these techniques
- The author's own experiences in learning and practicing some of the techniques

The list in no way indicates that these are recommended techniques. There are many other techniques that may be equally effective. Thus, while searching for a technique that is most suitable for oneself, the reader is encouraged to look beyond the list of techniques covered in this book.

Disclaimer:

The descriptions in this chapter are based on:

- Information available from published literature and websites.
- Experiences of some people randomly selected, who have practiced the technique.
- The contents may be biased by the author's own views and interpretations. Most masters insist on the purity of their

teaching and the dissemination of their message solely through trained teachers and the use of precise words approved by them. Hence, for accurate information on the techniques, it is recommended that the reader visit the official website, read the official publications, or get in touch with the offices of the organization in question.

• *The Official Description sub-section under each technique is the only one that has verbatim statements from the particular path's website or publications and has been included with their permission.*

I.   TRANSCENDENTAL MEDITATION OR TM (TAUGHT BY HIS HOLINESS MAHARISHI MAHESH YOGI)

a.   The Official Description of TM
Source: *www.tm.org*

> *"Transcendental Meditation opens the awareness to the infinite reservoir of energy, creativity and intelligence that lies deep within everyone.*

— Maharishi

> *"By enlivening this most basic level of life, Transcendental Meditation is that one simple procedure which can raise the life of every individual and every society to its full dignity, in which problems are absent and perfect health, happiness, and a rapid pace of progress are the natural features of life."*

— Maharishi

The Transcendental Meditation (TM®) technique is a simple, natural and effortless procedure which should be practiced for 15-20 minutes in the morning and evening, while sitting comfortably with one's eyes closed.

During the practice of this technique, the individual's awareness settles down and one experiences a unique state of restful alertness. As the body becomes deeply relaxed, the mind transcends all mental activity to experience the simplest form of awareness, Transcendental Consciousness, where consciousness is open to itself. This is the self-referral state of consciousness.

The experience of Transcendental Consciousness helps to develop the individual's latent creative potential while dissolving accumulated stress and fatigue through deep rest gained during the practice. This experience enlivens the individual's creativity, dynamism, orderliness and organizing power, which result in increasing effectiveness and success in daily life.

The Transcendental Meditation technique is scientific, requiring neither specific beliefs nor the adoption of a particular lifestyle. The practice does not involve any effort or concentration. It is easy to learn and does not require any special ability. People of all ages, educational backgrounds, cultures and religions in countries throughout the world practice the technique and enjoy its wide range of benefits.

Over 500 scientific research studies conducted during the past 25 years at more than 200 independent universities and research institutes in 30 countries have shown that the TM program benefits all areas of an individual's life which includes the mind, body, behaviour and environment.

The research has been published in such major scientific journals as *Science*, the *American Journal of Physiology, Scientific American, Lancet,* the *Journal of Counselling Psychology,* the *International Journal of Neuroscience,* the *Journal of the Canadian Medical Association,* the *British Journal of Educational Psychology,* and the *Journal of Conflict Resolution.*

Research indicates that those who follow the TM technique have the biological age of a person 5 to 12 years younger, on average, as well as a significantly reduced incidence of illness and risk of heart disease. Studies also show that those who follow the TM technique have warmer interpersonal relationships, less anxiety, increased self-esteem and self-confidence, increased problem-solving abilities and greater creativity. The individual spontaneously radiates a purifying and nourishing influence of positivity and harmony in society as a whole.

b.   How to learn TM:
     Source: *www.tm.org*

c.   How much times does it take to learn:

- **Step 1 – 3:** The introductory sessions that introduce Transcendental Meditation and its benefits explain the origin and the principle of TM and how it differs from other techniques. These take 1½ - 2 hours each.

- **Step 4:** Personal instruction in the technique, after which one returns home to enjoy the benefits. This takes 2 hours.

- **Step 5 – 7:** Seminars to offer further information about the technique take 1–2 hours each.

d.   For how long does one have to practice it?

     One needs to practice it for about 15 – 20 min in the morning and in the evening.

     Are there any refresher courses?

     Refresher courses are always beneficial and one must keep getting one's TM checked from time to time through a trained teacher.

     Is the program residential?

     The basic TM program can be done on a non-residential basis. However, advanced programs like TM – Siddhi and Yogic Flying are generally residential programs.

e.   Where does one learn it?

     Several TM centres exist throughout India and across major cities in the world.

f.   Where can one obtain more information?
     www.tm.org
     www.maharishi-india.org

The author's comments on TM

Positive Aspects:

- It is a very simple technique – easy to learn and to practice.

- It is very doable: It takes only about 20 minutes twice a day, once each in the morning and evening.
- Most people experience a deep restfulness even in the very early stages of practice.
- Deeper sleep, lower blood pressure, a more relaxed state of mind, and less stress are the results reported by many people even within the first few weeks of practice.
- Much scientific research and evidence is available.
- It is popular in the western world, which questions such methods with a scientific approach.

What if one is already practicing another technique?

- If it is purely a breathing technique, such as pranayama, then it may be okay to continue its practice. However, if one is practicing another meditation technique involving observation, concentration, or any other mental processes, it may be better to practice one method at a time.
- One should, however, go by the opinion and advice of the trained teacher.

Is there any scientific evidence available?

TM was perhaps one of the first techniques to subject itself to extensive scientific tests and experimentation at research labs and renowned universities in the US, Europe, and across the globe. Among all the techniques, TM perhaps has the distinction of having some of the largest number of published scientific results and findings.

II. ART OF LIVING

The Official Description

How does one Learn?

Basic Course:

- The basic course is non-residential, and is 6 days long, most of the sessions of which last approximately 2-3 hours.

Advanced Course

- The Advanced Course is a residential program of approximately 5-6 days.
- Sri Sri Ravi Shankar himself is present in some of the advanced courses
- It is recommended once every year for a serious seeker.

Sahaj Samadhi

- This takes much less time than the basic course and is comprised of only 3 sessions of 1 or 2 hours each.

How long does one have to practice?

For the Basic Course

- For those who have done the Basic Course, the entire process, including Sudarshan Kriya, takes approximately 20-25 minutes.
- This needs to be practiced at least once every day.

The Full Cycle

- For those who have done the Sahaj Samadhi Meditation and the Advanced Course, the total time required per day, including a set of exercises, breathing techniques, Sudarshan Kriya, and Sahaj Samadhi Meditation, is approximately 1 to 1½ hours.

Where can one obtain more information?
www.artofliving.org

Where does one learn?

Information on various courses is available at any of the centres, as well as on the website.

Author's Comments on AOL

Positive Aspects of AOL:

- It is very simple to learn, especially the Basic Course.
- It is very easy to practice even for a very busy person
- Most people experience the results within the first few days or

weeks of practice.

- People suffering from depression and anxiety have reportedly felt the benefits of this technique.

- The accessibility of the guru is a great positive factor of this technique, as one can see, meet, and even spend a few days with him in an advanced course.

- Another positive factor is the guru's sense of humour and light-heartedness, which demonstrates that life should not be taken too seriously. He teaches, by his own example, to smile, laugh, and celebrate love, which is an eye-opener for those who are tense about life. "Walk lightly, walk like a cloud," he says.

- It is a well-organized network. It is run and managed professionally. Courses are conducted regularly in several locations and printed schedules are available in advance from several centres.

- The organization has well-trained teachers, many of whom are practicing professionals and successful in their respective fields. It is generally easy to intellectually relate to them.

- The technique also has impressive brand ambassadors who can vouch for the tremendous transformation that AOL has brought about in their lives. Since these are intellectual, rational, and successful individuals, one's faith in the technique can be strengthened by this.

The results and good feelings that follow the Basic Course (without learning the Sahaj Samadhi meditation) may make the follower so content that he or she doesn't want to do anything beyond it. Many may say, "I have found what I wanted and am not keen on looking for anything else." However, in order to progress to higher levels of consciousness, it is desirable that one do the Sahaj Samadhi Meditation or any other technique the AOL teacher approves of.

What if one is already practicing another technique? Which of the following courses can the seeker undertake?

Basic course

- If one is practicing a meditation technique, there should be no problem. One may continue it.
- If one is already practicing a breathing technique and is then learning the Basic Course, there could be an issue.
- However, in each case, the teacher's advice should be sought.

Advanced Course

- The teacher will advise accordingly.

Sahaj Samadhi

- If it is a meditation technique, the teacher will decide whether to recommend that the individual continue the existing technique, or replace it with the Sahaj Samadhi Meditation.
- In a number of cases, the individuals may be advised to continue with the practice of the meditation technique they have already been following.

Is there any scientific evidence available?

Yes, medical reports and other experimental evidence supporting the positive effects of Sudarshan Kriya are available.

III. VIPASSANA

Official Description:

- This is one of the most ancient meditation techniques, which was taught by the Buddha.
- As compared to TM and AOL, as well as many other popular techniques today, Vipassana requires a far greater commitment in terms of learning and sustaining its practice. It is certainly a powerful technique.
- The technique is a combination of:
  - Certain guidelines for learning the technique and for follow up, applicable during the residential program.
  - Breathing techniques that focus on the breath.
  - Meditations through self-observation.

The official description of Vipassana

Sources:

i. www.vri.dhamma.org

ii. www.dhamma.org

iii. Other published material from the Vipassana International Academy, Igatpuri, Pin-422 403, Dist Nasik, Maharashtra, India.

1. The Historical Background:

The technique of Vipassana is a simple, practical way to achieve peace of mind and to lead a happy and useful life. Vipassana means "to see things as they really are". It is a logical process of mental purification through self-observation.

From time to time, we all experience agitation, frustration and disharmony. When we suffer, we usually do not keep our misery limited to ourselves. Instead we keep distributing it to others. Certainly this is not the proper way to live. We all long to be at peace with ourselves and with those around us. After all, human beings are social beings and we have to live and interact with others. How then, can we live peacefully? How can we remain harmonious ourselves and maintain peace and harmony around us?

Vipassana enables us to experience peace and harmony. It purifies the mind, freeing it from defilements and deep-seated causes of suffering. The practice leads step-by-step to the highest spiritual goal of full liberation from all mental defilements.

Vipassana is one of India's most ancient techniques. It was rediscovered 2500 years ago by Gautama Buddha, and is the essence of what he practiced and taught during his forty-five year ministry. During the Buddha's time, a large number of people in northern India were freed from the bonds of suffering by practicing Vipassana, allowing them to attain high levels of achievements in all spheres of life. Over time, the techniques spread to the neighbouring countries of Burma, Sri Lanka, Thailand and others, where it had the same ennobling effect.

Five centuries after the Buddha, the noble heritage of Vipassana had disappeared from India. The purity of the teaching was lost elsewhere as well. In the country of Myanmar (Burma), however, it was preserved by a chain of devoted teachers, for over two thousand years, this dedicated lineage transmitted the technique in its pristine purity, from generation to generation.

Vipassana has been reintroduced to India, as well as to the citizens of more than eighty other countries, by S. N. Goenka. He was authorized to teach Vipassana by the renowned Burmese Vipassana teacher, Sayagyi U Ba Khin. Before he died in 1971, Sayagyi was able to see one of his most cherished dreams come true. He had strongly desired that Vipassana return to India, the land of its origin, to help it come out of its manifold problems. He felt that from India it would then spread throughout the world for the benefit of all mankind.

S. N. Goenka began conducting Vipassana courses in India in 1969 and then after ten years he began teaching in foreign countries as well.

2.   Introduction of Vipassana

It is necessary to know one's true self – this is the advice every person has been given. One must know oneself not just at the intellectual level of ideas and theories, or the emotional and devotional level by blindly accepting what one has heard or read. Such knowledge is not enough. One must know reality at the actual level of a mental and physical phenomenon. This alone will help us emerge from suffering.

This direct experience of one's own reality, this technique of self-observation, is what is called 'Vipassana' meditation.

In the time of the Buddha, *'passana'* meant seeing with open eyes in the ordinary ways, but Vipassana refers to observing things as they really are, not as they seem to be. Apparent truth has to be penetrated until one reaches the ultimate truth of the entire mental and physical structure. When one experiences this truth, one learns to stop reacting blindly and learns to overcome suffering.

Gradually, the old suffering is eradicated and one comes out of all the misery to experience happiness.

Vipassana meditation leads to the total purification of the mind. It is the highest form of awareness and the total perception of the mind-matter phenomenon in its true nature. It is the observation of things as they are.

Vipassana is the meditation that Buddha discovered after trying all other forms of bodily mortification and mind control and finding them inadequate to free him from the seemingly endless cycle of birth and death, pain and sorrow. It is a technique so valuable that it was preserved in its pristine purity in Myanmar for more than 2,200 years.

Vipassana meditation has nothing to do with the development of supernormal, mystical, or special powers. Even though an individual may be awakened through its practice, nothing magical happens. The process of purification that occurs is simply an elimination of negativities, complex knots, and habits that have clouded pure consciousness and blocked the flow of mankind's highest qualities – those of selfless love, compassion, sympathetic joy, and equanimity. There is no mysticism in Vipassana. It is a science of the mind that goes beyond psychology by not only understanding, but also purifying the mental process.

The practice of it is an art that manifests its profound practical value in our lives by first lessening and finally eliminating the greed, anger, and ignorance that corrupt all relationships, from the family level to the level of international politics. Vipassana spells an end to daydreaming, illusion, and fantasy, which are mirages of the apparent truth.

Like the sizzling explosion of cold water thrown on a red-hot stove, the reactions after bringing the mind out of its hedonistic tendencies into the here and now are often dramatic and painful. Yet there is an equally profound feeling of release from tensions and complexes that have for so long held sway in the depths of the unconscious mind.

Through Vipassana, anyone – irrespective of race, caste, or creed, can eliminate those tendencies that have woven so much anger, passion, and fear into their life. During the training, a student concentrates on only one task, which is the battle with one's own ignorance. There is no guru-worship or competition amongst students. The teacher is simply a well-wisher pointing to the way he has charted out through his own practical experience.

With the continuity of practice, the meditation will quieten the mind, increase concentration, arouse mindfulness, and open the mind to the super-abundant consciousness, or the "peace of *nibbana* (freedom from all suffering) within."

As the Buddha experienced during his enlightenment, a student delves deep within his inner self, dispersing apparent reality, until he is able to penetrate even sub-atomic particles to discern the Absolute.

There is no dependence on books, theories, or intellectual games in Vipassana. The truth of impermanence *(anicca)*, suffering *(dukkha)*, and egolessness *(anatta)* is grasped directly by the enormous power of the mind rather than by the crutch of the intellect.

The illusion of a 'self' blinding the mental and physical functions is gradually broken.

The madness of cravings and aversions, the futile grasping of *I-me-mine*, the endless chatter and conditioned thinking, and the reactions of blind impulses gradually lose their strength. By his or her own efforts, the student develops wisdom and purifies the mind.

The foundation of Vipassana meditation is moral conduct. The practice is strengthened through *samadhi,* or the concentration of the mind. The purification of the mental processes is achieved through *panna,* or the wisdom of insight. We learn how to observe the interplay of the four physical elements within ourselves with perfect equanimity and find how valuable this ability is in our daily lives.

We smile in good times and are equally unperturbed when

difficulties arise around us knowing that we, like our troubles, are nothing but a flux of waves of *'becoming',* arising with incredible speed only to pass away with equal rapidity.

The Buddha repeatedly discouraged any excessive veneration paid personally to him. He said, "What will it profit you to see this impure body? Who sees the teaching, the 'Dhamma', sees me."

How does one learn the technique:

Sources:

v. www.vri.dhamma.org

vi. www.dhamma.org

vii. Other published material of Vipassana International Academy, Igatpuri, Distt Nasik, Maharashtra, India.

To learn Vipassana, it is necessary to take a ten-day residential course under the guidance of a qualified teacher. The courses are conducted at established Vipassana centres and other places. For the duration of the retreat, students remain within the course site, having no contact with the outside world. They refrain from reading and writing and suspend all rites and rituals. They follow a demanding daily schedule, which includes about ten hours of sitting in meditation. They also observe silence, not communicating with fellow students. However, they are free to discuss meditation questions with the teacher and material problems with the management.

There are ***three steps*** to the training which is given in a Vipassana Meditation Course:

(1) Firstly, one must abstain from any physical or vocal action which disturbs the peace and harmony of others. One cannot work to liberate oneself from defilement of the mind while one continues to perform physical and verbal deeds which only multiply those defilements. Therefore, a code of morality is the essential first step of the practice. One undertakes not to kill, steal, conduct sexual misconduct, tell lies, and use intoxicants. By abstaining from such actions, one allows the mind to

quieten down sufficiently so that it can proceed with the task at hand.

(2) The next step is to develop some mastery over this wild mind by training it to remain fixed on a single object – the breath. For the first three and a half days, students practice *Anapana* meditation, focusing one's attention on the breath. One tries to keep one's attention for as long as possible on the respiration. This is not a breathing exercise as one does not regulate the breath. Instead, one observes natural respiration as it is, as it comes in and as it goes out. In this way, one further calms the mind so that it is no longer overpowered by violent negativities. At the same time, one is concentrating the mind, making it sharp and penetrative and capable of deep insight.

(3) These first two steps of living a moral life and controlling the mind are very necessary and beneficial in themselves, but they will lead to self-repression unless one takes the third step – purifying the mind by developing insight into one's own nature.

The third step, undertaken for six-and-a-half days, is the practice of Vipassana, which is the experiencing of one's own reality by the systematic and dispassionate observation of the ever-changing mind-matter phenomenon manifesting itself as sensation within oneself.

One penetrates one's entire physical and mental structure with the clarity of insight. This is the culmination of the teachings of the Buddha, self-purification by self-observation.

How long does one have to practice it?

• One should continue the practice in one's daily life after the retreat to get optimum and continued benefit.

   Some of the components are:

   – Anapana (awareness of breath)

   – Vipassana (awareness of bodily sensations with the understanding of their impermanent nature)

   – Metta Bhavana (compassionate love, selfless love)

Are there any Refresher Courses?

It is recommended that the 10-day residential program be done at least once a year. There are also 1-day and 3-day refresher courses.

Where can one obtain more information:
www.vri.dhamma.org
www.dhamma.org

Where can one learn?

Vipassana courses are held regularly at permanent centres and rented sites in different countries. In addition to the frequent ten-day courses and special courses, extended courses of 20, 30, and 45 days are periodically offered for advanced students.

Author's comments on Vipassana

Positive Aspects:

- It is a very intense technique. For seekers with a strong urge to progress quickly and with the willingness to work towards it, this technique can provide immense satisfaction.
- The heritage of the technique is very strong.
- The purity, discipline, and sanctity of the teaching of the technique, as well as the residential course, the quality of the teachers, and the code of conduct are all impressive.
- The superior intellectual ability of teachers.
- The availability of brand ambassadors.

Challenges

- A disciplined 10-day regimen to learn the technique, which includes:
  - Silence for a long time.
  - Waking up very early in the morning
  - Meditating for many hours in a day.
  - Eating light and limited meals

- Later, after the course is completed:
  - Regular practice of approximately 2 hours per day
  - A 10-day refresher course every year is recommended for serious seekers

What if one is already practicing a technique?

No other technique should be practiced during those 10 days when one is going through the residential program. After this period, specific guidelines and instructions can be discussed with the trained teacher.

Scientific Evidence:

Several experiments have been conducted. The Vipassana Research Institute has documented several examples of the positive impact of Vipassana in fields such as health, education, drug addiction, and business management.

IV. THE MEDITATION TECHNIQUES TAUGHT BY OSHO

This section has been extracted from various published materials and public discourses by Osho. It has also been taken from information contained in the website www.osho.com.

Most of the quotes are taken from the book, 'Meditation – The First and Last Freedom", published by Tao Publishing Pvt. Ltd., 50, Koregaon Park, Pune: A Rebel Book. (The page number and chapter title is mentioned in brackets after the quote. Where reference is given in the book to another publication, the same is also mentioned).

Quotations by Osho in this book are used with permission from Osho International Foundation.

At the core of Osho's teachings of meditation, lie the precepts that:

- Meditation is not about doing – but about being and becoming. One does not have to strive or try hard to meditate. Just by learning to be natural and spontaneous, meditation happens.

- Meditation is about being natural. Being yourself. It is a discovery in which one does not have to strive too hard. Nor does one have to leave action behind. Meditation is not against action or against active life.

  - *"Nothing needs to be done; just be a witness, an observer, a watcher, looking at the traffic of mind – thoughts passing by desires, memories, dreams and fantasies. Simply stand aloof, cool, watching it, seeing it, with no judgment, with no condemnation, neither saying This is good,' nor saying, This is bad.'*

    — Osho Philosophia Ultima,
    Ch. 1 (Page xii, Introduction: Ref 3).

- Meditation is not about controlling or trying to stop one's thoughts. Nor is it about concentrating on an object or mantra or image. It is simply about observing what is going on inside one's mind and one's being. The ground rule of such observation is that it must be done without judging whether what is going on inside is good or bad. One must just be a detached and dispassionate observer.

  - *"A Buddha is not a man of concentration; he is the man of awareness. He has not been trying to narrow down his consciousness; on the contrary, he has been trying to drop all barriers so that he becomes totally available to existence."*

    — Osho
    From Ancient Music in the Pines, Ch. 3
    (Pg 225, Obstacles to Meditation: False Methods. Ref: 11).

- Physical renunciation of worldly objects or abstinence is not a necessary pre-condition to meditation or the inner journey.

- Meditation or the inner journey itself is not about repressing thoughts and desires. According to Osho, it is neither possible nor desirable to do so because, at best, one can stop the physical manifestation of the cravings, but one's mind might continue to yearn for them. By attempting to suppress or repress one's cravings at the mental level, one is embedding them deeper. They might just unexpectedly erupt one day. The important thing is to transcend these, not by repression or force, but in a gentler way by:

  (a) Internally experiencing their energy and their nature

  (b) Finding the source of joy that is greater than what one obtains by the gratification of these cravings

- *Osho also emphasizes in his various discourses that Living in the Past or the Future is equal to not living in the present moment.* Living in the present moment, according to him, is the only way to live. We hope that we will be happy when we achieve certain things, or on the occurrence of certain event(s), such as:

  – Becoming rich, getting promoted, or achieving financial security.

  – When one has retired from all work pressures and can do what one has always longed to do.

  – When one's kids have settled.

However, the day that one will be eternally happy never comes because when one milestone is achieved, another one creeps in. This deprives an individual from being able to rest peacefully or from enjoying the present moment, because happiness is the absence of desire. The state of non-craving and complete fulfilment cannot be attained by trying to kill desire superficially by force or repression. It has to happen inside one's being. One has to "become that" (by "becoming", Osho is perhaps implying reaching a state of permanent *Consciousness* or as Osho often calls it "Awareness"). Hence, by setting our own pre-conditions based on the fulfilment of which we alone would be happy, we are missing out on the creation and all its bounty, *which is happening in the here and now.*

- Meditation is not something sad, dull, or gloomy. In fact, it will recharge you and unleash tremendous energy. You will begin to live with more joy, fullness and intensity.

- Meditation must be practiced exactly as taught. Trying to innovate or mix and match techniques is not advisable. The methods are based on thousands of years of experiment, so any attempt to improve or improvise is more likely to do harm than good

- Meditation is not for those who are in a hurry and just can't wait to experience quick, tangible results. Its seed needs its own time to blossom.

  – Osho wanted us to be dependent only upon ourselves rather than on him or the master. Hence, while a master is needed to show us the right path, our growth and progress depends on ourselves:

"My approach to your growth is basically to make you independent of me.

Any kind of dependence is slavery, and the spiritual dependence is the worst slavery of all.

I have been making every effort to make you aware of your individuality, your freedom, your absolute capacity to grow without any help from anybody. Your growth is something intrinsic to your being. It does not come from outside; it is not an imposition, it is an unfolding.

All the meditation techniques that I have given to you are not dependent on me – my presence or absence will not make any difference – they are dependent on you. It is not my presence, but your presence that is needed for them to work.

It is not my being here but your being here, your being in the present, your being alert and aware that is going to help."

— Osho

Beyond Enlightenment # 11

The techniques:

Among the many techniques Osho has taught, some have been mentioned in this section:

Osho Active Meditations

- Osho Dynamic Meditation
- Osho Kundalini Meditation

These meditations involve body, breath, and voice. With the practice of these, the silent meditative techniques become easier.

Osho Meditative Therapies

- Osho Mystic Rose
- Osho No mind
- Gibberish

Other Methods

- Osho Nataraj Meditation
- Osho Whirling Meditation
- Vipassana

Where does one learn the methods?

Online at osho.com or at any of the Osho Centres in the world. In places where no centres exist, meditation camps and classes are held from time to time.

For more information on the methods, please log on to www.osho.com or contact:

Osho International Meditation Resort
Osho International,
17 Koregaon Park,
Pune - 411 001 Maharashtra - (INDIA)
Tel: +91 (20) 5601 9999
Fax: +91 (20) 5601 9990
Email: resortinfo@osho.net

Author's comments

Osho is undoubtedly one of the greatest mystics and enlightened masters of our time. He can be credited for revolutionizing the concept of teaching spirituality, or *inner science,* as he calls it. He broke the conventional mindset by bringing this science from obscure places to the doorstep of the common man.

He was among the first masters to challenge the concepts of renunciation, self-control, and repression. He did not believe in sticking to any rules, so much so that he did not proscribe any one particular meditation technique. Though meditation is an integral part of the path shown by Osho, he allows seekers to experiment with a wide array of techniques before deciding which one to stay with. Seekers are not asked to sacrifice or give up any of the duties or even the desires of the material world.

"Religiousness is something that is absolutely scientific. I propose scientific methods to my people. I don't give them any belief system, I just give them methods of meditation which need no beliefs, no God, no heaven, no hell, no reincarnation – simply a method how to make your mind more and more silent. An atheist can do it, a communist can do it, and a theist can do it. It doesn't matter what you believe or disbelieve."

"The method is absolutely scientific. It has nothing to do with your beliefs. You just do the method and you discover your own godliness. You will not find any God sitting there, but you will find a fragrance that is only expressible in the word godliness. No other word can express it"

— Osho
The Last Testament Vol. 3 Chapter 30

The positive aspects:

- No specific technique is forced or prescribed. Since each one of us is unique, no single method can apply to all or can be as effective for all. Freedom is given to the student to decide. By letting someone else decide what is good for us, we are forsaking the freedom to choose. When we discover and choose what is good for us, the real transformation will take place.

- The techniques taught by Osho are based on his own experiences, as well as the experiments of millions of people. Hence, they can be undoubtedly trusted.

- The institutional support and the wide network of Osho centres.

- Abundant reading and listening materials are available, which directly and penetratingly deal with each of the aspects of 'Inner Science'. (In fact, simply listening to Osho can send you into a meditative state).

Challenges and Concerns:

- Not having one fixed method also poses its own challenge: namely, the onus of deciding which one to learn. However, enough help and guidance is available on this.

- The possibility of disillusionment exists. If the first few methods the seeker experiments with don't click, he or she may become disheartened.

- The seeker has to find a set of criteria while deciding whether to stay with, or move on from one's chosen method. One is one's own guide.

    "Really, when you try the right method, it clicks immediately. The right method, whenever you happen to hit upon it, just clicks. Something explodes in you, and you know that, "This is the right method for me." But effort is needed, and you may be surprised that suddenly one day one method has gripped you.

    "Take one method: play with it for at least three days. If it gives you a certain feeling of affinity, if it gives you a certain feeling of well being, if it gives you a certain feeling that this is for you, then be serious about it. Then forget the others. Do not play with other methods; stick to it at least for three months."

    — Osho
    Meditation: The First and the Last Freedom
    (Page 15, The Science of Meditation: The right method
    will click")

- The important thing is to take up one technique, practice it exactly as advised, and give it a reasonable amount of time – about 21 days. Your own being will guide you to the right answer and you will discover whether or not it is the right technique for you.

V. ISKCON

ISKCON stands for International Society for Krishna Consciousness. Founded by his Divine Grace A.C. Bhaktivedanta Swami Prabhupada, "Hare Krishna" has become a household word across the world.

(a) Description

The chanting of the mantra lies at the heart of all the teachings of ISKCON.

Hare Krishna, Hare Krishna, Krishna Krishna, Hare Hare;
Hare Ram, Hare Ram, Ram Ram, Hare Hare.

Along with the chanting of the mantra, a certain code of conduct in life is also recommended.

How does one chant?

There are no rules regarding chanting. One can chant at any time and anywhere – at work, in the car, in public transport, or at home. However, the best time for chanting is in the early morning, just before and after sunrise. Setting aside a certain fixed time is beneficial for chanting.

Types of chanting

- Personal or individual chanting is done with beads that can be purchased from any Hare Krishna temple.
- Kirtana, which is done in a group and is usually accompanied by musical instruments and clapping.

According to the book, *Chant and Be Happy,* published by the A.C. Bhaktivedanta Trust: "One may hold a kirtana at home with family and friends, with one person leading the chanting and the others responding. Kirtana is more of a supercharged meditation process, where in addition to hearing oneself chant, one also benefits by hearing the chanting of others. Musical instruments are nice, but not necessary. One may sing the mantra to any melody and clap his or her hands. (Especially recommended are the traditional melodies). If you have children, they can sing along as well and make spiritual advancement. You can get the whole family together every evening for chanting."

Both forms of chanting are recommended and beneficial.

(b) The Official Description

(Extracted from various publications of ISKCON, particularly *Chant and Be Happy* and the website: www.iskcon.com, Copyright ISKCON Communications, 2004).

"The more one chants, the more easily he will be able to follow the principles listed below because he will gain spiritual strength and develop a higher taste. When one begins to relish spiritual pleasure from chanting, giving up bad habits that may hinder, one's spiritual progress becomes much easier."

(1) Just by chanting Hare Krishna, one will automatically want to follow the four regulative principles of spiritual life:

A. No consumption of meat, fish, or eggs.

B. No intoxication.

C. No gambling.

D. No illicit sex (sex outside of marriage, or not meant for the procreation of God-conscious children).

(2) One should regularly read Vedic literature, especially the Bhagavad Gita and Srimad- Bhagavatam. If one simply hears about God, His uncommon activities, and transcendental pastimes, the dust accumulated in the heart due to the long association with the material world will be cleansed.

(3) In order to be more fully immunized against material contamination, one should eat only vegetarian food that has been spiritualized by being offered to the Supreme Lord. There is a karmic reaction involved when one takes the life of a living being (including plants), but the Supreme Lord states in the

Gita that if one offers Him vegetarian food, He will nullify that reaction.

(4) One should offer the fruit of one's work to the Supreme Lord. When one works for his own pleasure or satisfaction, he must accept the karmic reactions to his activities, but if one dedicates his work to God and works only for his satisfaction, there is no karmic reaction. Work performed as service to the Lord not only frees one from karma, but awakens one's dormant love for Krishna.

(5) As much as possible, one who is serious about chanting Hare Krishna, should associate with other like-minded persons. This provides great spiritual strength.

Eventually, serious chanters will want to take initiation from a legitimate spiritual master. In the Vedic scriptures, initiation is recommended for it dramatically helps one chant Hare Krishna and assists in the awakening of one's original spiritual consciousness. There are qualified spiritual masters in the International Society for Krishna Consciousness throughout the world who are willing to assist anyone sincere about becoming God-conscious.

(c) How does one learn?

The mantra is simple and known to all. There is no secrecy about it and no elaborate initiation is required. However it would be best to associate with any of the teachers of the ISKCON temple or centres nearby.

How long does one have to practice it?

There is no pre-set minimum amount of time. Please see "How does one chant" under section a) Description.

Where can one obtain more information? Where does one learn?

www.iskcon.com

Author's Comments

The Positive aspects

1. The people who have dedicated themselves to this cause on a full-time basis include celebrities, professionals, intellectuals, and highly-educated men and women.
2. It has a well-organized network through which help, inspiration, and guidance are available.
3. It is simple, direct, and easy.

Possible Concern for some Seekers

Even though a large number of spiritual paths focus on meditation as the key to spiritual progress, according to ISKCON, chanting is the only panacea in the present times. This therefore implies that it encompasses mediation and its benefits within it.

Quoting from *Chant and Be Happy*:

"According to Vedic cosmology, the material creation eternally passes through cycles of four ages. Each begins with a Golden Age (Satya-yuga), then conditions progressively deteriorate, ending in the Kali-yuga, an age characterized by quarrel and hypocrisy. For each of the four ages, the Vedas prescribe a universal method of self-realization just suited for that particular age.

For instance, in the Sata-yuga, the recommended path was that of the mystic yoga system, which involved a lifetime of unbroken yoga practice, accompanied by strict vows of penance and austerity. We are presently at the beginning of last age, Kali-yuga. In this age people no longer have endurance, will power, or sufficient life span necessary to successfully practice the original yoga system described in the Vedas. The Vedic scriptures therefore advise,

"In this age of Kali there is no alternative, for spiritual progress other than chanting the holy name, of the Lord."

— Brhan-naradiya Purana"

However, if we compare it with other spiritual paths, the following questions may emerge:

i. Is only chanting the mantra enough? Is it not one of the steps on the ladder of the spiritual path?

ii. Can one do it consistently, with feeling and fervour?

iii. Can one feel benefits like relaxation and de-stressing after *japa*?

Reading the published literature and interacting and associating with the followers and teachers from ISKCON can offer convincing answers to the aforementioned concerns and queries that may arise in the mind of a seeker.

These doubts will disappear when the actual experience and inner transformation is triggered, after one starts on the path of chanting and the other precepts suggested by ISKCON. After all, each path has the potential to reach us to the goal, and ISKCON can provide enough brand ambassadors to reinforce this.

An implicit message given by ISKCON is that chanting provides similar or better effects as well as the experience of a higher state of consciousness which is promised by so many meditation techniques.

What if one is already practicing a technique?

If one wants to continue a meditation technique along with the teachings of ISKCON, one may decide based on (a) what the teachers of the earlier method say (b) the advice of ISKCON teachers, and (c) one's own experiences.

VI. KRIYA YOGA - AS TAUGHT BY YOGODA SATSANGA SOCIETY, FOUNDED BY SRI PARAMAHANSA YOGANANDA

One of the most famous books on spirituality, which in fact serves as a guide to innumerable seekers, is *Autobiography of a Yogi* by Sri Paramahansa Yogananda. This book, with its familiar cover with the picture of Paramahansaji (a young, vibrant yogi with long, flowing hair) is an all-time masterpiece and is widely available — from pavement stalls to the best bookshops in any town.

Note: The material in this section has been taken from

* Autobiography of a Yogi by Paramahansa Yogananda
* www.yogananda-srf.org
* Inputs received from YSS, Ranchi

(a) Introduction

Paramahansaji learned, practiced, and imparted knowledge about the ancient and sacred technique of Kriya Yoga. There are many Kriya Yogis worldwide and the Yogoda Satsanga Society (YSS) and the Self-Realization Fellowship (SRF) were the organizations established by Paramahansa Yogananda in 1917 and 1920 respectively to disseminate Kriya Yoga to sincere seekers. The headquarters are located at Ranchi and Los Angeles, but they also have centres and temples in other cities. Sri Daya Mata, a direct disciple of Paramahansa Yogananda since the 1930s, is currently the spiritual head of YSS/SRF.

Kriya Yoga is a systematic approach of attaining oneness with Brahman through life-force control.

Kundalini Jagran is one of the things that happens during the practice of Kriya Yoga.

The aim of Kriya Yoga is to feel the unity between the individual and the all-embracing consciousness and to finally merge with the Divine Consciousness.

(b) The Tradition & Science of Kriya Yoga

The tradition of Kriya Yoga was passed on to Paramahansaji by his guru Swami Sri Yukteswar, who was bestowed this sacred technique by Lahiri Mahasaya. Lahiri Mahasaya had received it from his master, Saint Mahavatar Babaji.

Quoting from Paramahansaji's Autobiography of a Yogi, chapter 26, 'The Science of Kriya Yoga':

* *"Kriya is an ancient science. Lahiri Mahasaya received it from his great*

guru Babaji, who rediscovered and clarified the technique after it had been lost in the Dark Ages. Babaji simply, renamed it, Kriya Yoga."

- *"The Kriya Yoga that I am giving to the world through you in this nineteenth century," Babaji told Lahiri Mahasaya, "is revival of the same science that Krishna gave millenniums ago to Arjuna and that was later known to Patanjali and Christ and to St. John, St. Paul and other disciples."*

- *"Kriya Yoga is an instrument through which human evolution can be quickened," Sri Yukteswar explained to his students. "The ancient yogis discovered that the secret of cosmic consciousness is intimately linked with breath mastery. This is India's unique and timeless contribution to the world's treasury of knowledge. The life force which is ordinarily absorbed in maintaining the heart action must be freed for higher activities by a method of calming the ceaseless demands of breath."*

- *"Kriya Yoga is a simple psycho-physiological method, by which human blood is de-carbonized and recharged with oxygen. The atoms of this extra oxygen are transmuted into life current to rejuvenate the brain and spinal centres."*

- *"Kriya Yoga has nothing in common with the unscientific breathing exercises taught by a number of misguided zealots. Attempts to hold breath forcibly in lungs are unnatural and decidedly unpleasant. Kriya practice, on the other hand, is accompanied from the very beginning by feelings of peace and by soothing sensation of regenerative effect in the spine."*

(c) How does one learn?

The tradition of Kriya Yoga has been kept rather secretive. In *Autobiography of a Yogi*, Paramahansaji says *"Because of certain yogic injunctions, I may not give a full explanation of Kriya Yoga in a book intended for the general public."*

How, then, does one go about learning Kriya Yoga?

Step 1: Register or enrol with the Yogoda Satsanga Society (YSS)

Q: *How does one register?*

Ans: Get in touch with any of the centres. The list of centres is available at:

i. www.yogananda-srf.org

ii. www.ranchi.com/tourism/views/ylession.asp

iii. www.ranchi.com/tourism/views yogodasatsanga.asp

Step 2: After registration, one receives 182 lessons over 5 years, at the rate of 3 lessons per month.

Q: What are these lessons?

Ans: In an attempt to use the methodical perfection of the West, Paramahansaji put his teachings and techniques in a series of lessons. These lessons are sent by post to the person who has enrolled. It may be noted that even the lessons are a secret and they are only for the eyes of true seekers. However, anyone can enrol to receive them.

Q: Is it all learning by correspondence?

A: Initially, it largely is. However, monks (swamis) keep travelling to the centres and there are opportunities to interact with them. Also, please see Step 3 below.

Step 3: Apart from theoretical inputs on life and yoga contained in the lessons, in the first year, the seeker will also be taught three basic techniques:

1. Energizing Exercises: A series of exercises developed by Paramahansa Yogananda in 1916 to prepare the body for meditation.

2. A Concentration Technique that helps to develop one's latent powers of concentration.

3. The Aum Technique: A powerful technique of meditation that expands one's awareness beyond the limitations of the body and mind and leads to a direct personal experience of that Divine Consciousness, which underlies and upholds all life.

After one has practiced the above for 1½ years, one is eligible for initiation into the main technique of Kriya Yoga.

Before being given the main technique, the pupil's level of understanding and progress, as well as readiness, is assessed.

Step 4: If found ready, the pupil goes through an initiation process in which his energy system is raised to a new level. In the course of his initiation, he is taught the secret yoga technique, which he is allowed to practice from that point. By practicing, he qualifies himself sooner or later for the next initiation.

In this, an even larger energetic opening is carried out and more advanced yoga techniques are provided. Thus, the pupil gradually advances.

(d) The Specifics

Q: How long does it take to learn? How long does one have to practice?

Ans: This is revealed at an appropriate time after enrolment.

Q: What is the essence of the technique?

Ans: There is no one thing that can be ascribed to being the essence of the technique, but an approximate, though incomplete, way to understand Kriya Yoga is that the main technique is related to pranayama, or life-force control.

Q: Does one have to take sanyas? Can I be a sincere seeker and practitioner of Kriya Yoga and yet be fully involved in my material duties?

Ans: Becoming a monk or sanyasi is not necessary to progress on the path of Kriya Yoga.

However, for those who wish to commit themselves completely to this spiritual quest, practicing the Yogoda sanyas tradition would help. This is not an easy task. One has to be unmarried, with no financial or social responsibilities. One has to formally apply to join the order, providing all the reasons for joining. Escapists are not accepted. One is asked to initially stay at the ashram for one month, almost on a trial basis, where the pupil and the organization get to know each other better. The monk order, or sanyas, is not undemanding. One has to lead a life of abstinence, brahmacharya, and follow a strict schedule of meditation and work.

(e) The Positive aspects:

- The lineage of the method comes directly from the enlightened masters who have been a living testimony of the reality of spirituality and the tangibility of the experiences.

- Paramahansa Yogananda, in his life and in his maha-samadhi, demonstrated to the doubting mind that transcendental experiences, cosmic consciousness, miracles, and the union with the Almighty Force, were as real and as doable as acts that we perform to sustain our material bodies.

- A wide network of YSS exists, which imparts the true knowledge of Kriya Yoga in its pristine form.

(f) Challenges & Concerns

The book, *Autobiography of a Yogi,* talks about miracles and the theory behind them. Rationalists may not be very comfortable with these ideas. However, they may do well to understand that:

- Miracles are only one of the innumerable and unfathomable aspects of spirituality. They are neither the essence nor the goal of spirituality.

- The book explains the theory behind the occurrence of miracles in the chapter, *Law of Miracles,* in a rational, analytical, and scientific way. The explanations are comprehensive enough to dispel the doubts of most sceptics.

- Even so, in order to begin learning Kriya Yoga or to enrol to receive the lessons, one need not internalize or agree with the possibility of miracles or their theory. One can begin, even with these doubts being present. Over a period of time, they will be addressed.

- The other concern may be whether Kriya Yoga is a technique for the ambitious householder. Or is renunciation the recommended way to progress faster? Is it true that not joining the monk order is a suboptimal and compromised way of pursuing this path?

To answer this, we can refer to Paramhansaji's words that the positive effects of Kriya will be experienced by anyone practicing it, irrespective of whether or not he has become a monk:

"The Kriya Yogi uses this technique to saturate and feed all his physical cells with undecayable light and thus to keep them in a spiritually magnetized condition".

Also that, with Kriya Yoga,

"...life force is mentally guided to the inner cosmos and becomes re-united with subtle spinal energies. By such reinforcement of life force, the yogi's body and brain cells are renewed by spiritual elixir."

The issue of renunciation versus leading an active professional and family life has been discussed in several other chapters of the book. The principles mentioned there are largely applicable here as well.

It is not as though one will progress faster only as a monk if one chooses Kriya Yoga as his or her path towards gaining spiritual growth. However, more clarity on this aspect will emerge after one enrols for the course with YSS and goes through the repository of knowledge penned by Paramhansaji for the benefit of the true seekers.

Note: The following web links contain valuable information about YSS:

www.yogananda-srf.org
www.ranchi.com/tourism/views/ylession.asp
www.ranchi.com/tourism/views/yogodasatsanga.asp

VII. SAHAJ YOGA (AS TAUGHT BY SHRI MATAJI NIRMALA DEVI)

Sahaj mean spontaneous. It also means natural and without too much exertion. Hence Sahaj Yoga is a technique that is simple and spontaneous. This method was discovered by Shri. Mataji Nirmala Devi in 1970.

(a) Introduction

The essence of the Sahaj Yoga method can be explained based on the following precepts that lie at its very core:

When a child is born, a great amount of energy is blocked or lies dormant at the base of the spine, in the sacrum bone. This energy is supposedly "coiled" into three-and-a-half loops and is called the 'kundalini'. Kundalini is the power of "pure desire" within us.

The kundalini instrument consists of:

- Kundalini
- Three Nadis
- Three Chakras

The three Nadis are channels of energy and are components of our sympathetic nervous system.

The Chakra is a subtle energy centre corresponding to the autonomic nerve plexuses. These centres are meant for our physical, mental, emotional, and spiritual requirements and well-being.

The essence of Sahaj Yoga lies in awakening the kundalini from the base of the spine (sacrum bone) through the central channel, piercing through the six chakras (which are our energy centres in the spinal cord). It finally reaches the seventh chakra – on top of the head (the fontanel bone area). The rising of the kundalini to the seventh chakra at the top of the head leads to self-realization.

According to Shri Mataji, *"Kundalini cures you, she improves you, she bestows all the blissful things upon you. She takes you away from the worries at the grosser level. She nourishes and revitalizes the centres (chakras)"*.

One of the causes of suffering is our lack of knowledge about ourselves, and the block of energy through the Chakras. Hence the Nadis and Chakras are in a state of imbalance. Due to this imbalance, we tend to become detached from Mother Nature, who takes care of us relentlessly.

Hence, Sahaj Yoga helps us attain three objectives:

- To balance the Nadis
- To raise the energy from the *Mooldhara* Chakra
- To connect ourselves with Mother Nature – the ever loving "Param-Chaitanya"

It does this by helping us purify ourselves, release negatives, and correct imbalances.

(b) What is the practice like?

The practice is quite simple. One has to sit, preferably on the floor with legs crossed, as in *sukhaasan*. Our *Mooldhara Chakra* thus touches the ground. This is recommended, as the earth and sky have the ability to take away a lot of negativity from within us.

There is also a very simple posture that can be done along with affirmations and visualizations. The affirmations are for removing the negative stresses, energy, and prarabhdha from our system, aided by Mother Nature.

They also aid in making us:

- Slowly realize our true nature
- Experience our true spirit
- Imbibe positive feelings of compassion and forgiveness
- Become our own master

(c) How long does it take to learn?

It does not take very long if the seeker has a true desire for self-realization.

(d) How long does one have to practice it?

The entire process takes approximately 10 minutes. One should practice it 2-3 times a day. Even twice a day, once in the morning and once in the evening, will be beneficial.

(e) From where does one get more information?
www.sahajayoga.org

Author's Comments

(f) The positive aspects

- It is simple to learn and to practice
- There are tangible results
- One experiences positive energy flowing, almost akin to a cool breeze, within weeks of practice.

Note: Faith and spiritual connection with Shri Mataji Nirmala Devi is helpful in reaping the benefits. Even if, at the onset, it is not strong enough, later, with the practice of the technique, the bond or connection with the master is very likely to happen.

(g) Possible concern from some seekers

- When one reads the literature on the theory and the background of the Sahaj Yoga technique taught by Shri Mataji, one comes across the mention of spine, nadis, chakras and the kundalini. This can create a bit of a concern in some seekers. For example, they may react as follows:
  - "I do not want to take any risks with my spine and nerves, given their extremely sensitive nature".
  - "Is kundalini really there? I just want to progress spiritually and I am not keen on making any energy rise inside me through my backbone. I am uncomfortable with doing any such thing with my spine or mind, as they are so tender and important for my normal existence."
  - "Is raising the kundalini really necessary for spiritual growth? Why do so many other masters and techniques not talk about kundalini at all?"

The answer to the above reactions may be:

- There is no conscious physical, mental, or emotional effort required to visualize chakras, nadis, the kundalini, or to make the kundalini rise through one's spine. One has to simply follow the various steps of the technique, which do not require any complex visualization. It is, in fact, simpler than most other meditative techniques. All things happen completely naturally:

— With regards to whether raising kundalini is the only way to spiritual growth: it is difficult to precisely or confidently say so since many masters do not mention it, while some others stress its importance.

— The important thing is for the seekers to know that their belief in kundalini or its rising is immaterial. This is because, as mentioned earlier, spiritual progress, even through this path, does not require any visualization or mental and intellectual effort with respect to one's kundalini. It happens naturally, of its own accord, if one simply follows the precepts of the path.

• The path selection can be independent of whether or not it talks about kundalini. Each path has its own merits and the masters have their own valid reasons for either talking about kundalini or not mentioning it at all. Irrespective of this, each path is capable of leading us to the goal. One has to decide which path or technique goes well with one's own mindset and conviction.

• Some seekers who come with the expectation or notion that meditation is a long, complex process to learn and practice may find that after learning the Sahaj Yoga technique, it is, in fact, very simple. They might even begin to wonder, "Do I need to add on another meditation technique to Sahaj Yoga in order to progress faster?"

It may be said that a mix and match approach of techniques is not the ideal thing for one's spiritual journey. Each path, including Sahaj Yoga, would in itself be complete and equipped enough to take one to the goal of self-realization. However, each one's needs and pace of progress is different and hence, one can consider adding any other technique if that appears to be a more satisfying approach.

However, to arrive at the correct decision, it is best to take the advice of a teacher of Sahaj Yoga if one would like to add a technique.

SUMMARY

This chapter discusses the basics of the following 7 techniques, including their core beliefs, the key aspects of the methodology, how to learn it, and other related topics.

1.   Transcendental Meditation
2.   Art of Living
3.   Vipassana
4.   Techniques taught by OSHO
5.   ISKCON
6.   Kriya Yoga
7.   Sahaj Yoga

GLOSSARY OF TERMS

A sana: Yoga position or yoga pose, also called yogasana. A balanced position for the smooth flow of energy in specific areas of the body and mind.

Ashram: Residential location for people living together in yogic tradition.

Ashtanga Yoga: The eightfold path of yoga as outlined by Patanjali: yama, niyama, asana, pranayama, pratyahara, dharana, dhyana, samadhi.

Atman: Soul.

Bhagavad Gita: A part of the famous Hindu epic *Mahabharata.* Includes the teachings of Lord Krishna to his disciple, Arjuna, at the commencement of the battle of Kurukshetra, with explanations on sannyasa yoga, karma yoga, bhakti yoga, and jnana yoga.

Bhakti: Devotion.

Bhakti yoga: The yoga of devotion.

Bhastrika: 'Bellows' breathing technique in which the breath is forcibly drawn in and out through the nose in equal proportions, like the pumping action of the bellows.

Brahman: Supreme consciousness, absolute reality.

Chakra: Literally meaning circle or wheel, in yoga this refers to the energy centers lying along the confluence of the nadis (energy channels).They are centers of radiating life force or energy that are located between the base of the spinal column and the crown of the head. Sanskrit for "wheels". There are seven chakras that store and release the life force (prana).

Dharna: Practice of concentration; sixth step of the eightfold path in ashtanga yoga.

Dharma: Duty, righteous path.

Dhyana: Meditation; single-pointed focus of the mind on either a form, thought, or sound.

Diksha: Initiation given by the guru.

Guna: Quality of nature with regards to tamas, rajas, and sattwa.

Guru: Spiritually enlightened soul who can dispel darkness, ignorance, and illusion from the mind, and enlighten the consciousness of a devotee/disciple.

Japa: Continuous chanting, i.e. repetition of a mantra.

Jnan or Gyana: Knowledge, understanding, wisdom.

Jnana Yoga: The yoga of knowledge – attained through spontaneous self-analysis and the investigation of abstract and speculative ideas.

Kapalbhati Pranayama: A breathing technique aimed at cleaning the frontal part of the brain; also called skull polishing – done through rapid breaths with more force on exhalation.

Karma: Action; the act of doing.

Karma Yoga: The yoga of action – aims at supreme consciousness through action; discussed in the Bhagavad Gita.

Kriya: Activity, dynamic yogic practice.

Kundalini: Man's retained energy, or potential energy, and consciousness.

Kundalini Shakti: Refers to the human's potential energy lying dormant in the mooladhara (base) chakra like a coiled serpent. When awakened, it rises up through the sushumna nadi.

Kundalini Yoga: Philosophy expounding the awakening of potential energy and inherent consciousness within the human body and mind.

Mantra: Subtle sound vibration, which, through repetition, aims at expanding one's awareness or consciousness.

Moksha: Liberation from the cycle of birth and death.

Moola: Root.

Mudra: Literally means 'gesture' - mudra expresses and channels cosmic energy within the mind and body.

Nadi: Energy channels in the body.

Niyam: Rule; there are 5 rules described in the Ashtanga Yoga of Patanjali.

Om: The universal mantra; cosmic vibration of the universe; represents the four states of consciousness.

Patanjali: Author of the Yoga Sutras and preacher of the eightfold (ashtanga) yoga. The Yoga Sutras of Patanjali succinctly outlines the art and science of Yoga meditation for Self-Realization. It is a process of systematically encountering, examining, and transcending each of the various gross and subtle levels of false identity in the realm of mind, until the true Self comes shining through. When Patanjali compiled the Yoga Sutras, no new system was created, but rather, the ancient practices were summarized in an extremely organized and terse way.

Prakriti: Nature

Prana: Vital energy force sustaining life and creation

Pranayama: Technique of breathing and breath control that regulates the flow of energy and aims at maintaining a balance of energy. It is the fourth of the eight rungs of Yoga, and involves regulating the breath so as to make it slow and subtle, leading to the experience of the steady flow of energy (prana), which is beyond or underneath exhalation, inhalation, and the transitions between them.

Samadhi: The final stage of ashtanga yoga, in which concentration becomes one with the object of concentration; supreme union. *Samadhi* is the eighth of the eight rung in the Yoga Sutras of Patanjali. *Samadhi* is the deep absorption in the object of meditation, wherein only the essence of that object, place, or point shines forth in the mind, as if the mind were devoid even of its own form. With *Meditation*, there is still an observer observing an object. When the observer becomes extremely absorbed in the process of observing the object, the three collapse such that the observer, the process of observation, and the object being observed all become one, and only pure awareness remains. This is when *Meditation* becomes *Samadhi*.

Samskaras: Those actions that come from the deep impressions of habit that are called *Samskaras*.

Sanyasi: One who has renounced the world in search of self-realization.

Shishya: Disciple; student.

Soham: Represents a mantra in meditation; literally means, 'I am That'. Represents the psychic sound with the sound 'so' during inhalation and 'ham' during exhalation.

Swami: Title of respect for a spiritual master.

Tapas: Self-discipline or austerity (one of the niyamas).

Vedas: Four ancient texts – Rig, Yajur, Sama, Atharva – that are further divided into Samhita, Brahmana, Aranayaka, and Upanishads. They were revealed to the sages and saints of India and explain and regulate every aspect of life from supreme reality to worldly affairs. They are the oldest books in the library of mankind.

Yoga: Derived from the Sanskrit word for "yoke" or "join together." Essentially, it means union. It is the science of uniting the individual soul with the cosmic spirit through physical disciplines (postures) and mental disciplines (meditation). It is state of union between two opposites – body and mind; individual and universal consciousness; a process of uniting the opposing forces in the body and mind in order to achieve supreme awareness and enlightenment.

Yogi: Someone who practices yoga.

Sources for the above definitions:

1. www.healthandyoga.com
2. Other reference material

SEEKERS INTERVIEWED

Among the many seekers met and interviewed, the insights provided by the following were particularly useful for this book:

1. *Mr. Sanjay Sharma, PGDM* – Supply Chain Mgt., Purchase Manager, Anand Nishikawa Company Pvt Ltd. An avid follower of Osho since 1989. Was named as Swami Devpat by Osho commune. (For Osho, his philosophy, meditation techniques etc.).

2. *Mrs. Jaya Agarwal, BE (Hons)* – Chemical, from BITS, Pilani; working as Senior Process Engineer with KBR Singapore. Earlier with Bechtel and ABB. Trained Teacher of AOL for Part I. (For Art of Living, TM and spirituality as a way of life).

3. *Mr. Ajay Goyal, B Tech., Vice President* – Commercial, Reliance Industries Ltd. (for Art of Living and Sahaj Yoga).

4. *Mr. Manish K Jar, BE, MBA* – Founding partner and Managing Director of Idea7 Consulting Services, an auto consulting firm specializing in training, marketing processes mapping, research etc.. His company's client list includes Toyota, Skoda, Mahindra & Mahindra, Tata Motors etc.. (For Vipassana).

6. *Mr. Amit Varma, B. Tech (IIT-D), PGDM (IIM -A), ex-Group Manager* – Corporate Planning, Hindustan Lever Ltd.. Currently Vice President & Head of Rural Business of a large corporate house. (For Vipassana and relevance of spirituality in a corporate manager's life).

7. *Mr. Venu Krishna Das, B.Com, LLB,* ex Claims Manager with Royal & Sun Alliance Insurance Company, Dubai. Currently

self employed and based at Mumbai. He is associated with ISKCON since 1992 and is actively involved in promoting Krishna Consciousness and philosophy. (For ISKCON).

8. *Ms. Anuradha Iyer, MBA, ex Vice President* – CRM, HSBC-Mumbai. Ex-Account Director and AVP at J Walter Thomson. (For thoughts on preparing for the spiritual journey).

9. *Mr. Manoj Jain, Promotor of Nice Girl,* one of the largest manufacturer & wholesale sellers of children's garments in northern India. (For relevance of Jainism, lessons from penance of Jain munis in a modern and ambitious person's life).

10. *Mr. Ajay Garg, Promoter & Director, Vaniki Herbs,* a leading manufacturer and distributor of Ayurvedic medicines in North Indian States. (For need of scientific proof of God and other aspects important for rationalists and disbelievers)

BIBLIOGRAPHY

1. Meditation – the First and Last Freedom, Osho
2. Chant and Be Happy, ISKCON
3. The Science of Being and The Art of Living by Maharishi Mahesh Yogi
4. Selected Works of Swami Vivekananda
5. The Bhagwad Gita
6. An Autobiography of a Yogi by Yogananda Paramhansa
7. Various publications of Vipassana Research Institute, Igatpuri
8. Various writings, books, speeches of Osho.
9. The Story of My Experiments with Truth, An Autobiography, M.K. Gandhi
10. Ideas & Opinions, Albert Einstein
11. The Tao of Physics, Fritjof Capra
12. For The Brotherhood of Man, Under the Fatherhood of God – Biography of Mother Teresa.
13. Gitanjali by Rabindranath Tagore
14. The Prophet, Kahlil Gibran
15. God Loves Fun, Sri Sri Ravishankar ji
16. You Can Win, Shiv Khera
17. Search into Secret India, Dr. Paul Brunton
18. The Razor's Edge, Somerset Maugham
19. The Alchemist, Paulo Coelho
20. The Monk Who Sold His Ferrari, Robin S Sharma

FEEDBACK FORM

Please email us what you think about this books by answering some or all of the questions below:

☞ Please write your answer only by mentioning the appropriate question number.

☞ Please send email to: guptarajivr@gmail.com.

☞ Each feedback will be gratefully acknowledged by the author.

☞ Any valuable suggestions/insights will be mentioned with sender's name in future writings:

1. How did you obtain this book?
   (a) Gifted by someone
   (b) Purchased
   (c) Borrowed from the library
   (d) Other (please specify)

2. If you purchased the book, please specify the city, locality, and the name of the bookstore.
   (a) City/Town
   (b) Locality
   (c) Name of the bookstore

3. Had you heard about the book before you picked it up for reading
   (a) Yes
   (b) No
   If yes, from where:

4. What were the most important things that made you decide to buy or read this book.
   (a) Cover
   (b) Title
   (c) Contents
   (d) Book Reviews
   (e) Recommended by bookstore
   (f) Display at bookstore

5. What was the single most important factor in deciding to pick up the book?

6. What were your expectations before reading the book?

7. Which of your expectations *were not* fulfilled?

8. Which of your expectations *were* fulfilled?

9. Suggestions for improvement.

10. Would you recommend this book to anyone?
    (a) Yes
    (b) No

11. Would you like to Promote Spiritual Awareness?
    Your Profile:
    (a) Name: (Optional)
    (b) Gender:
    (c) Age:
    (d) Qualifications:
    (e) Occupation:
    (f) City/Country:
    (g) Do you practise meditation?
        Yes/No
    (h) Do you have any unresolved doubts or queries?
    (i) Your favourite books on related subjects?